Drudgery Divine

Chicago Studies in the History of Judaism
Edited by
William Scott Green and Calvin Goldscheider

Drudgery Divine

*On the Comparison of Early
Christianities and the Religions of
Late Antiquity*

Jordan Lectures in Comparative Religion, XIV
School of Oriental and African Studies
University of London

JONATHAN Z. SMITH

THE UNIVERSITY OF CHICAGO PRESS

JONATHAN Z. SMITH is the Robert O. Anderson Distinguished Service Professor of the Humanities and in the College, and a member of the Committee on the History of Culture at the University of Chicago. His books include *Imagining Religion: From Babylon to Jonestown* and *To Take Place: Toward Theory in Ritual*, both published by the University of Chicago Press.

The University of Chicago Press, Chicago 60637
School of Oriental and African Studies, University of London
© 1990 by School of Oriental and African Studies
All rights reserved. Published 1990
Printed in the United States of America

99 98 97 96 95 94 93 92 91 90   5 4 3 2 1

Library of Congress Cataloging-in-Publication Data

Smith, Jonathan Z.
   Drudgery divine : on the comparison of early Christianities and the religions of late antiquity / Jonathan Z. Smith.
   p.   cm. — (Jordan lectures in comparative religion ; 14) (Chicago studies in the history of Judaism)
   Lectures delivered at the School of Oriental and African Studies, University of London, 1988.
   Includes bibliographies and indexes.
   ISBN 0-226-76362-5 (cloth). — ISBN 0-226-76363-3 (pbk.)
   1. Christianity and other religions—Roman—Study and teaching—History.
2. Christianity and other religions—Greek—Study and teaching—History.
3. Rome—Religion—Study and teaching—History.   4. Greece—Religion—Study and teaching—History.   5. Mysteries, Religious—Study and teaching—History.   6. Christianity and other religions—Judaism—Study and teaching—History.   7. Judaism—Relations—Christianity—Study and teaching—History.
8. Christianity—Origin—Study and teaching—History.   9. Apologetics—History.   I. Title.   II. Series.   III. Series: Chicago studies in the history of Judaism.
BR128.R7S55   1990
291'.09'015—dc20   90-38519
                                                                          CIP

CONTENTS

For Siobhan and Jason, a daughter and a son *sans pareil*

A patient pursuit of facts, and a cautious combination and comparison of them, is the drudgery to which man is subjected by his Maker, if he wishes to attain sure knowledge.

Thomas Jefferson
Notes on Virginia (1781)

PREFACE

WHEN, in the first two decades of this century, Louis H. Jordan presented his classic briefs for the defence of comparative religion to the courts of both academic and public opinion, he could appeal to the widely shared assumption that comparison was the scientific method par excellence. He could point, by way of analogy, to its triumphs in the fields of comparative anatomy and philology and could promise the same for religious research.[1] There appears to be no such consensus or confidence today. Indeed, it may be argued, comparison has come to be, for many in the field, the sign of unscientific procedure, abjured in the name of responsibility towards the concrete specificity of their objects of study. This *crise de conscience* makes all the more urgent the task of rethinking the comparative enterprise in modes appropriate to the academy's self-understanding as well as to its perception of the processes and goals of disciplined inquiry.

In what follows, I shall be reflecting on the comparative endeavour by means of a classic and privileged example: the comparison of early Christianities and the religions of Late Antiquity, especially the so-called mystery cults.

I have chosen this example for reasons having little to do with its possible intrinsic interest. Rather, I have selected it because there is an unusually thick dossier of the history of the enterprise. Literally thousands of monographs, dissertations and articles have been addressed to the question,[2] so that one is able to compare the comparisons and undertake archaeological work in the learned literature in such a way as to highlight both theoretical and methodological issues as well as matters of 'interest', queries as to what is 'at stake' in the various comparative proposals.

[1] See, J. Z. Smith, *Map Is Not Territory: Studies in the History of Religions* (Leiden, 1978): 254–56.

[2] See, among others, the rich bibliographies by K. J. Prümm, *Religionsgeschichtliches Handbuch für den Raum der altchristlichen Umwelt* (Freiburg im Breisgau): 215–356; R. Pettazzoni, 'Bibliographie des religions à mystères dans l'antiquité,' *Cahiers d'histoire mondiale*, 2(1954–55): 661–67; B. M. Metzger, 'A Classified Bibliography of the Graeco-Roman Mystery Religions, 1924–1973, with a Supplement, 1974–77,' *ANRW*, 2.17.3:1259–1423.

I have selected this privileged example as well because, for the almost four centuries of this enterprise here passed in review, the data brought to the comparison, both from early Christianities and from the religions of Late Antiquity, have remained remarkably constant. This is an area of scholarly inquiry, not unlike others within the human sciences, where progress is made not so much by the uncovering of new facts or documents as by looking again with new perspectives on familiar materials. For this reason, matters of methods and models ought to be central. In the pages which follow, 'what interests us here is not so much the connections between phenomena as the connections between problems'[3].

[3] V. N. Vološinov (M. Bakhtin), *Marxism and The Philosophy of Language* (Cambridge, Mass., 1973): xv.

ACKNOWLEDGMENTS

THIS book contains the revised texts of the Louis H. Jordan Lectures in Comparative Religion as delivered at the School of Oriental and African Studies (University of London) in March, 1988. I am grateful to the School for the invitation to prepare these lectures and for providing a stimulating series of seminars in which they could be discussed. I am especially indebted to Professor J. E. Wansbrough, the Pro-Director of the School, and to Professor J. R. Gray, Chairman of the Centre of Religion and Philosophy, for many courtesies and good conversations. Miss N. C. Shane did much to make our visit to London a memorable one both for my wife and myself.

Three of the chapters were delivered, in a somewhat different form, as the Selma Pilavin Robinson Lectures at Brown University, sponsored by the Judaic Studies Program, in March, 1988. As they have on other occasions, Professors J. Neusner and E. Frerichs were both generous hosts and gentle goads in enabling me to clarify the relationships between these particular studies and other investigations shared with members of the Program. There is no other Judaic Studies program in America which is consistently hospitable to this sort of generic discourse.

The graduate students of the Early Christian Literature program at the University of Chicago, organized by Colleen Stamos, hosted a series of evening seminars in which the several chapters were discussed at an early stage of their drafting.

In preparing this text, most especially the first chapter, I have often envied the printed catalogue of Dr. Williams Library (London). This distress was considerably eased by the fine holdings and extraordinary assistance of the staffs of the Department of Special Collections at the Joseph Regenstein Library (University of Chicago) and of the Meadville/Lombard Theological School (Chicago).

Jason Smith served as my mystagogue, initiating me into the intricacies of word-processing and rescuing me on more than one occasion.

My deepest intellectual debt is to Professor Burton L. Mack (Claremont) who has been my constant conversation partner from the inception of this project. He has provoked and stimulated me through innumerable discussions and carefully read the original draft of each chapter. I am grateful to Professor Mack, as well, for sharing with me, prior to its publication, the manuscript of his work, *A Myth of Innocence: Mark and Christian Origins* (1988) which allowed me to complete the experimental comparisons proposed in the final chapter.

It is appropriate, in a work devoted to matters of genesis and growth, to acknowledge and celebrate the excitement and joy generated by Siobhan and Jason in their different but equally wonderful ways.

ABBREVIATIONS

AARDS	*American Academy of Religion Dissertation* (or *Academy*) *Series* (Missoula, 1974–).
Adams	Ch. F. Adams, ed., *The Works of John Adams* (Boston, 1850–56), 1–10.
ANRW	*Aufstieg und Niedergang der Römischen Welt* (Berlin-New York, 1972–).
AOAT	*Alter Orient und Altes Testament* (Neukirchen, 1969–).
ASNU	*Acta seminarii neotestamentici Upsaliensis* (Stockholm, 1940–).
ASORD	*American Schools of Oriental Research, Dissertation Series* (Missoula, 1975–).
ATANT	*Abhandlungen zur Theologie des Alten und Neuen Testaments* (Zürich, 1944–).
BHTH	*Beiträge zur historischen Theologie* (Tübingen, 1929–).
BZET	*Beiträge zur evangelischen Theologie* (Münich, 1940–).
BZNTW	*Beihefte zur Zeitschrift für die neutestamentliche Wissenschaft* (Berlin, 1923–).
Cappon	L. J. Cappon, ed., *The Adams-Jefferson Letters: The Complete Correspondence between Thomas Jefferson and Abigail and John Adams* (Chapel Hill, 1959), 1–2.
CBOTS	*Coniectanea Biblica, Old Testament Series* (Lund, 1967–).
CCCA	M. J. Vermaseren, ed., *Corpus Cultus Cybelae Attisdisque* (Leiden, 1977–) = EPRO, 50.
CR	*Corpus Reformatorum* (Halle, Brunswick, Berlin, 1834–).
EHPRS	*Etudes d'histoire et de philosophie religieuses de l'Université de Strasbourg* (Paris, 1922–).
EPRO	*Etudes préliminaires aux religions orientales dans l'empire romain* (Leiden, 1961–).

Ford	P. L. Ford, ed., *The Writings of Thomas Jefferson* (New York, 1892–99), 1–10.
FRLANT	*Forschungen zur Religion und Literatur des Alten und Neuen Testaments* (Göttingen, 1903–).
GIUM	*Gnosis: Collana di studi storico-religiosi pubblicata a cura dell'Instituto di studi storico-religiosi dell' Universitá di Messina* (Palermo, 1979–).
Glawe	W. Glawe, *Die Hellenisierung des Christentums in der Geschichte der Theologie von Luther bis auf die Gegenwart* (Berlin, 1912).
HDR	*Harvard Dissertations in Religion* (Missoula, 1975–).
JPTW	J. Rutt, ed., *The Theological and Miscellaneous Works of Joseph Priestley, LLD, FRS, etc.* (London, 1819–31), 1–25.
Lipscomb-Bergh	A. A. Lipscomb and A. E. Bergh, eds., *The Writings of Thomas Jefferson* (Washington, 1903), 1–20.
MPG	J.-P. Migne, *Patrologiae cursus completus, Series Graeca* (Paris, 1857–66), 1–167.
MVAG	*Mitteilungen der vorderasiatischen Gesellschaft* (Leipzig, 1896–).
MVAW	*Mededelingen van de koninklijke vlaamsche Academie voor Wetenschappen, Letteren en schoone Kunsten van België* (Anvers-Brussels, 1939–).
NTTS	*New Testament Tools and Studies* (Leiden, 1960–).
RGVV	*Religionsgeschichtliche Versuche und Vorarbeiten* (Giessen, 1903–).
Rutt, *Life*	J. Rutt, *The Life and Correspondence of Joseph Priestley* (London, 1831–32), 1–2 = *JPTW*, Vols. 1.1 and 1.2.
RV	*Religionsgeschichtliche Volksbücher für die deutsche christliche Gegenwart*, series I, *Religion des Neuen Testament* (Tübingen, 1904–1911), 1–23.
SBLD	*Society for Biblical Literature Dissertation Series* (Missoula, 1974–).
SBT	*Studies in Biblical Theology* (London, 1950–).

SD	*Studies and Documents* (London, 1934–).
SHR	*Studies in the History of Religions = Supplements to Numen* (Leiden, 1954–).
SNTSM	*Society for New Testament Studies, Monograph Series* (Cambridge, 1965–).
SSEA	*Schriften der Studiengemeinschaft der evangelischen Akademien* (Tübingen, 1952–).
SVT	*Supplements to Vetus Testamentum* (Leiden, 1953–).
TDNT	*Theological Dictionary of the New Testament* (Grand Rapids, 1964–76), 1–10.
TR	*Theological Repository* (London, 1769–84), 1–4.
TU	*Texte und Untersuchungen zur Geschichte der altchristlichen Literatur* (Berlin, 1882–).
Turchi	N. Turchi, *Fontes historiae mysteriorum aevi hellenistici e graecis et latinis scriptoribus selegit* (Rome, 1930), in the series, Biblioteca di scienze e filosofia, 5.
UNT	*Untersuchungen zum Neuen Testament* (Leipzig, 1912–38), 1–25.
VVAW	*Verhandelingen van de koninklijke vlaamesche Academie voor Wetenschappen, Letteren en schoone Kunsten van België* (Brussels, 1941–).
WUNT	*Wissenschaftliche Untersuchungen zum Neuen Testament* (Tübingen, 1950–).

I

On The Origin of Origins

It must surely stand as one of the most touching moments of rapprochement in western history. Two men, once close friends and colleagues, then bitter political opponents, had drifted apart. For some dozen years they had exchanged no word. Now, although destined never to meet again face to face, through the intervention of a mutual friend and participant in their earlier collaboration, they became correspondents and left a bulky record of fourteen years of shared intimacies. The one was seventy-seven years of age when the letters recommenced; the other was sixty-nine. They had both been signers of America's Declaration of Independence. Each had served both as Vice-President and President of the United States – indeed, one had served as Vice-President during the term of the other. Their renewed correspondence was terminated only by their deaths, within five hours of each other, on July 4, 1826. I refer, of course, to John Adams and Thomas Jefferson.

As might well be expected, these two old men had much to write about: family matters, politics, political philosophy, and religion. Of the 158 letters that have survived, 47 are chiefly centered on this latter topic. As early as the fifth letter of their exchange, Adams had pronounced several contemporary millenarian writers to be 'evidently cracked', and their writings to be 'irrational', 'impious', 'unphilosophical', and 'superstitious' – a brief catalogue of Enlightenment and Deist invective (Cappon 2:297–8). Jefferson, in his turn, reminded Adams of the passage in Jeremiah 29.26 (Authorized Version): 'for every man that is mad, and maketh himself a prophet, that thou shouldst put him in prison and in the stocks' (Cappon 2:299), while Adams, after thanking Jefferson for the reference which he confirmed in 'the concordance', opined:

It may be thought an impiety by many, but I could not help
wishing that the ancient practice had been continued down
to more modern times and that all the prophets at least from
Peter Hermit to Nimrod Hess inclusively, had been confined
in the stocks and prevented from spreading so many
delusions and shedding so much blood. (Cappon 2:302)

While their discourse on religion ranged freely from conjecture
on Amerindian 'Antiquities' (Cappon 2:305) to the texts of the
'sacred Sancrists', (Cappon 2:412) the bulk of their exchanges
centered on Christianity. Despite the disclaimer, their project is
best captured by Jefferson: 'We must leave, therefore, to others,
younger and more learned than we are, to prepare this euthanasia
for Platonic Christianity, and it's restoration to the primitive
simplicity of it's founder.' (Cappon 2:385)

The first and most extended set of interchanges between
Adams and Jefferson concerning Christianity, taking up the bulk
of twelve letters, took place between July and December, 1813.
The beginning of this discourse was not auspicious as it reawak-
ened old controversies and wounds between the two men. Adams
had been sent, two months earlier (May, 1813), a copy of Thomas
Belsham's *Memoirs of the Late Reverend Lindsey*, which contained,
in an appendix, two letters from Jefferson to the British scientist
and theologian, now newly an immigrant to America, Joseph
Priestley, written in 1801 and 1803, and a letter from Priestley
transmitting Jefferson's second letter to Lindsey.[1] After reading
these documents, Adams was furious. The first letter from
Jefferson to Priestley (March 21, 1801), was written just seventeen
days after Jefferson was inaugurated as President, having defeated
Adams in a bruising campaign. After conveying concern for
Priestley's failing health, Jefferson savagely attacks Adams and his
administration. He characterizes it as a period of 'bigotry in
politics and religion' when 'barbarians really flattered themselves
that they should be able to bring back the times of Vandalism,
when ignorance put everything in the hands of power and
priestcraft'. As Jefferson interprets the Federalist rule, everything
was regressive. 'We were to look backwards not forwards, for

---

[1] Th. Belsham, *Memoirs of the Late Reverend Lindsey* (London, 1812): 535–40 (Appendix no. 12).

improvement' in education and science. Adams himself, Jefferson claims, had said that we would never go beyond our 'ancestors'. This conservatism, he writes to Priestley:

> was the real ground of all the attacks on you. Those who live by mystery and charlatanerie, fearing you would render them useless by simplifying the Christian philosophy – the most sublime and benevolent, but most perverted system that ever shone on man – endeavoured to crush your well-earned and well-deserved fame.

Therefore, as 'one of the first moments' of his new administration, Jefferson declares:

> I can hail you with welcome in our land, tender you the homage of its respect and esteem, cover you under the protection of all those laws which were made for the wise and good like you, and disdain the legitimacy of that libel on legislation, which, under the form of a law, was for some time placed among them. (Ford 8:21–23)[2]

This latter, refers to the Alien and Sedition Acts of 1798, the passage of which so deeply divided Federalists and Republicans, and under which Adams, while President, had briefly considered prosecuting Priestley,[3] only to dismiss the recommendation with the harsh judgement: 'I do not think it wise to execute the Alien Law against Priestley. He is as weak as water, as unstable as ... the wind. His influence is not an atom in the world.' (Adams 9:14)

Adams strongly responded to the various political matters in Jefferson's letter to Priestley on seven occasions after reading the Lindsey *Memoirs*, and Jefferson is clearly embarrassed. All he can do is to insist at length that the letters were published without his permission, that they were intended to be private, and that the

[2] Jefferson's letter, along with Priestley's reply (April 10, 1801), and a brief historical background is given in D. McKie, 'A Note on Priestley in America,' *Notes and Records of the Royal Society of London*, 10 (1952):51–9. See also, E. P. Smith, *Priestley in America: 1794–1804* (Philadelphia, 1920): 122–24, 145–46.

[3] In his copy of the letter, next to the phrase 'that libel on legislation, which, under the form of a law ...,' Jefferson wrote, 'Alien law'. (Lipscomb-Bergh 10:229n). It was fortunate for Adams's equanimity that Belsham did not publish the first letter of Jefferson to Priestley (January 19, 1800) which is, if anything, even ruder on the subject of the Federalists and their 'persecutions' of Priestley (Lipscomb-Bergh 10:138–43).

'renewal of these old discussions, my friend, would be ... useless and irksome'. (Cappon 2:337) Adams finally moves off the subject because he is plainly even more intrigued by the brief statement concerning Christianity in Jefferson's first letter to Priestley: 'simplifying the Christian philosophy – the most sublime and most benevolent, but most perverted system that ever shone on man'. He quotes the phrase back to Jefferson, in a letter of July 16th, having twice before promised to turn to the 'subject of religion in your letters to Priestley'. (Cappon 2:359, 354, 358) Adams agrees quickly to the proposition that Christianity is 'the most sublime and most benevolent ... system', but balks at the claim that it is the 'most perverted', stolidly insisting that he would have to do a large number of detailed studies in comparative religion before accepting the notion![4] However, what clearly piques his interest and curiosity even more than Jefferson's judgement in the first letter, is Jefferson's second letter to Priestley (1803) and Priestley's comments on it.

Jefferson's second letter to Priestley (April 9, 1803) is to 'acknolege' the gift of Priestley's *Socrates and Jesus Compared* (1803) which had just been published in Philadelphia. Jefferson goes on to recollect that in 1798–9, after conversations with Benjamin Rush, he had promised 'some day to write him a letter giving him my view of the Christian system'. It was to be a comparative work, beginning first with the 'moral doctrines of the most remarkable of the ancient philosophers', doing 'justice to the branches of morality they have treated well' and pointing out 'those in which they are deficient'. Next, he would turn to the 'deism and ethics of the Jews', showing how they became 'degraded' and required 'reformation'. Finally, he would explore the 'life, character & doctrines of Jesus', focusing on their 'pure deism' and Jesus's endeavour to reform Judaism by bringing it into closer conformity 'to the standard of reason, justice & philanthropy, and to inculcate the belief of a future state'. Because Jesus did not write, he continued, 'much was forgotten', and early

---

[4] Adams to Jefferson, July 16, 1813: 'But whether it has been more perverted than that of Mosse, of Confucious, of Zoroaster, of Sanchoniathan of Numa, of Mahomet of the Druids, of the Hindoos etc. etc. etc. I cannot as yet determine; because I am not sufficiently acquainted with those systems or the history of their effects to form a decisive opinion of the result of the comparison.' (Cappon 2:359)

representations of his thought were 'much misunderstood & presented in very paradoxical shapes'. Later, 'his character & doctrines have received still greater injury from those who pretended to be his special disciples and who have disfigured and sophisticated his actions & precepts'. The result has been to lead many to 'throw off the whole system in disgust'. For this reason, were he to undertake such a project, he would 'purposely omit the question of his divinity, & even his inspiration'. Having sketched out these theses (which are thoroughly congruent with the arguments of Priestley's *Socrates and Jesus Compared*), Jefferson goes on to press Priestley to undertake a full-blown comparison of Greek thought and Christianity. Priestley, he writes, has 'all the materials at hand' to 'extend' his work 'to the whole subject'. (Ford 8:224–5) This resulted, one year later, in the posthumous publication of Priestley's, *The Doctrines of Heathen Philosophy Compared with those of Revelation* (1804).

Adams's letter to Jefferson of July 16, 1813, is almost entirely taken up with quoting back to Jefferson a long extract from the latter's letter to Priestley and assuring Jefferson that, having read the outline of his proposed project, in his opinion, 'you are as good a Christian as Priestley and Lindsey'. (Cappon 2:360) This initial interchange spurs Adams to begin a complex discourse on Jefferson's planned 'view of the Christian system', the works of Priestley and the issue of the comparison of Greek and Christian thought. This set will be brought to a close, twelve letters later, with a letter from Adams to Jefferson on Christmas Day, 1813.

The name of Joseph Priestley served as a trigger for this extended discourse and recurs throughout. Priestley's association with Adams was long-standing, Jefferson was a newer acquaintance,[5] but, of far more significance for our undertaking, both

---

[5] Adams met Priestley for the first time in London, April 19, 1786 (J. Butterfield, ed., *Diary and Autobiography of John Adams* [Cambridge, Mass., 1961] 3:189). It is unclear, from the record, how many times they met or corresponded, but it was clearly more than once. Adams heard Priestley preach at the Essex Street Chapel on April 23, 1786 (Adams 3:397). Upon Priestley's arrival in New York in June 1794, H. Wansey delivered an oral message from Adams to Priestley that Boston 'would be better calculated for him [Priestley] than any other part of America' and that he would be well received if he settled there. In his turn, Priestley sent Adams a letter back with Wansey (H. Wansey, *An Excursion to the United States in the Summer of 1794*, 2nd ed. [London, 1798]: 82; cf. J. Rutt, *Life*, 1.2:234n). Choosing to settle in Northumberland, Pennsylvania, a small town, a post-office was established there for Priestley's convenience by Adams's executive directive (J. Binns,

were equally familiar with the range of Priestley's writings, especially those devoted to religion.[6] Adams bragged to Jefferson of the depth of his readings in Priestley; Jefferson, in turn,

Recollections of the Life of John Binns [Philadelphia, 1854]: 173). During 1795, Priestley apparently wrote several letters to Adams concerning the naturalization laws (Rutt, *Life*, 1.2:304, 312). Beginning in February, 1796, Priestley gave a series of addresses at the Universalist Chapel in Philadelphia. Many members of government attended, including Vice-President Adams, who was, according to Priestley, 'most punctual in his attendance, and an old acquaintance and friend' (Rutt, *Life*, 1.2:333, 336). The first volume of these lectures, Priestley's *Discourses relating to the Evidences of Revealed Religion* (1796), was dedicated to Adams who received a presentation copy from Priestley. In the long dedication, Priestley refers to his 'acquaintance and correspondence ever since your embassy to England', their 'common friendship' for Dr. Price of the Gravel-Pit Meeting in Hackney, and Adams's role in providing Priestley with 'asylum from the persecution which obliged me to leave England' (*JPTW* 16:3–5). Adams was uneasy with the dedication, fearing 'it will give me the character of a heretic', but he consoled himself with the thought that 'dedicating a book to a man will not imply that he approves everything in it' (Adams 1:488). By 1798–9, relations between the two men had deteriorated, largely as a result of the Thatcher polemics and the threat of the Alien and Sedition Acts. Priestley writes to Th. Belsham, January 11, 1798: 'Mr. Adams only attended on me once, the last winter. When my lectures were less popular, and he was near his presidentship, he left me, making a kind of apology, from the members of the principal Presbyterian church having offered him a pew there. He seemed to interest himself in my favour against Mr. Volney, but did not even subscribe to my Church History. Had he done that, and recommended the subscription, it would have succeeded [Priestley returns to this complaint in a letter to Russel, April 3, 1800 in Rutt, *Life*, 1.2:430–1] ... but that any statesman would risk his popularity on account of religion is not to be expected. He would have been the first in any similar situation if he had done it. I suppose, too, he was not pleased that I did not adopt his dislike of the French' (Rutt., *Life*, 1.2:390). The only subsequent direct contact may have been a warning from Adams to Priestley to be discrete in his politics. (Priestley's son, in his *Continuation* of Priestley's *Memoirs* [London, 1806]: 201–2, states that such a communication occurred. Priestley, writing to Belsham, March 2, 1801, states only that Adams 'desired ... to write me to be on my guard' (Rutt, *Life*, 1.2:454–55).

Priestley's relations with Jefferson were of a quite different character. The two men first met in 1797 on Jefferson's trip to Philadelphia for the inauguration. Jefferson went to hear Priestley preach (Rutt, *Life*, 1.2:373; D. Malone, *Jefferson and his Time* [Boston, 1948–81], 3:449). The two commenced a long correspondence, beginning in January, 1800 (Ford 7:406), mostly concerning education and Jefferson's plans for the University of Virginia. (Perhaps the most important of these exchanges was Priestley's 'Hints Concerning Public Education,' sent to Jefferson, May 8, 1800. See G. Chinard, *The Correspondence of Jefferson and Dupont de Nemours* [Baltimore, 1931]: 16–18.) With Jefferson's election, Priestley wrote, 'you will rejoice with the friends of liberty on the election of Mr. Jefferson' (Rutt, *Life*, 1.2:454–55), and Jefferson, for his part, in the letters cited above (pp. 2–3), becomes almost indiscrete in his sympathy for Priestley's 'persecution' under Adams. Priestley dedicated his *A General History of the Christian Church from the Fall of the Western Empire to the Present Time* (1802) to Jefferson, praising him as an 'advocate of religious as well as of civil liberty', and, noting his 'apprehension' caused by the actions of the 'late administration here [i.e., Adams]', thanks Jefferson for having provided him with 'security' (*JPTW* 9:5–6).

[6] The following works by Priestley were certainly owned by either Adams (JA) or Jefferson (TJ) or both. I cite them in short-title form in alphabetical order: 1) *An Address to*

declared his religious views to 'rest' on Priestley's works. They form, he writes, the 'basis of my own faith'. (Cappon 2:361, 369)

What Adams and Jefferson both learned from Priestley – as well as other writers, chiefly English, such as Lord Bolingbroke, who may be located in the broad spectrum of eighteenth century Deist and Anti-Trinitarian thought – may be displayed in a few passages from their exchange. They agreed that Jesus's 'pure principles' had been 'muffled by priests'. One must dismiss the writings of the Christian 'Platonists and Plotinists', and return to the 'simple evangelists', the teachings of the 'unlettered apostles, the Apostolic fathers, and the Christians of the Ist. century', selecting, 'even from them, the very words only of Jesus' (Cappon 2:384). This latter project, as is well-known, was taken up in the so-called 'Jefferson Bible'.[7] Continuing the exchange: 'Their Platonizing successors, indeed, in after times, in order to legitimize the corruptions which they had incorporated into the doctrines of Jesus, found it necessary to disavow the primitive Christians, who had taken their principles from the mouth of Jesus himself, of his Apostles, and the Fathers cotemporary with

---

Protestant Dissenters (TJ); 2) *A Description of a Chart of Biography* (TJ); 3) *A Comparison of the Institutions of Moses with those of the Hindoos* (JA); 4) *Discourses on the Evidences of Revealed Religion* (JA); 5) *Doctrine of Phlogiston* (TJ); 6) *The Doctrine of Heathen Philosophy* (JA/TJ); 7) *An Essay on the First Principles of Government* (JA/TJ); 8) *Experiments and Observations on Different Kinds of Air* (JA); 9) *A Harmony of the Evangelists in English* (TJ); 10) *A Harmony of the Evangelists in Greek* (TJ); 11) *A History of the Corruptions of Christianity* (JA/TJ); 12) *An History of the Early Opinions Concerning Jesus Christ* (JA/TJ); 13) *Institutes of Natural and Revealed Religion* (TJ); 14) *Lectures on History* (TJ); 15) *Letter to the Rev. J. Linn* (TJ); 16) *A Second Letter to the Rev. J. Linn* (TJ); 17) *Letters to the Inhabitants of Northumberland* (TJ); 18) *Letters to Burke* (TJ); 19) *Memoirs* (TJ); 20) *Originality and Superior Excellance of the Mosaic Institutions* (TJ); 21) *Philosophical Empiricism* (JA); 22) *The Present State of Europe Compared with Ancient Prophecies* (TJ); 23) *Socrates and Jesus Compared* (TJ); 24) *The Triumph of Truth* (TJ); and 25) *The Use of Christianity in Difficult Times* (TJ). See L. Swift, ed., *Catalogue of the John Adams Library in the Public Library of the City of Boston* (Boston, 1917) and E. M. Sowerby, *Catalogue of the Library of Thomas Jefferson* (Washington, D.C., 1952–59). It must be stressed that, due to the distribution of the libraries both men created, the above list is minimal. (See, on this, D. L. Wilson, 'Sowerby Revisited,' *William and Mary Quarterly*, 3d ser., 41[1984]: 615–28.) Adams's annotations in his copies of Priestley were published by Z. Haraszti, 'John Adams on Dr. Priestley: His Marginal Notes on Priestley's Theological Works Now First Published,' *More Books: The Bulletin of the Boston Public Library*, 10(1935): 301–318, and reprinted (in less satisfactory form) in Haraszti, *John Adams and the Prophets of Progress* (Cambridge, Mass., 1952): 280–99.

[7] See now the splendid edition and commentary, D. W. Adams, ed., *Jefferson's Extracts from the Gospels* (Princeton, 1983).

them.' But, their 'Platonism' resulted in 'nonsense'. The names
for this corrupting force vary, but most usually it is identified as
'Platonic Phylosophers, Platonic Jews or Christians' (Cappon
2:410–11). In opposition to the 'genuine system' of either Judaism
or, more markedly, Christianity, there stands 'the Platonizing
Philo or the Philonizing Plato'[8] whose doctrines are 'at least as
absurd ... [and] less intelligible' than those of the Amerindians.
Behind Plato stands the 'doctrines of the Oriental and Egyptian
Philosophers' from whom he 'borrowed' (Cappon 2:309). Plato,
as a philosopher of his own time, was bad enough. He had an
habitually 'foggy mind'. In comparison to Xenophon, 'his
dialogues are libels on Socrates.' His *Republic* is 'nonsense',
characterized by 'whimsies ... puerilities, and unintelligible jargon ... sophisms, futilities, and incomprehensibilities' (Cappon
2:432–3).[9] Far worse, was his baleful influence on later Christian
thinkers:

> The Christian priesthood, finding the doctrines of Christ
> levelled to every understanding, and too plain to need

[8] Adams, here, repeats the tag, variously given as *hē Platōn philōnizei, hē Philōn
platōnizei* or *hē Platōn ephilōnisen, hē Philōn eplatōnisen* in the *Suda*, s.v. *Platōn* (*Lexicon
graecae et latine* [Cambridge, 1705], 3:613); Photius, *Bibliotheca* 105; Jerome, *De viris
illust.* 11 and elsewhere. This tag was much repeated in seventeenth and eighteenth century
antiquarian literature; see, for example, J. Healey, *St. Augustine, Of the Citie of God, with
the learned comments of J. L. Vives* (London, 1616), 17:20, 'It was a proverbe, Philo either
Platonized or Plato Philonized.' Priestley employed the tag as least once (*TR* 4:409).

[9] Jefferson on Plato (and Priestley) is consistent. See, among others, Jefferson to
William Short, October 31, 1819: 'Plato ... dealing out mysticisms incomprehensible to
the human mind, has been deified by certain sects usurping the name of Christians;
because, in his foggy conceptions, they found a basis of impenetrable darkness whereon to
rear fabrications as delirious, of their own invention. These, they fathered blasphemously
on Him who they claim as their founder ... The establishment of the innocent and genuine
character of this benevolent moralist [Jesus], and rescuing it from the imputation of
imposture, which has resulted from artificial systems (e.g. the immaculate conception of
Jesus, His deification, the creation of the world by Him, His miraculous powers, His
resurrection and visible ascension, His corporeal presence in the Eucharist, the Trinity,
original sin, atonement, regeneration, elections, orders of Hierarchy, &c.) invented by
ultra-Christian sects, unauthorized by a single word ever uttered by Him, is a most
desirable object, and one to which Priestley has successfully devoted his labors and
learning. It would in time, it is to be hoped, effect a quiet euthanasia of the heresy of
bigotry and fanaticism which have so long triumphed over human reason and mankind ...
this work is to be done by winnowing the grain from the chaff of the historians of His life'
(Lipscomb-Bergh 15:383–85). The anti-Platonism of Jefferson is well treated in K. Leh-
mann, *Thomas Jefferson: American Humanist* (Chicago, 1947): 84–86, et passim., and
D. J. Boorstein, *The Lost World of Thomas Jefferson*, 2nd ed. (Chicago, 1981): 159–62.

explanation, saw, in the mysticisms of Plato, material with which they might build up an artificial system which might, from it's indistinctness, admit everlasting controversy, giving employment for their order and introduce it to profit, power and preeminence. The doctrines which flowed from the lips of Jesus himself are within the comprehension of a child; but thousands of volumes have not yet explained the Platonisms engrafted on them: and for this obvious reason that nonsense can never be explained. (Cappon 2:433)

Most pernicious of these 'Platonisms' was the 'fabrication of the Christian Trinity' (Cappon 2:411; cf. Cappon 2:368, 'it is too late in the day for men of sincerity to pretend they believe in the Platonic mysticisms that three are one and one is three; and yet the one is not three and the three are not one'). Faced with these 'corruptions', the task becomes, in Jefferson's striking phrase, already quoted, 'to prepare this euthanasia for Platonic Christianity, and it's restoration to the primitive simplicity of it's founder' (Cappon 2:385).

In forty-three years of theological disputation, Joseph Priestley worked at an agendum first set out with clarity in his *Free Address to Protestant Dissenters* in 1768: he will 'first, exhibit the genuine scripture doctrine upon the [given] subject, and then ... trace the corruptions of it in an historical manner; accounting for them as well as we can' (*JPTW* 21:252). He credits Nathaniel Lardner with teaching him this approach when the latter argued, in his *Letter* on the Logos (1730) that the first 'corruptors' of 'primitive' Christianity were the Christian Pythagoreans and Platonists; their chief corruption, the doctrine of the Trinity; and their motivation, the attempt to make Christianity more 'palatable' to pagan converts.[10] In Priestley's writings, this brief narrative yielded a model employing a diverse vocabulary in order to state six relatively simple historical claims:

A) A group, variously called 'philosophical Christians' as

---

[10] N. Lardner, *A Letter Written in the Year 1730 Concerning the Question Whether the Logos Supplied the Place of a Human Soul in the Person of Jesus Christ*, 1st ed. (London, 1759); I cite its convenient reprint in *The Works of Nathaniel Lardner, D.D.* (London, 1838), 10:73–185. For the summary above, see esp., 10:85–86, 103 and 164. For Priestley's testimony to Lardner's influence on his work, see Rutt, *Life* 1.1:69; *JPTW* 18:40. Indeed, Lardner edited Priestley's first published theological work (Rutt, *Life* 1.1:48; *JPTW* 3:9).

opposed to 'simple' or 'illiterate' Christians (*JPTW* 2:404; 5:27, 28, 43, 44; 6:167; 8:138–40; 18:19), or 'platonizing Christians' (*JPTW* 6:204, 245; 8:118, 198, 284; 18:86; *TR* 4:409)

B) 'adapted' (*JPTW* 5:234, 241; 6:152), 'accomodated' (*JPTW* 5:157; 13:10), 'added' (*JPTW* 2:405; 5:233; 18:9; 21:227; *TR* 4:307), 'adopted' (*JPTW* 1.2:16; 3:357–8, 399; 5:20, 40, 47, 217, 243; 6:196; 13:9), made 'agreeable' (*JPTW* 13:9), 'annexed' (*JPTW* 5:234), 'applied' (*JPTW* 5:234; 18:19), 'borrowed' (*JPTW* 6:65; 18:40, 50), 'brought forward' (*TR* 4:89), 'built [on]' (*JPTW* 5:97, 121, 225), 'caught at' (*JPTW* 5:30), '[allowed to] come in' (*JPTW* 5:4), 'converted' (*JPTW* 5:26, 33), 'copied' (*JPTW* 5:200), '[allowed to] creep in' (*JPTW* 21:252, 375), 'derived' (*JPTW* 3:391, 397), 'diffused' (*JPTW* 3:388), 'extended' (*JPTW* 5:183), 'formed' (*JPTW* 6:361), 'gave a handle to' (*JPTW* 6:168; *TR* 4:383), 'got' (*JPTW* 5:27), 'got the idea' (*JPTW* 5:60), 'incorporated' (*JPTW* 3:389 – the phrase is 'unnaturally incorporated'), 'inferred' (*JPTW* 5:93, 97), 'introduced' (*JPTW* 3:208, 220, 404, 416; 4:466; 5:18, 19, 21, 30, 45, 63, 91, 159, 183, 188, 233; 8:137; 13:9; 21:254), 'learned' (*JPTW* 5:27, 181), 'were led' (*JPTW* 5:60, 180; 21:375), 'mixed' (*JPTW* 3:256, 413; 5:26; 8:198; 21:375), 'modified' (*JPTW* 5:59), 'received' (*JPTW* 3:336), 'substituted' (*JPTW* 5:198), '[had] suggested' (*JPTW* 21:305), 'superadded' (*JPTW* 5:232; 21:277; *TR* 4:307), 'took up' (*JPTW* 6:160), or 'went into' (*JPTW* 3:358 – the phrase is 'went into the depths')

C) religious ideas and practices taken from 'Heathenism' (*JPTW* 3:389; 5:18, 181; 21:375), 'Oriental Philosophy' (*JPTW* 3:386, 391, 399, 403; 5:24, 217; 7:221; 8:119; 21:375), 'Pagan Philosophy' (*JPTW* 5:188; 18:50 – sometimes 'Greek philosophy', e.g. 5:24–25), or 'Platonism' (*JPTW* 5:19, 25, 161, 181, 188; 6:9, 44, 63, 152; 8:19, 44; *TR* 4:97, 383)

D) thus 'contaminating' (*JPTW* 8:119), 'corrupting' (the most common single term, e.g. *JPTW* 2:79, 146, 395, 407; 3:257, 258, 417, 446; 4:466; 5:3, 4, 7, 8, 9, 18, 23, 27, 90, 91, 179, 180, 192, 243; 6:62; 8:120, 137; 13:9; 14:29–31), and 'infecting' (*JPTW* 3:389; 5:25)

E) 'ancient doctrine' (*JPTW* 5:23) or, more commonly, 'apostolic' (*JPTW* 3:304; 8:198; *TR* 4:71), 'genuine' (*JPTW* 2:407; 5:8, 52, 220; 14:480; 21:374, compare the phrases: 'genuine doctrine of revelation' [5:91], 'genuine Christian principles' [5:27] and 'primitive and genuine doctrine' [5:92]), 'original' (*JPTW* 1.1:362; 5:8, 9, 232), 'plain' (*JPTW* 5:14, 18, cf. 'naked' 5:100), 'proper' (*JPTW* 5:138), 'primitive' (*JPTW* 5:22, 58, 163, 237, 239; 8:120; 18:9; 21:277, 374), 'pristine' (*JPTW* 3:209), 'pure' (*JPTW* 2:407; 3:146; 5:3, 4, 7; 8:119), 'received' (*JPTW* 5:125), 'simple' (*JPTW* 5:21; 21:251), 'true' (*JPTW* 5:104), 'virgin' (*JPTW* 8:119) Christianity

F) resulting in 'absurdities' (*JPTW* 7:223), 'abuses' (*JPTW* 2:407; 5:7, 187, 231, 237, 243; 6:196; 8:120; 21:254), 'additions' (*JPTW* 5:232), 'change' (*JPTW* 5:27, 163, 232, 238), 'confusion' (*JPTW* 6:180 ['strange confusion'], 196; *TR* 4:90), 'corruptions' (see above), 'darkness' (*JPTW* 5:90, 243), 'debasements' (*JPTW* 3:327; 5:4, 7; 21:375), 'defections' (*JPTW* 5:23), 'departures' (*JPTW* 5:8, 9, 23, 92), 'disfigurements' (*JPTW* 5:92), 'depravities' (*JPTW* 5:92, 231), 'deviations' (*JPTW* 5:8, 232; 21:277), 'embarrassments' (*JPTW* 5:90), 'errors' (*JPTW* 5:238; 21:251), 'false [notions]' (*JPTW* 21:375), 'foreign [ideas]' (*JPTW* 3:209, 252, 257; 4:466; 5:4), 'Christian idolatry' (*JPTW* 5:23, 180, 205; 6:375; 8:120; 21:262) or 'Christian polytheism' (*JPTW* 5:40; 6:373, 375), 'incumberances' (*JPTW* 21:252), 'influences' (*JPTW* 17:442), 'infringements' (*JPTW* 5:91), 'innovations' (*JPTW* 1.1:362; 5:8, 20, 22, 196), 'leaven' (*JPTW* 3:209 ['corrupt leaven'], 404), 'loads' (*JPTW* 3:446), 'mischief' (*JPTW* 17:442), 'misleadings' (*JPTW* 5:105), 'misrepresentations' (*JPTW* 5:92; 13:10), 'mixtures' (*JPTW* 3:207 ['heterogenous mixture']; 17:442 ['unnatural mixture'], 'modern [notions]' (*JPTW* 5:122), 'modifications' (*JPTW* 5:92), 'novelties' (*JPTW* 5:18, 31, 40, 45, 232, 233), 'obscurisms' (*JPTW* 5:4), 'superstructures' (*JPTW* 5:121), 'superstitions' (*JPTW* 5:232, 238; 21:249, 251), 'taints' (*JPTW* 2:406; 3:392), 'tinctures' (*JPTW* 3:416; 21:251), and 'tinges' (*JPTW* 6:152).[11]

To restate the model in its simplest terms, Priestley held that A) philosophical or platonizing Christians, in the early Christian centuries, B) adopted C) religious ideas taken from contemporary

---

[11] In the above, I have sought to provide only a few instances of each term, including the most striking, rather than a complete concordance. I have occasionally altered the grammatical form of a given word in constructing the list.

Greek thought – of either 'Oriental' or 'Platonic' derivation[12] – which D) corrupted E) the purity of primitive Christianity F) so as to result in either Christian idolatry (i.e., 'Papism' embarrassing to post-Reformation Christians as well as 'Jews and Mahommedans') or philosophical absurdities which made Christianity seem ridiculous in the eyes of 'unbelievers' and critics of the 'Left'.[13]

[12] Although Priestley is not wholly consistent, he often appears to distinguish between two models of origination, the one an 'Oriental-Gnostic' model, the other a 'Platonic-Philonic' one. The 'Oriental-Gnostic' model is more diffuse (see, among other passages, *JPTW* 2:74; 3:220, 336, 388–96, 403–4; 6:63–65; 8:119; 17:458; 18:50; 21:375). Ultimately transmitted from India ('Indostan') to Egypt and thence to Greece, it is antimaterialistic, especially with respect to the nature of the soul (this latter being a crucial concern of Priestley's more philosophical works, especially his *Disquisitions Relating to Matter and Spirit* [1777]) and dualistic with regard to the world and creation. It appears to have been generally 'in the air' in antiquity. The 'Platonic-Philonic' model has a more specific etiology (see, among other passages, *JPTW* 3:404–413; 6:152–204; 8:118, 138–42; Rutt, *Life* 1.2:16; *TR* 4:72, 77). It is most massively developed in *Corruptions* (*JPTW* 5:13–90). It largely focuses on the preexistence and divinity of Jesus (through connecting him with the Logos – an identification which, according to Priestley, does not antedate Justin [*JPTW* 3:359; 5:29–30; 6:63, 198, 201]) and is the result of 'philosophical Greeks' converting to Christianity. 'Ashamed of being the disciples of a man who had been crucified, they *naturally* gave a distinguished rank to the soul of Christ before he came into the world' (*JPTW* 2:404–5, emphasis added; see further, *JPTW* 2:216; 3:405, 416; 5:24; 6:201, 259–61; 18:19). The 'Oriental-Gnostic' model is, ultimately, one of 'world view,' and hence, framed in terms of a generic history of ideas; the 'Platonic-Philonic' model, on the other hand, is framed in terms of a specific psychological explanation. It is the latter model which is most highly developed in Priestley's mature works. Note that both of these models refer to doctrine and theologoumena. When speaking of (Roman Catholic) ritual practices, Priestley almost always simply asserts, without further explanation, that they were borrowed from 'paganism' (most massively in *JPTW* 5:217–311) resulting in 'Christian idolatry' (e.g. *JPTW* 21:262). Occasionally, he offers a psychological explanation similar to that of the 'Platonic-Philonic' model, e.g., 'heathen converts wishing to have what they had in paganism' introduced these 'borrowed' practices (*JPTW* 21:277–8). It should be noted that Priestley's frequent use of the term 'idolatry' to describe contemporary Christian praxis disturbed some of his stoutest supporters. See, among others, Th. Lindsey, to whom Priestley's *Corruptions* was dedicated, *Conversations on Christian Idolatry in the Year 1789* (London, 1791): viii, where Lindsey insists that the 'idolatry' of present Christians is 'of a very different nature from the heathen idolatry, so severely condemned in the sacred writings' (cf. Lindsey, *Conversations*: iii, 69–70). Why God should have 'permitted' doctrinal and cultic 'corruptions' remained an insoluble problem for Priestley (*JPTW* 2:407), although he affirms that 'this corrupt state of Christianity has, no doubt, been permitted by the Supreme Governor of the world for the best of purposes' (*JPTW* 5:4, cf. R. A. Schaberg, *Providence and Necessity: The World View of Joseph Priestley*, diss. St. Louis University [St. Louis, 1979]: 86–88).

[13] On this latter point, see the shrewd remarks on Priestley's 'two-fold apologetic' in E. W. Chapin, *The Theology of Joseph Priestley: A Study in Eighteenth Century Apologetics*, diss. Union Theological Seminary (New York, 1967): 50. For Priestley on 'papism' or 'popery,' see, among others, *JPTW* 2:79, 217; 3:220, 389; 11:7; 21:249, 251, 281; for his comments on 'Jews and Mahommedans,' see *JPTW* 2:395, 414; 5:90; 7:223; *TR* 1:124.

What is required is a 'further Reformation' (*JPTW* 5:7, cf. 15:74; 21:249), one which will employ 'the historical manner' (*JPTW* 21:252) in a thorough-going fashion.

This outline of the Priestley model of the course of Christian history, for all of its occasional eccentricities, should be thoroughly familiar to the reader. It is but a variant of the regnant, Protestant, apologetic, historiographical project described, more than a century ago, with provocative economy, by one of its most profound English students, Mark Pattison:

> The German reformation is imperfectly described as an appeal to scripture *versus* tradition. It was rather an appeal to history. The discovery had been made that the church, as it existed, was an institution which no longer corresponded to its original, that it was a corrupted, degraded, perverted institution. The appeal to scripture was not itself the moving spring of the reformation, it was the consequence of the sense of decay and degeneracy. As the doctrine of the fall of man was the key of human, so the doctrine of the corruption of the church was the key of ecclesiastical history. The reformation appealed to the bible, because in this earliest record of the church, it had a measure of the deviation from type which had been brought about.[14]

The scattered polemic references in the early reformers – a Melanchthon or a Calvin – to the 'pagan imprinting' on Roman Christianity, to this or that detail of Catholic praxis being the result of syncretism,[15] gave way to a full-blown history, to the

(On this aspect of the Unitarian apologetic, see, among others, the counter-polemic, [anonymous], *Historical and Critical Reflections upon Mahometanism and Socinianism in Four Treatises Concerning the Doctrine, Discipline and Worship of the Mahometans* [London, 1712]; 151–244. D. A. Pailin reprints a brief extract in his *Attitudes to Other Religions: Comparative Religion in Seventeenth- and Eighteenth-century England* [Manchester, 1984]: 270–3.) For Priestley's comments on contemporary 'unbelievers', see, among others, *JPTW* 3:99; 4:466; 10:535; 21:88, 252; Rutt, *Life* 1.1:198–200, 255–56.

[14] M. Pattison, *Isaac Casaubon: 1559–1614*, 2nd ed. (Oxford, 1892): 322. The same point is made by F. C. Baur, *Die Epochen der kirchlichen Geschichtsschreibung* (Tübingen, 1852): 39–40. See further, the important monograph by P. Polman, *L'Élément historique dans la controverse religieuse du XVIe siècle* (Gembloux, 1932), esp. pp. 1–277, in the series, Universitas Catholica Lovaniensis: Dissertationes, ser. 2, vol. 23.

[15] For Melanchthon, see, among others, *Apologia Confessionis Augustanae* (1530, in *CR* 27: cols. 419–644): cols. 515, 540, 543–555, 569, 587–95, et passim; *Oratio de Platone* (1538, in *CR* 11: cols. 413–25): esp. cols. 424–25. For Calvin, see, among others, *Institutio*

quest for origins and the narration of progressive degradation, whether as a result of 'infiltrations' from the non-Christian environment, or diabolical 'intervention' or 'invention'. The former historiographical task was first undertaken, in a sustained way, in the treatises on the origin of cultic 'errors' by Heinrich Bullinger (1528–9), Zwingli's successor at Zurich.[16] The latter was raised as the key to the interpretation of the entire sweep of Christian history in the thirteen folios of the *Magdeburg Centuries* (1559–74) by Mathias Flacius Illyricus and his colleagues.[17] The first model lays prime emphasis on external causality (and, frequently, adopts a lay perspective); the second model, while positing Satan as the ultimate cause, has an internal focus, with the papacy (or the AntiChrist) as the efficient cause of 'Christian error', and always adopts an institutional or sacerdotal perspective.

While Priestley was not immune from the latter model, with its apocalyptic unfolding of the *mysterium iniquitatis* (= *to mystēr-ion ... tēs anomias* of 2 Thess. 2.7) and the workings of the Antichrist as portrayed in Revelation 17 (*JPTW* 2:189; 5:393; 22:93; 25:324–25),[18] he was more profoundly influenced by the

---

christianae religionis (1530, in *CR* 30): cols. 80–90, 500, 867–91, 924–5, 1081–89, et passim.; cf. *Traité des reliques* (1543) in *CR* 34:405–42.

[16] H. Bullinger, *De origine erroris libri duo* (Zürich, 1539), esp. fols. 107v–113r. See, Polman: 98–109.

[17] M. Flacius, et al., *Ecclesiastica historica* (Basel, 1559–74). While the focus of the work is primarily on the 'blemishing' of doctrine and Church institutions through the arrogance of the satanically inspired Roman papacy, a section (usually the sixth) of each *Century* is devoted to ritual 'corruption'. It is in the initial description of this, as occurring in the second century, that the dominant phrase, *mysterium iniquitatis* first occurs (2:109). It is not until the volume devoted to the fourth century, that there is a clear statement of external influence as both Jewish and gentile elements are borrowed into the Christian ritual (4:406). This process culminates in what is the thickest ritual description in the *Centuries*, the actions of Boniface IV in consecrating the Pantheon to '*omnium deorum gentilium*' in 7:229. On the *Centuries*, the classic treatment remains that of F. C. Baur, *Die Epochen der kirchlichen Geschichtschreibung*: 39–71; see further, R. Polman, 'Flacius Illyricus, Historien de l'église,' *Revue d'histoire ecclésiastique* 27(1931):27–73. It is, perhaps, of significance that when the Jesuit scholar, H. Pinard de la Boullaye, in his magisterial, *L'Étude comparée des religions* (Paris, 1922–25), 1–2, strongly criticized what he termed the '*méthode des antécédents*' in the study of Christian materials, he devoted considerable space to the *Centuries* as the progenitor of the method (2:117–26).

[18] There has yet to be a full study of Priestley's millenarianism. As with Newton, so with Priestley, the topic has been an embarrassment to his more scientifically inclined biographers. The best treatment, to date, is that by C. Garrett, *Respectable Folly: Millenarians and the French Revolution in France and England* (Baltimore, 1975): 126–43.

former, especially as developed by generations of anti-Trinitarian scholars and polemicists. Fortunately, we do not have to rehearse this intellectual history here. Much of the work has already been undertaken in Walter Glawe's important monograph, *Die helleni-sierung des Christentums* (1911)[19]; we need only pause at a few way-stations.

The first two points of rest, unaccountably overlooked by Glawe, would have to be the intellectual father of 'Unitarianism', the author of 'a new system of belief', Michael Servetus[20], and, secondly, the one with whom 'the history of the Unitarian movement in England properly [begins]',[21] Joseph Biddle.

Servetus's work on the *Trinity* (1531) is replete with scornful references to 'philosophers' (e.g., I.28, 29, 60; II.18, 20, 21; III.12), they are 'sophists' (I.15), 'lawyers' (I.24) and 'quibblers' (I.16); he charges that Christians have been 'led astray by your philosophy' (I.23).[22] This latter is especially the case with the doctrine of the Trinity. 'It arose out of Greek philosophy', rather than the gospel; it 'incurs the ridicule of the Mohammedans and the Jews' (I, argument; Wilbur: 3. Cf. I.58–59 where this 'horrible invention' causes 'Mohammedans to laugh' and Jews to dismiss Christianity as 'fancy', 'foolishness' and 'blasphemies' [Wilbur: 66–67]). The Trinity, with its 'cabbalistic metaphysics' (II.28) is a 'gross perversity' (II.16) by those who 'take pride in Platonizing' (II.4), an 'addition' or 'superimposition' (I.60) wrought by 'the plague of philosophy ... brought upon us by the Greeks' (I.60) who have forgotten that 'Christ was not speaking to philosophers ... but to the common people' (II.9; Wilbur: 83), and prefer allegory which 'is exceedingly silly and savours somewhat of Plato' (I.49; Wilbur: 43).

Writing a little more than a century later, Joseph Biddle, in his

---

[19] W. Glawe, *Die hellenisierung des Christentums in der Geschichte der Theologie von Luther bis auf die Gegenwart* (Berlin, 1912), in the series, Neue Studien zur Geschichte der Theologie und Kirche, 15.

[20] E. M. Wilbur, *A History of Unitarianism* (Boston, 1945), 1:49.

[21] Wilbur, *A History of Unitarianism*, 2:222.

[22] M. Servetus, *De Trinitatis erroribus libri septem* (The Hague, 1531), esp. books I–II. I have followed, throughout, the translation by E. M. Wilbur, *The Two Treatises of Servetus on the Trinity* (Cambridge, MA., 1932), in the series, Harvard Theological Studies, 16. For the circumstances surrounding the publication of this treatise, see Wilbur, *A History of Unitarianism*, 1:58–67.

Confession of Faith Touching the Holy Trinity (1648),[23] praises the reformers for cleansing Christianity from the 'Pollutions' and 'Filth of their [Roman Catholic] Superstition', while noting that further reformation is required: especially with respect to 'this Absurdity', the Trinity, which 'lying at the bottom corrupteth almost our whole Religion' (unpaginated p. 1). This 'Error', which is traceable to Justin Martyr, 'coming out of Plato's School' (unpaginated p. 5), 'partly came to pass' because the 'Fathers' were:

> great Admirers of Plato, and accordingly ... did in outward profession so put on Christ, as that in Heart they did not put off Plato, wittingly applying his high notions ... to what was simply and plainly spoken of the Man Christ Jesus ... partly, that they may thereby avoid the Scandal of worshipping a crucified man. (30)

This causality, which we have already encountered, at a later date in Priestley, was formulated, a few years after Biddle, in a set of four crisp propositions by Daniel Zwicker (1648). Justin was motivated, in Zwicker's account, to substitute a Platonic understanding of Christ for the gospel one 1) because of his love of Platonic philosophy, 2) because the memory of his 'Gentile' past was not wholly obliterated, 3) because of the hellenistic custom of elevating preeminent individuals to the rank of the gods, and 4) because of a 'horror' at worshipping one who was a mere man.[24]

This sort of anti-Trinitarian controversy literature grew until, in 1710, George Bull could complain, with acerbity, of the endless soundings of the Unitarians's battle-alarm. "Platonism, Platonism," say they, "first corrupted the pure tradition of the apostles."[25]

It has been worth our spending some time briefly recalling this

---

[23] J. Biddle, *A Confession of Faith Touching the Holy Trinity, According to the Scripture* (London, 1648). I cite the reprint from the so-called *Unitarian Tracts* (London, 1691), 1.1 (separately paginated) = *The Faith of One God ... Asserted and Defended, In Several Tracts Contained in this Volume* (London, 1691–1702), 1–2. For the circumstances surrounding the publication of this treatise, see Wilbur, *A History of Unitarianism*, 2:193–208.

[24] D. Zwicker, *Irenicum Irenicorum* (Amsterdam, 1648): 16–17. See further, Glawe: 38–41.

[25] G. Bull, *The Primitive and Apostolic Tradition*, in G. Bull, *Works on the Trinity* (Oxford, 1855), 3:270.

tradition in order to note its chief characteristic. With the rare exception of an Isaac Casaubon on *mystērion*,[26] or a George Bull on historical theology,[27] the comparisons it makes are largely matters of surface – 'Platonism' is employed as a generic noun, often triggered by a single word, most frequently *logos*, shorn of literary or intellectual context and historical situation. In this sense, 'Platonism' is a parallel to the generic notion of 'heathen' or 'pagan idolatry' or to that of 'superstition' employed with respect to Catholic cultic practices in the early reformers. From another perspective, these early essays may be seen as largely *comparing Christianity with itself*, or, more precisely, with an idealized version of itself (the 'simple gospel'). Any remainder was considered a 'corruption' for which the covering term was, most frequently, 'Platonism'. If queried as to the reason for this internal discrepancy between 'simple' and 'platonic Christianity', the answer given by the authors of these essays was, usually, a hypothetical, psychological one – the embarrassment of Christianity's philosophical converts.

The needed sophistication began to enter the theological discussion in 1700 with the anonymous publication of N. Souverain's, *Le Platonisme devoilé, ou Essai touchant le Verbe Platonicien*,[28] which has been termed, 'a landmark ... in the development of the notion of the hellenization' of Christianity (Glawe:115).

At first glance, Souverain may appear to be merely much, much more of the same. The vocabulary of vituperation we have

---

[26] I. Casaubon, *De rebus sacris et ecclesiasticus: Exercitationes XVI ad Cardinalis Baronii* (London, 1614); I cite a later edition, (Geneva, 1663): 477–500 (= Exercit. 16).

[27] G. Bull, *Defensio Fidei Nicaenae* (Oxford, 1685); Bull, *The Primitive and Apostolic Tradition ... Concerning the Divinity of Our Saviour Jesus Christ* (1710), in Bull, *Works on the Trinity*, 3:209–315.

[28] [N. Souverain], *Le Platonisme devoilé, ou Essai touchant le Verbe Platonicien* (Cologne, 1700). I have also consulted the German translation by J. F. C. Loffler, *Versuch über den Platonismus der Kirchenväter, Oder Untersuchung über den Einfluss der platonischen Philosophie in den ersten Jahrhunderten*, 2nd ed. (Züllichau and Freystadt, 1792). To judge from copies in libraries, the German translation is far more common than the French original. Glawe:115–32 provides a publication history, an invaluable outline of the argument of the entire work, and a suggestive statement (p. 130) of its controversial place in the history of hellenization research, being attacked, equally, by both 'Unitarians' and 'Trinitarians'. However, my interests in Souverain's work, chiefly methodological, as reflected above, differ from his. See further the important monographic article by H. Stein, 'Der Streit über den angeblichen Platonismus der Kirchenväter,' *Zeitschrift für die historische Theologie*, 31(1861): 319–418, esp. 319–64.

grown used to recurs in every chapter: the sharp contrast between
the later 'platonic faith' and the original 'simple faith' (277,
291–2, 297, 318, 345, 355, 386, 389); the presence of a cabal of
'platonic Christian fathers' (115–6, 141, 335) and their *platonisme
outré* (75); the notion of the 'Christian-Platonic Trinity' (115),
and other 'abuses' (269), which represented 'tinctures' (1), 'fanati-
cisms' (75), 'impostures' (160), 'innovations' (316), 'embellish-
ments' (317) and 'corruptions' (318) which must be removed by
the application of the 'historian's method' (1). Likewise, familiar
from his predecessors is the claim that Justin was 'the first of the
platonizing fathers' (280, cf., 12, 187, 318, 385), and the explanation of the reasons for 'platonizing' being the conversion of Greek
philosophers to Christianity (92) and their embarrassment at the
'obscurity' of Jesus's birth and his 'shameful' death on the Cross
(246). He introduces, as well, the old patristic explanation (e.g.,
Justin, *Dial.* XIX) of God's 'accomodation' or 'condescension'
(50, 142, 315, 357). Yet, all is most certainly not the same. Simply
put, Souverain recognizes *difference*. He offers specific historical
explanations which provide context. For example, Justin's doctrine of the *logos*, Souverain asserts, was developed as a response
to a contemporary issue, the attempt to prove that Christianity
was not a novel religion. For Justin, 'the Christ has preexisted,
just as Christianity and Christians have preexisted' (187–8). On
another matter, Souverain writes, the Prologue of John, rather
than being influenced by Platonism, borrowed the term and the
understanding of *logos* from Jewish wisdom speculation where it
is a 'figurative' language 'never extended to persons'. It is foolish
to think of the Prologue as growing out of 'platonic dualism', he
continues, because its major purpose is 'anti-docetic' (11–14,
25–28, 140–52). Of greater significance to our inquiry, and
suggested by this latter example, Souverain recognizes *semantic
difference*, that is to say, the same word can have different
meanings, or, more pointedly, 'this is the comedy played by the
Trinitarians', to keep the words and change the meanings
(233–35, cf., 117). Neither language nor meaning is stable. Thus:

> The three Hypostases had one meaning among the Platon-
> ists, another meaning among the Athanasians, another
> meaning among the disciples of Arius, and ten other

[meanings] among us ... *The term is a Proteus*, which assumes all sorts of forms and significations. (236–7, emphasis added.)

Subsequent scholarly discussions by anti-Trinitarians concerning the 'corruptions' of 'Platonism', up through Priestley, will continue to follow the directions pioneered by Souverain, with, however, the added difficulty of confronting the contemporary revival of Platonic theology by the Cambridge Platonists and others. Mosheim remains an extremely sophisticated eighteenth century example of this latter endeavour;[29] Lord Bolingbroke, a

[29] J. L. Mosheim, *De rebus christianorum ante Constantinum Magnum Commentarii* (Helmstadt, 1753); I cite the English translation, *Historical Commentaries on the State of Christianity during the First Three Hundred and Twenty-five Years of the Christian Era* (New York, 1856), 1–2. In this work, Mosheim is most interesting for developing an insight first strongly brought to bear on the issue of 'Platonism' and early Christianity in Souverain (68–90, et passim) – the influence of Christian gnosticism. See the large blocks of exposition, for the *first two* centuries, in Mosheim, 1:228–56, 405–512, and, especially, 1:32(nn. 2, 3), 48, 78, 118 n. 1, 288, 230, 232, 233 n. 1, 234 n. 2. The most significant passage, for our purposes, reads: 'The early Christian fathers, who were acquainted with none other besides the Grecian system of philosophy [in Mosheim's view, the two modes of ancient philosophizing were the 'Grecian' and the 'Oriental' (1:30–48)], perceiving that some of the dogmas of the Gnostics coincided with the principles of the Platonists, were induced to conclude that the discipline of the former had been altogether generated by a conjunction of the platonic philosophy with Christianity: to this opinion great numbers of the learned of modern days have likewise subscribed, so many indeed, that they are scarcely to be enumerated. After having, however, examined the subject with every possible degree of impartiality and attention, I am most thoroughly convinced that the founders of the Gnostic schools cannot, with the least propriety, be reckoned among the followers of Plato. *With regard to certain particulars taken separately, I am very ready to admit that there is no great want of resemblance between the Platonic philosophy and the doctrine of the Gnostics; but only let the two systems be compared together, as they ought to be, in toto*, and the great dissimilarity that exists between them becomes at once conspicuous' (1:233 n. 1 – emphasis added). A major methodological principle is here enunciated.

Another persistent element in Mosheim's history is the centrality he gives to Alexandrian Neo-Platonism (particularly, and in this he resembles Souverain, its heavy reliance on allegory) as the source of 'error': 'Nearly all those corruptions, by which, in the second and subsequent centuries, Christianity was disfigured, and its pristine simplicity and innocence almost wholly effaced, had their origin in Egypt' (1:369). In this, the Christians were followers of Philo (1:384–6, 379–80[n. 2, cont'd], et passim). At other points, Mosheim is more conventional: the mysteries were borrowed from 'paganism' and introduced into Christian worship to make Christianity more palatable to 'heathen converts' (1:19–20 [and n. 5], 390–393 [and nn. 1–2]); relics and statues of martyrs, and the notion of their intercession, were 'accomodations' to popular piety which 'degenerated into a pernicious kind of superstition ... becoming a source of corruption in the true religion ... nearly similar to those which the heathens of old were accustomed to pay to their demi-gods and heroes' (1:135, 136 n. 2).

See further Mosheim's annotated translation of Cudworth, *Systema intellectuale huius*

more savagely polemic instance,[30] deeply influential, however, on figures such as Jefferson.[31]

To this collection of anti-Trinitarian writers concerned with 'Christian Platonism' and its 'corruptions', must be added a second group, signaled by Jefferson's astonishing declaration to Adams that:

> I have read his [Priestley's] Corruptions of Christianity, and Early Opinions of Jesus, over and over again; and I rest on them, and on Middleton's writings, especially his letters from Rome, and [his letter] to Waterland, as the basis of my own faith. These writings have never been answered ... therefore I cling to their learning, so much superior to my own. (Cappon 2:369)

The name of Middleton, here joined with that of Priestley, introduces us to the literature of 'Pagano-papism', a term first

---

universi (Jena, 1733): 674, 682, et passim, and Mosheim's dissertation, *De turbata per recentiores Platonicos ecclesia Commentatio* (1725) bound in with the *Systema* and separately paginated (pp. 1–47). In evaluating Mosheim on gnosticism from our present vantage point, it should be recalled that central texts such as Hippolytus's *Philosophoumena* were not yet available to the scholar (A. Momigliano, *Essays in Ancient and Modern Historiography* [Middletown, 1977]: 317), let alone the Coptic-Gnostic materials. Glawe: 150–76 has a lengthy treatment of Mosheim, whom he terms the 'qualitative highpoint' in the development of the notion of hellenization in contrast to Souverain, whom he terms the 'quantitative highpoint'.

[30] Although brutal, John Leland's comment on Bolingbroke is not far off the mark: '[He is] seized with a sort of madness, when certain subjects come his way – metaphysics – artificial theology – Plato and Platonic philosophy ... but above all, the Christian divines and clergy. These, when he happens to meet with them, bring one of his fits upon him, and often set him a raving for several pages together.' (J. Leland, *A View of the Principal Deistical Writers that have Appeared in England during the last two Centuries*, 4th ed., rp. [London, 1836]: 249). Examples of Bolingbroke's frenzy on the subject of 'the lofty madness of Plato' and his baleful influence on Christian thought abound. See the edition by G. Mallet, *The Philosophical Works of the Late Honorable Henry St. John, Lord Viscount Bolingbroke* (London, 1754–77), 1–5, among other passages, 1:7–8, 46, 57, 66, 71, 73, 122, 131, 146, 148, 224–5, 240–1, 332, 341; 2:22–3, 61, 71–2, 80, 83–114, 120, 124, 180, 332–3, 358–9, 363, 368, 382; 3:5, 128–9, 135, 140–1, 307, 347–8; 4:34, 344, 357, 501. For all his lack of sympathy for Bolingbroke's philosophical presuppositions, D. G. James, *The Life of Reason: Hobbes, Locke, Bolingbroke* (London, 1949): 241–67 has some shrewd observations.

[31] See the lengthy set of extracts copied out from Bolingbroke by a youthful Jefferson in his 'Commonplace Book' as reprinted in G. Chinard, *The Literary Bible of Thomas Jefferson: His Commonplace Book of Philosophers and Poets* (Baltimore-Paris, 1928): 40–71. Chinard's judgement that 'no single influence was stronger on Jefferson's formation and none was more continuous' than Bolingbroke (p. 20) has proved controversial.

employed in English by John Corbet in 1667,[32] a quarrelsome post-Reformation literature with titles such as *Heydnisches Papstthum* and *Ethnico-Pontifica Conformitate*.[33] As I have discussed this subject elsewhere,[34] it is possible, here, to be brief.

Growing out of the work of Humanist antiquarians, a considerable collection of 'similarities' between 'pagan' and Christian practice became available.[35] In their earlier form, such as in the *De rerum inventoribus* of Polydorus Vergil (1499 and 1517), these parallels were used, sporadically, to indicate Christian 'borrowing', usually by the laity who were assumed to be prone to 'superstition'.[36] As such, this was the opposite of the explanation

[32] J. Corbet, *A Discourse of the Religion of England* (London, 1667): 17.

[33] Titles cited in J. G. Walch, *Bibliotheca Theologica Selecta* (Jena, 1758), 2:371–73. The actual works are unavailable to me.

[34] J. Z. Smith, *To Take Place: Toward Theory in Ritual* (Chicago, 1987): 96–101.

[35] A good example would be Guillaume du Choul, *Discours de la religion des anciens romains* (Lyons, 1556), a work largely constructed as a commentary on a collection of coins and medallions. There are a dozen instances of brief, parenthetical, comparisons – much as one finds in travellers' reports – between some Roman praxis and 'what we do today'. I would consider such parallels to be chiefly pedagogical. See, among others, *Discours*: 7, 216, 217, 219, 220, 229, 237, 250, 262, 274, 280, 284, 302, 309. However, there may be more here than meets the eye. At one point, du Choul refers to the 'ridiculous superstitions of the Gentiles' which 'we have transferred to our Christian religion' (263). See, further, the useful over-view of the antiquarian tradition by A. Momigliano, *Studies in Historiography* (New York, 1966): 1–39.

[36] I have been able to consult only a later edition of the 2nd version, *De rerum inventoribus liber octo* (Gryphium, 1546). See, among the several translations, *The Works of the Famous Antiquary, Polidore Virgil ... English't by John Langley* (London, 1663, rp. New York, 1868): 142, 143, 148–52, 161, 162, 166–7, 172, 178, 189, 191, et passim. Some indication of the wide circulation of this work can be gained from J. Ferguson, *Handlist of Editions of Polydore Vergil's De inventoribus Rerum* (New Haven, 1944) who cites 90 editions of the two versions of the Latin text.

The theme of the 'superstitious' laity was further developed by another sort of antiquarian, representative of what G. Cocchiara terms, 'folkloristic theology' (*The History of Folklore in Europe* [Philadelphia, 1981]: 58). At times, their works are simply Herodotus-like ethnographies, presenting the curiousities of 'popish' church and folk practice as if describing a foreign tribe. Th. Kirchmeir (=Neogeorgus), *Das Päpistisch Reich* (n.p., 1555), esp. Bks. I and IV is a characteristic example. There is no suggestion here of borrowing. The one reference, describing Shrove Tuesday customs as constituting a 'Bacchic feast'(IV.10, unpaginated) is a characterization, not a genealogy. The English translation of Kirchmeir's work, by the Puritan author, B. Googe, *The Popish Kingdome or reigne of Antichrist* (London, 1570; rp. London, 1880) adds a number of these characterizations, none of which are found in the original German text. See, for example: 'Their feasts and all their holidayes they kepe throughout the yeare! Are full of vile Idolatrie, and heathenlike appeare' (44r). More closely related to the themes we have been tracing is the sort of folkloristic tradition represented by the work of H. Bourne, *Antiquitates Vulgares; or, the Antiquities of the Common People* (London, 1725). While many customs are treated as

offered by the anti-Trinitarians who located the centre of 'borrowing' among the elite, the 'Christian-Platonic philosophers'. In the writings of the Protestant polemicists against 'Pagano-papism', the two were joined, along with the old anti-Catholic perspective of the *Centuries*: it was the Roman Catholic hierarchy who introduced novel practices, for their own self-aggrandisement, having borrowed them from 'paganism'.[37]

'heathenish' popular survivals, they are also linked to direct Catholic borrowing; for example: 'There need be no Question, but as this Custom is practically Heathenish, so it is also originally: For the Heathens were wont to worship Streams and Fountains, and to suppose that the Nymphs, whom they imagin'd the Goddesses of the Water, presided over them. As the Papists have borrowed many of their silly and superstitious Ceremonies from the Religion of the Heathens, so this in particular, a sottish, stupid, and abominable Custom, they could borrow no where else' (69). Bourne's work was incorporated, in its entirety, in the first edition of John Brand's influential book, *Observations on Popular Antiquities: including the whole of Mr. Bourne's Antiquitates Vulgares* (Newcastle-on-Tyne, 1777). Subsequent editions of Brand's book have reduced Bourne to one of Brand's sources and removed the polemics. Like Bourne, Brand, in the first edition of *Observations*, argues both survival and 'papal' borrowing from 'heathen Rome' (iii–ix, as reprinted in R. M. Dorson, *Peasant Customs and Savage Myths* [Chicago, 1968], 1:6–12). See further, R. M. Dorson, *The British Folklorists: A History* (Chicago, 1968), chapter 1, esp. 10–22.

[37] See, among others, [J. Poirée (?)], *Traité des anciennes cérémonies: ou Histoire contenant leur naissance & accroissement, leur entrée en l'Église & par quels degrez ont passé iusques à la superstition* (n.p., 1662): 8–9, 14, 15, 38–9, 41, 56 for 'imitations' during the first four centuries, largely attributed to 'the common people.' After the fourth century, in a manner reminiscent of the ideology of the *Centuries*, a succession of Popes 'ordain' each successive 'corruption' (56–83) as the 'simplicity of Christianity' is transformed, by the Roman Church, into the 'magnificence of paganism' (23). An interesting feature of this work is its rigid chronological framework. See the summary table of ceremonial innovation in chronological order (unpaginated, sig. uij). I regret that I have been unable to obtain the English translation (by T. Douglas), *Vitis Degeneris: or, the Degenerate-Plant, Being a Treatise of antient Ceremonies. Containing an historical Account of their Rise and Growth, their first Entrance into the Church, and their gradual Advancement to Superstition therein* (London, 1668).

Two other representative works may be cited, each of which displays a characteristic, and influential, variation on the same polemic theme. 1) P. Mussard, *Les Conformitez des cérémonies modernes aves les anciennes. Où il est prouvé par des authoritez incontestables que les Cérémonies de l'Église Romaine sont empruntées des payens* (n.p. [Geneva], 1667), which sets out to juxtapose the 'simplicity' of the Christian cultus of the first three centuries with the 'confusion' and 'illness' of the Roman Church with its 'pomp and ceremonies' (235–6, 239, 252, 257). It employs an unusually rich vocabulary of similarity between 'pagan' and Catholic rituals. Analyzing just two chapters, Mussard states that the one: 'parallels' (12), is 'the same' or 'the same thing' (12, 23, 27, 36, 39, 45), 'resembles' (13–14), 'is comparable' (14), 'conforms' (14, 16, 24, 25, 28, 49, 56), 'is like:' (35), 'imitates' (25, 47, 49, 52, 56, 59), 'follows' (55), 'has also' (33, 35, 41), 'takes its origin from' (53, 55), 'is built on the model of' (59) the other. The comparisons range across the full dossier: papal names and functions (12–28), ecclesiastical habits (34–5), monasticism and asceticism (40–60), the mass (60–86), religious processions (86–102), feasts (102–27), saints (128–45), temples (146–68), relics (168–84), images (184–221), etc. An unusual element is Mussard's appeal to linguistic data:

Conyers Middleton, *A Letter from Rome Shewing an Exact Conformity between Popery and Paganism* (1729),[38] is a different sort of work than those we have been considering in at least one important respect. Its genre is that of ethnography rather than of the encyclopaedia,[39] that is to say, it is based, self-consciously, on first-hand experience rather than on book learning. 'My Observations are grounded on Facts, which I have been a Witness to myself' (ii). As such, the text is dominated by verbs of seeing – e.g., '[when one] begins to look about ... he will find his Eyes and Attention attracted ...' (21, cf. ii, 7, 8, 9, 11, 13, 14, 15, 21, 29, 37, 45, 50, 51, 54, 61) – and by the notion of 'printed figures' (10–11), 'sculptures' (16, 18), and 'coins' (18). Thus, his initial description:

> The very first thing that a Stranger must necessarily take Notice of, as soon as He enters their Churches, is the use of Incense or Perfumes in their Religious Offices: The first Step he takes within the Door will be sure to make him sensible of it ... A custom received directly from Paganism; and which presently called to my Mind, the Old Descriptions of Heathen Temples and Altars, which are seldom or never mention'd by the Ancients without the Epithet of perfumed or incensed ... In the Old Bas-Reliefs, or Pieces of Sculpture, where any Heathen Sacrifice is represented, we never fail to observe a Boy in Sacred Habit, which is always white,

'the name, Pope, which is the same as that which the Scyths gave to Jupiter, their chief idol, according to Herodotus' (12); 'the word, mass, is taken from the superstitious rituals of Isis' (60, cf. Polydorus Vergil, V.9 [Langley:166–7]). 2) Th.Gale, *The Court of the Gentiles*, vol. 3, *The Vanity of Pagan Philosophy Demonstrated* (London, 1677), which announces the general thesis that 'all the great Errors brought into the Christian Church, both before and after the rise of the Antichrist, had their origins from Pagan Philosophie' (3:123). While chiefly focusing on doctrine, Gale makes a number of ritual parallels, see: 3:128–30, 171–214.

[38] C. Middleton, *A Letter from Rome Shewing an Exact Conformity between Paganism and Popery: Or, The Religion of the Present Romans to be derived entirely from that of their Heathen Ancestors* (London, 1729).

[39] See, Smith, *Map Is Not Territory* (Leiden, 1978): 244–53 and Smith, *Imagining Religion: From Babylon to Jamestown* (Chicago, 1982): 22–23. Perhaps the most revealing passage in Middleton on this point occurs early on in his exposition: 'Many of our Divines have, I know, with much Learning ... effectively prov'd the Crime of Idolatry on the Church of Rome: but these Controversies ... are not capable of giving that Conviction, which I immediately received from my Senses, the surest Witnesses of Fact in all Cases; and which no Man can fail to be furnished with, who sees Popery, as it is exercised in Italy ... This Similitude of Popish and Pagan Religion, seemed so evident and clear ...' (14).

with a little Chest or Box in his Hands, in which this Incense
is kept for the Use of the Altar. In the same manner still in
the Church of Rome, there is always a Boy in Surplice,
waiting on the Priest at the Altar ... (15–16.)

Between 1724 and 1725, Middleton undertook a journey to Italy,
most especially to Rome.[40] Middleton was already an anti-
Papist. He travelled, not out of 'any Motive of Devotion':

> My Zeal was not that of visiting the Holy Thresholds of the
> Apostles or kissing the feet of their Successor: I knew that
> their Ecclesiastical Antiquiaries were mostly fabulous or
> legendary; supported by Fictions and Impostures, too gross
> to employ the Attention of a Man of Sense.(9)

Rather than wishing to gaze at 'ridiculous Fictions of this Kind',
Middleton hoped to encounter the 'genuine Remains and vener-
able Reliques of Pagan Rome; the authentic Monuments of
Antiquity'. He keenly anticipated his 'Joy at viewing the very
Place and Scene of these important [ancient] Events ... treading
on that ground ... [where the] Great Heroes of Antiquity had
been personally engaged', (11) and he was uninterested in the
'present Religion of the Place' (13). But his plan was to prove
impossible. For it was the present rather than the antique Roman
rituals which occupied the foreground of his vision. To his (at
least, claimed) surprise, the new turned out to be all but identical
to the old. 'All these [Roman Catholic] Ceremonies appear
plainly to have been copied from the Ritual of Primitive
Paganism, as if handed down by an uninterrupted Succession
from the Priests of Old to the Priests of New Rome' (13). As he
called to mind some ancient passage, portrait or coin, he
discovered, 'the same Ceremony was described, as transacted in
the same Form and Manner, and in the same Place ... where I
now saw it before my eyes' (13–14). It was 'the same Temples, at
the same Altars, sometimes [before] the same Images, and always
with the same Ceremonies' (69–70). He goes on to describe, in
colourful detail, eleven such areas of parallelism (15–67), all of
which he has been 'a Witness to myself' (ii).
What had occurred, Middleton believes, reviving an old

---

[40] I have taken this paragraph, with some revision, from Smith, *To Take Place*: 96–98.

reformer's charge,[41] was a process of linguistic sleight-of-hand. He returns to this theme insistently throughout the *Letter*. The present, Catholic ritual activities are but 'verbal Translations of the old Originals of Heathenism' (26). 'By a Change only of Name they have found the means to return to the Thing' (31). They have 'changed the Name rather than the Object of their Worship (33, cf.36–37). The issue is not one of similarity, but of persistence and identity.

To the two major polemic traditions we have reviewed – the anti-Platonic/anti-Trinitarian controversialists who focused on matters of thought and the history of ideas, and the 'Pagano-papists' who concentrated on ritual parallels – the same sort of comments can be brought. With a few notable exceptions, their comparisons between Christianity and the religions of Late Antiquity were based on the co-occurrence of a single word or a single image, largely shorn of all context, be it historical or literary. This is an effective rhetorical tactic. It reduces one's opponent to thinness and transparency. It raises no questions as to meaning and interpretation. Lacking 'thick description', the 'other' lacks recognizable humanity as well. Nothing is seen as problematic; all is surface, possessing utter self-evidence. There is, thus, no parity between the two terms of the comparison. This problem, to which we shall return in later chapters, is exacerbated in the traditions we have been considering in that both terms of the comparison, the 'pagan' and the 'papist', were considered 'other' with respect to 'genuine' Christianity by their Protestant opponents. Nevertheless, the broader issues remain even when their apologetic context is less overt, when one term – the early Christian – is more highly valued than the other, as, for example, in the footnotes in biblical commentaries up to the present day.

With these observations, we have concluded our introduction to what the *Philadelphia Aurora* in 1790 termed 'the Priestleyan Age'.[42] However, historical periodizations require at least two

[41] See, among others, Martin Chemnitz, *Examiniis Concilii Tridentini* (Frankfurt, 1565–73), I cite a modern edition (Berlin, 1861): 711. 'Between pagan idolatry and the invocation of saints, there is only a difference of names ...'

[42] I have taken this quote from Priestley's savage American opponent, William Cobbett. See Cobbett, *Porcupine's Works containing various Writings and Selections exhibiting a faithful Picture of the United States ... from the Ends of the War, in 1783, to the Election of the President in March, 1801* (London, 1801), 7:169.

terms to be interesting. For the second, we must return to the
Adams–Jefferson correspondence.

II

Rather late in their exchange (September 30, 1816), a new name
enters into the discussions on religion between Adams and
Jefferson, although still linked, at least initially, with that of
Priestley. After noting the affects of increasing age, Adams writes:
'When I read Dr. Priestley's Remarks upon *Du Puis*, I felt a
Curiousity to know more about him' (Cappon 2:489).[43] This
curiousity carried a high price: the reading of twelve octavo
volumes. Jefferson answers that he is in awe of Adams's industry,
but that he is content to have read an abridged edition of Dupuis
by his friend and correspondent, Destutt de Tracy;[44] besides, it

[43] These 'Remarks' are unidentified by the editor of the correspondence, but clearly
refer to Priestley's *A Comparison of the Institutions of Moses* (see below). As best as I can
determine, Priestley's first mention of Dupuis is in his *Observations on the Increase of
Infidelity* (1795) in which he notes: 'Just before I left England, I had sent to me (I believe
with the consent of the author) the plan of a very large and elaborate work, entitled, A
History of all the Forms of Worship and of all the Religions in the World … I shall be
glad to see this curious volume' (*JPTW* 17:87). Within a few years, Priestley has read and
attacked the book, most especially in *A Comparison of the Institutions of Moses with those of
the Hindoos and other Nations with Remarks on Mr. Dupuis's Origin of all Religions* (1799), a
copy of which Adams owned and lightly annotated (L. Swift, *Catalogue of the John Adams
Library*:201). Priestley devotes a substantial section of his monograph to these 'Remarks'
(*JPTW* 17:320–59). Dupuis's book is the 'plus ultra of infidelity,' 'the most extraordinary
production of the present or of any other age,' 'no man living has advanced more
extraordinary' opinions than Dupuis whose principle object 'is the overthrow of
Christianity' (*JPTW* 17:320, 325, 344). He complains that Dupuis, in his comparisons
between Christianity and other religions (discussed below) fails to distinguish between the
'original' and later 'corrupt' Christianity: 'One would think that a person who wrote in
this manner could never have read the New Testament, but must have taken his idea of
Christianity from the practices of Roman Catholicism only' (*JPTW* 17:347). Finally, he
notes that 'what is quite original to Mr. Dupuis … is that Christianity is derived from
Persian' religion (*JPTW* 17:346).

[44] Antoine Louis Claude Destutt de Tracy, *Analyse raisonée de l'Origine de tous les
Cultes, ou religion Universelle; Ouvrage publié en l'an III, par Dupuis, citoyen français* (Paris,
1804). Jefferson received his copy as a gift from the author on February 21, 1804 (letter
published in G. Chinard, *Jefferson et les idéologues d'après sa correspondance inédite avec Destutt
de Tracy, Cabanis, J.-B. Say, et Auguste Comte* [Paris–Baltimore, 1925]: 37) and acknowl-
edged the book and arranged for a copy to be given to the American Philosophical
Society in 1806 (Chinard:40 n. 1 and 41; cf. *Early Proceedings of the American Philosophical
Society, 1744–1838* [Philadelphia, 1844]: 381 and Sowerby, *Catalogue of the Library of
Thomas Jefferson*, 2:27). There was further correspondence between Destutt de Tracy and
Jefferson concerning the book in 1816–17 (printed in Chinard:168–9).

seems to him that the result of Dupuis's work has been to 'smother all history under the mantle of allegory' (Cappon 2:491). Adams, as usual, persists. It is 'the most entertain[in]g And instructive' history he has read (Cappon 2:494).[45] Indeed, Adams goes so far as to fantasize:

> We have now, it seems, a National Bible Society, to propogate King James's Bible, through all the Nations. [Although it would] be better to apply these pious Subscriptions, to purify Christendom from the Corruptions of Christianity; than propogate these Corruptions in Europe, Asia, Africa and America! Suppose, We should project a Society to translate Dupuis into all languages ... (Cappon 2:493–4, cf. 2:608.)[46]

If it is the case, as Richard M. Dorson states, that 'we smile condescendingly today at the solar mythologists'[47] associated with Max Muller and his, preeminently British, colleagues, how much more so is it possible to find the work of Charles François Dupuis ridiculous. Yet, we do well to recall that Dupuis served for the early nineteenth century comparative religionists much as Frazer (who nowhere cites Dupuis) served for the early twentieth century. His work 'was to be a major mine of mythic detail'[48] for generations of scholars, with or without explicit acknowledgment. Dupuis's work, as Anatole France wittily reminds us,[49] was subject to the same sort of parodic criticism as Muller's[50]: in 1817, Jean Baptiste Pérès demonstrated that, by an application of

---

[45] However, it should be noted that Adams's 'notes in the twelve volumes of Dupuis are rather sparse, consisting for the most part of repetitions in the margin of key names from the text.' Occasionally, he broke 'loose to express his irritation with Dupuis's atheism' (F. E. Manuel, *The Eighteenth Century Confronts the Gods* [Cambridge,MA., 1959]: 272).

[46] Chinard, *Jefferson et les idéologues*:233–57 has some analysis of this interchange between Adams and Jefferson; see also, Manuel:271–80.

[47] R. M. Dorson, 'The Eclipse of Solar Mythology,' in Th. A. Sebeok, ed., *Myth: A Symposium* (Bloomington, 1958): 25.

[48] B. Feldman and R. D. Richardson, *The Rise of Modern Mythology: 1680–1860* (Bloomington, 1972): 277.

[49] A. France, 'Dialogues sur les contes de fées,' in *Le Livre de Mon Ami* (1885). I cite the splendidly annotated edition by J. Heywood Thomas, *Anatole France: Le Livre de Mon Ami* (Oxford, 1942): 147–49.

[50] The relevant bibliography is given in Dorson, 'Eclipse of Solar Mythology,' 55, n. 22.

Dupuis's approach, Napoleon could be shown to have been a solar deity who never existed as an historical figure.[51] Nevertheless, we ought to be cautious. Dupuis's work was not only deeply influential on such diverse thinkers as Volney[52] and Saint-Simon[53] (not to speak of John Adams), but it was praised by contemporaries for accomplishing precisely what we have noted as lacking in the intellectual traditions already reviewed, – a shift from happenstance comparisons to systemic work.[54] The balanced judgement of Morris Jastrow, Jr., who devoted several pages to Dupuis in his classic work, *The Study of Religion* (1901) is apt, and raises issues that will preoccupy us throughout these pages:

> This fondness for comparisons is a characteristic of the comparative method in its infancy, whereas a matured comparative method is as much concerned with determining where comparisons should not be made as with drawing conclusions from comparisons instituted. But the weakness

---

[51] J.-B. Pérès, *Comme quoi Napoléon n'a jamais existé, ou grand erratum* (Agen, 1836). Cf. H. R. Evans, *The Napoleon Myth, containing a Reprint of The Grand Erratum* (Chicago, 1905).

[52] C. F. C. Volney, *Ruines ou méditations sur les révolutions des empires* (1791). I cite a later edition (Paris, 1826). Volney explicitly states his debt to 'the learned Dupuis' in a long note (325–6, cf. 327). Indeed, almost the whole of chapter 22, 'Origine et filiation des idées religieuses', from the second section on 'The Worship of Stars or Sabeism' (170–75) to the last section, 'Christianity, or the Allegorical Worship of the Sun' (212–22) owes much to Dupuis. It was in response to Volney that Priestley first took up a study and critique of Dupuis. See n. 43, above, and G. Chinard, *Volney et l'Amérique d'après des documents inédits et sa correspondance avec Jefferson* (Baltimore–Paris, 1923): 71–80.

[53] H. Saint-Simon, *Mémoire sur la science de l'homme* (posthumously discovered and published [1858]), in the *Oeuvres de Saint-Simon et d'Enfantin* (Paris, 1865–78), 40:28–31; see further, F. E. Manuel, *The New World of Henri Saint-Simon* (Cambridge, MA., 1956): 135.

[54] See, among others, J. A. Dulaure, *Des Cultes qui ont précédé et amené l'idolâtrie* (Paris, 1807): iii–iv, where he notes that myths had been reduced to a 'chaos', to a 'confused mass of heterogenous elements', by scholarship prior to Dupuis. I may note that, although Dulaure's name is often linked with Dupuis by writers on the history of the study of myth, I find little direct influence, either in *Des cultes*, or in his better known monograph on phallic worship, *Des Divinités génératrices* (Paris, 1805). Indeed, though Dulaure states, in *Des cultes*, that the three cults which have preceeded idolatry are 'Fetichism, Sabeism and Heroism' (18) – the second clearly derived from Dupuis – Sabeism is only discussed in one paragraph, the bulk of the book being devoted to the other two; nor does Dulaure mention Dupuis in his lengthy section on the zodiac (79–109). Dulaure's conclusion, that sky deities were created in imitation of heroes (462), directly contradicts a central contention of Dupuis.

of Dupuis is in itself a sign of progress, and in tracing the rise of the historical school in the study of religions, an honourable place must be assigned to him as one of its precursors.[55]

In 1795, year III of the Revolution, Citizen Dupuis, fifty-three years old, Professor of Latin Rhetoric at the Collège de France, member of the Académie des Inscriptions, and Secretary of the revolutionary National Convention, published his *Origine de tous les cultes*[56] and dedicated it to his colleagues in the Convention. It is a great, sprawling work: two-thousand and seventeen printed pages, plus a volume of twenty-two plates. In 1798, having retired from a series of legislative offices, he produced a more manageable abridged edition.[57]

The central quest of the work is for an understanding of that 'original deity, beyond material objectification' (1:viii, n. 2). By means of a lengthy – indeed, a remarkable – review of both antiquarian and ethnographic literature, Dupuis believes that this is to be found in 'the God-Universe', *l'Univers-Dieu*, seen as a single living being, which later develops (or degenerates), at a

---

[55] M. Jastrow, Jr., *The Study of Religion* (New York, 1902; rp. Chico, 1981): 28. Jastrow devotes pp. 25–28 to Dupuis, and cites, approvingly, Priestley's criticism of it (27, n. 1).

[56] Ch. F. Dupuis, *Origine de tous les cultes, ou, Religion universelle* (Paris, III = 1794–5), 1–6 + Atlas, in four quarto volumes; I cite this edition. An octavo edition (the one owned and read by Adams) of 12 volumes and a quarto Atlas was published simultaneously. A new edition, edited by P.-R. Augius, was published in 1822 and reprinted in 1834 (*non vidi*). The Atlas volume has been photographically reprinted in Florence in 1985. Despite Adams's suggestion, the full work has never been translated into English.

All biographical notices of Dupuis that I have seen are ultimately dependent on B. J. Dacier, 'Notice historique sur la vie et les ouvrages de M. Dupuis', *Histoire et mémoires de l'Institut Royale de France, Academie des inscriptions et belles-lettres* 5(1821): 121–41. Mme. Dupuis published a brief, 26 page, *Notice sur la vie littéraire et politique de M. Dupuis* (Paris, 1813), which I have not seen.

[57] Ch. F. Dupuis, *Abrégé de l'Origine de tous les cultes*, (Paris, VI = 1798). I know of 22 subsequent editions of this work published in France (1820–97), including the 'augmented edition' first issued in 1831. I cite an edition published in Paris in 1869. The abridged edition was anonymously translated into English, *The Origin of All Religious Worship, Translated from the French of Dupuis* (New Orleans, 1872; rp. New York, 1984). There are three further, anonymous, partial English translations, one by F. J. B., *Natural Religion; or, The Secret of All the Creeds* (London, 1908); the other two are translations of chapter 12, *A Translation of Dupuis' Explanation of an Apocalyptical Work of the Initiated into the Mysteries of the Light, or Sun Adored under the Symbol of the Lamb of Spring* (New York, 1849), and chapter 9, *Christianity, A Form of the Great Solar Myth, from the French of Dupuis* (London, 1873), in the series, T. Scott's Publications, 10. (All three of these partial translations are unavailable to me.)

secondary stage, into the mythology and worship of the heavenly bodies and, at a tertiary stage, into the myths and cults of heroes (1:1–124). This singularity could, at times, be represented as a variety of separate powers and principles, often hierarchically arranged (1:99–124); at other times, this singularity is represented as dual: active/passive, stable/changing, masculine/feminine, heaven or the sun/earth or the moon (1:124–39, et passim). A second dualism is often superimposed upon the first – a moral one: light and goodness/darkness and evil (1:223–41). This second duality underlies all ancient theogonies (1:223) and is especially clear in the Persian system which forms the 'basis' for all the developed religions of the west (1:229–41). From this systemic perspective, 'it matters very little whether he [the good god] is called Oromaze, Osiris, Jupiter, the Good God, the White God, etc … [or whether his opponent] is named Ahriman, Typhon, the chief of the Titans, the Devil, Satan, or the Black God' (*Abrégé*: 66). As Dupuis develops this theme, it appears that this struggle is best expressed by means of what later scholars will term a 'seasonal pattern'.

> The Sun … the mighty luminary, the depository of the whole force of nature … which, by its gentle heat in the Spring calls everything into fertility …Two points may be distinguished … which limit the duration of the creative action of the Sun [i.e., the two solstices] … all vegetative activity seems to be included within these two limits … Scarcely has the Sun in its annual route attained one of these points, when an active sexual force emanates from its rays … This is the time of the resurrection of the great god, and with him, the resurrection of all of nature. As soon as the Sun arrives at the opposite point, this power seems to abandon the deity, and nature experiences a decline. This is the mutilation of Attis … the wounding of Adonis … the killing of Osiris … What spectacle, indeed, could be more moving than that of the earth, when through the absence of the Sun is divested of its greenery … when we behold the remains of withered plants … Is the god going to plunge nature again into the eternal dark of Chaos … Such were the doubts of the ancients … when they saw the Sun withdrawing … hence those feasts of hope and joy, celebrated at the

winter-solstice, when men saw the Sun stop in its with-drawal and begin to return, again, towards them ... [as if the Sun] chased the darkness which had usurped part of his empire ... A new order of things, as beautiful as the previous, is reestablished ... The earth smiles again, and man forgets the sadness and mourning with which winter had covered the earth. Venus has found, again, her lost Adonis ... her lover, the conqueror of winter and the darkness of night, has finally risen from his tomb. (*Abrégé*: 93–95, cf. *L'Origine*: 2.1:1–27.)

With this as background, Dupuis turns, in the subsequent volumes, first to a 'Treatise on the Mysteries' (2.2:1–304), and then to the 'part of this work that the public has been most waiting for' (3.1.i), the relevance of all of this to an interpretation of Christianity.

The long section on the mysteries is, from one perspective, entirely conventional. Dupuis asserts that, while their ultimate origins are lost in obscurity, the Egyptians had 'the most ancient' mysteries, and that 'it was from them that they passed to the rest of the world' (2.1:1). This is most apparent, he claims, in the case of the Egyptian derivation of the Eleusinian Mysteries to which he devotes the longest exposition in the section (2.1:4–48). However, as already suggested by the long 'seasonal' passage quoted above, what makes this 'Treatise' interesting to the modern reader is Dupuis's polyonomy. One may compare Osiris (2.1:1–48), Adonis or Tammuz (2.1:50–60), Bacchus (2.1:60–75), Attis (2.1:75–89), and Mithra (2.1:89–109) as different manifesta-tions of the same deity (i.e., the solar Good God of Light) or, as I would translate, using modern vocabulary, as different manifesta-tions of the same mythic 'pattern'. Thus, when he is being most provocative, Dupuis insists on synonymy, even in the case of details, for example, 'it was during the night that one wept for the death of Tammuz, just as it was during the night that one wept for Christ, Osiris, Mithra and Bacchus' (2.1:59). Dupuis is least interesting when he suggests that this *analogy* may be reduced to causality, to borrowing or filiation, as in the case of his repeated formula, 'that branch of Mithraics known under the name of the Christian sect' (2.1:93; 3.1:1).

The final volume, devoted largely to Christianity, opens with a polyonomous affirmation, 'Christ will be, for us, what Hercules, Osiris, Adonis and Bacchus have been', that is to say, a form of the solar deity, an affirmation followed by the more radical claim, 'if he [Christ] seems to have assumed a mortal body, like the heroes of ancient poems, this will be only the fiction of legend' (3.1:iv), – in the language used earlier, a tertiary development or degeneration. At another point, he writes:

> We conclude that, despite the differences in stories and names, there is nothing that belongs to Christ which does not belong to Bacchus and Osiris, that is to say, which does not belong to the Sun honored under his various names. (3.1:69)

As with the mysteries, so too here, he can suggest a synonomy, which seems to depend on borrowing and filiation (e.g. 3.1:136–37), especially from Mithraism (for example, 3.1:69, where the phrase *comme Christ* occurs four times; cf. 3.1:45, 84–85, et passim), or the notion that Christianity is best 'understood as a branch of universal [solar] religion' (3.1:153). As with the mysteries, he is most intriguing, here, when he argues for the interpretation of Christ as an instance of a universal, 'seasonal' pattern.

> In order to understand the Christian legend concerning Christ, we have collected the legends of the different religions which have appeared in the west contemporary with Christ. We have shown that they have common characteristics and that they can be reduced, totally, to a singular idea: salvation by the Sun, supposedly born at the time of the Winter solstice and triumphant over darkness at the Spring solstice, after having been mourned as dead and then celebrated as the conqueror of the shadows of the tomb. Thus we have seen that the religion of Christ is nothing other than these [same] cosmic allegories which we find among the Mithraists, in the mysteries of the Great Mother, etc. Likewise, we have shown that the Christian theology is founded on the same principles as those of the Pagans, Egyptians, Greeks, Chaldeans, [and] Indians. (3.1:92.)

What has a consideration of the sort of approach to the comparative enterprise represented by Dupuis gained for our inquiry? It will be recalled that, when reviewing the intra-Christian comparisons of the anti-Trinitarians and the ritual comparisons of the Pagano-Papists, the same general criticism was made: that, with the partial exception of figures such as Souverain, these were largely surface comparisons, triggered by the co-occurrence of a single word or image, largely shorn of all context, be it literary or historical. (See above, pp. 17 and 25.) What Dupuis has added, for all the thorny problems with his data, is some rudimentary sense of depth. In a word, he has added the notion of *story*. Whether through the device of polyonomy, synonomy, or his 'monomythic pattern', it is important to note that he has not just compared this or that item in two traditions, but rather a total ensemble to a total ensemble: the Christian myth to the myth of other 'mystery religions', as well as to the religious system of more 'primitive' peoples. Indeed, he has done more. For there is always a third term to his comparisons. Christianity is compared to some other religion (or, another religious system is compared to some other religious system) with reference to his overall 'seasonal pattern', to the figure of the 'Solar Deity', or to his even more generalized structure of *l'Univers-Dieu*, in terms of which each religious tradition is but an instance. For Dupuis, the comparative enterprise is not just a horizontal one, it is a vertical process as well. To use, somewhat loosely, more contemporary terminology, religious systems can be studied synchronically as well as diachronically. There is depth to the scholar's comparative activities as well as depth within his or her data.

It will be apparent, I trust, to my readers that this chapter has largely been constructed around a conceit. That is to say, I have taken a particular moment in time, the Jefferson-Adams correspondence, as a snapshot in order to record what more properly belongs to the realm of the motion-picture. By taking two educated laymen and dissolving the presuppositions that informed their strongly felt denunciations of 'Platonic Christianity', we have been able, with extreme economy, to gain some sense of the beginnings and initial developments of the enterprise of comparing (early) Christianity to the religions of Late Antiquity. If there is one story-line that runs through the various figures and strategems briefly passed in review, it is that this has been by no means an innocent endeavour. The pursuit of the origins of the question of Christian origins takes us back, persistently, to the same point: *Protestant anti-Catholic apologetics.* It will be my contention, in the subsequent chapters, that this is by no means a merely antiquarian concern. The same presuppositions, the same rhetorical tactics, indeed, in the main, the very same data exhibited in these early efforts underlie much of our present-day research, with one important alteration, that the characteristics attributed to 'Popery', by the Reformation and post-Reformation controversialists, have been transferred, wholesale, to the religions of Late Antiquity. How else can one explain, for example, the fact that the most frequent distinction drawn in modern scholarship between the early Christian 'sacraments' (especially the Pauline) and those of the 'mystery cults' is that the latter exhibit a notion of ritual as *ex opere operato*?[58] The

---

[58] I cite only a few representative instances culled from a far longer list. It should be emphasized that these only include passages which employ the phrase, *ex opere operato*. The list could have been enormously expanded if it took into account scholars who closely paraphrase the term (e.g. F. V. Filson, *The New Testament Against Its Environment* [London, 1950]: 94) or those who use parallel terms, created by Protestant anti-Catholic apologetics, such as 'magical', 'external' or 'merely ceremonial'. On this latter point, see Smith, *To Take Place*: 96–103.

The scholars employing the phrase, *ex opere operato* to distinguish the rituals of the 'mysteries' from the 'sacraments' of early Christianity include: H. A. A. Kennedy, *St. Paul and the Mystery Religions* (London, 1913):254, cf. Kennedy, 'Mysteries, Christian,' Hastings, *Encyclopedia of Religion and Ethics* (1917), 9:74; H. Weinel, *Biblische Theologie des Neuen Testaments: Die Religion Jesu und des Urchristentums*, 3d ed. (Tübingen, 1921):304; S. Angus, *The Mystery Religions: A Study in the Religious Background of Early Christianity*, 2nd ed. (London, 1928): 96; C. C. McCown, 'The Sources of Pauline Mysticism,' in T. S. Kepler, ed., *Contemporary Thinking about Paul* (Nashville, 1950): 120; E. Klaar, *Die Taufe nach paulinischen Verständnis* (Münich, 1961): 17; E. O. James, *Sacrifice and Sacrament* (London, 1962): 258; O. Küss, *Der Römerbrief*, 2nd ed. (Regensburg, 1963), 2:371; B. M. Metzger, 'Methodology in the Study of the Mystery Religions and Early Christianity,' rp. in Metzger, *Historical and Literary Studies: Pagan, Jewish, and Christian* (Grand Rapids, 1968): 14; A. di Nola, 'Mistero e misteri', *Enciclopedia delle Religioni* (Florence, 1972), 4:477.

The distinguished scholar of New Testament philology and of Persian religions, James H. Moulton, in *Religions and Religion* (New York, n.d. [1913]): 39–41 is uncommonly blunt about the anti-Catholic basis of this sort of distinction, e.g., p. 40: 'But granted what is fairly obvious, that the so-called "Catholic" idea of the sacraments has an exceedingly close relation to the old Mystery Religions, we have to ask on which side Paul stands ...' There is a useful note on this matter in K. Prümm, *Religionsgeschichtliches Handbuch für den Raum der altchristlichen Umwelt* (Rome, 1954): 355, n. 2.

comparison of the enterprise of comparison with respect to early Christianity, then and now, leads one to voice the same sorts of criticisms and queries with respect to methods, periodizations, data, and, above all, to those tacit assumptions, to those matters which are taken as self-evident, which govern the scholar's work.

Before pursuing this theme, however, we need to pause and consider the endeavour of comparison itself, the genus to which the species, the comparison of early Christianities and the religions of Late Antiquity, belongs. The second chapter is dedicated to this more generic undertaking.

On Comparison

I

In 1611, when John Donne, in 'An Anatomie of the World', penned, as part of his surprisingly modern description of 'the world's condition now', the poignant well-known lines:

> 'Tis all in peeces, all cohaerence gone;
> All just supply, and all Relation:
> Prince, Subject, Father, Sonne, are things
> forgot,
> For every man alone thinkes he hath got
> To be a Phoenix, and that then can bee
> None of that kinde, of which he is, but hee.

he described a radical and solitary individualism under the sign of the phoenix, a unique being, *sui generis* in both the popular and technical sense of the term, self-generated and belonging to no wider class. In the words of Isidore of Seville, 'in the entire world, [the phoenix] is *unica et singularis*' (*Etymologies* 12.7.22), so the phoenix became, in Late Antiquity, at one and the same time, a rhetorical topos for the exceptional (e.g. Aristides, *Oration* 45.107; Synesius, *Dio* 9.3) as well as an early figure for the death and resurrection of Jesus (1 Clement 25).

Although the latter will preoccupy us in later chapters, it is with the question of the 'unique' that we are here concerned. Despite Henry J. Todd's view, in his revision of Samuel Johnson's *Dictionary* (1818), that 'unique', was an 'affected and useless term of modern times', it has proved to be both resistent and resilient. The 'unique' is an attribute that must be disposed of, especially when linked to some notion of incomparable value, if progress in thinking through the enterprise of comparison is to be made.

Let us be clear at the outset. There is a quite ordinary sense in which the term 'unique' may be applied in disciplinary contexts. When the historian speaks of unique events, the taxonomist of the unique *differentium* that allows the classification of this or that plant or animal species, the geographer of the unique physiognomy of a particular place, or the linguist of each human utterance as unique, he or she is asserting a reciprocal notion which confers no special status, nor does it deny – indeed, it demands – enterprises of classification and interpretation. *A* is unique with respect to *B*, in this sense, requires the assertion that *B* is, likewise, unique with respect to *A*, and so forth. In such formulations 'uniqueness' is generic and commonplace rather than being some odd point of pride. In my language, I would prefer, in such instances, the term 'individual', which permits the affirmation of difference while insisting on the notion of belonging to a class.

It is when the notion of superlative value is conjoined to the unique – an association that the *Oxford English Dictionary* blames on the French (who else!) – that one begins to verge on problematic modes of speech. As William James has reminded us:

> The first thing the intellect does with an object is to classify it along with something else. But any object that is infinitely important to us and awakens our devotion feels to us also as if it must be *sui generis* and unique. Probably a crab would be filled with a sense of personal outrage if it could hear us class it without ado or apology as a crustacean, and thus dispose of it. 'I am no such thing,' it would say, 'I am *myself, myself alone*.'[1]

The irony of this passage, which recognizes the genuineness of the impulse, the affirmation of individuality, but asserts, nevertheless, the probity of class, continues in a host of formulations which merge the notion of the unique and the special, while relativizing the former: a formula of 'unique, but ...' As irony, the mood has been precisely captured in a fragment of dialogue between Edward Chamberlayne and Sir Henry Harcourt-Reilly in T. S. Eliot's, *The Cocktail Party*:

Edward: Mine is a very unusual case.
Reilly: All cases are unique, and very similar to others.

---

[1] W. James, *The Varieties of Religious Experience* (New York, 1929): 10.

Consider two further examples from widely divergent British texts where the ironic 'unique, but ...' appears far less conscious, but is no less present. The first is from the Preface to the *Guinness Book of World Records* (1979 edition):

> It should be stressed that unique occurrences and interesting peculiarities are not in themselves necessarily records.

The second is from the epigraph of a science fiction anthology, *England Swings SF* (1968), edited by Judith Merril:

> You have never read a book like this before, and the next time you read anything like it, it won't be *much* like it at all.

Such irony is wholly displaced in the typical way in which 'unique' is spoken of in religious studies (and in some other fields within the human sciences). Here the 'unique' is more phoenix-like, it expresses that which is *sui generis*, *singularis*, and, therefore, *incomparably* valuable. 'Unique' becomes an ontological rather than a taxonomic category; an assertion of a radical difference so absolute that it becomes 'Wholly Other', and the act of comparison is perceived as both an impossibility and an impiety.

While the history of the 'unique' in religious discourse has yet to be written – unlike the history of paradoxography, of singularities and prodigies, within the natural sciences, which is a story well-told – I am willing to hazard the guess that when it is, it will reveal that the 'unique' is a thoroughly modern notion, one no earlier than those same nineteenth century German Protestant discussions which yielded, in reaction to comparative religious data, such diverse innovations as the notion of 'universal Christianity', the World Parliament of Religions ... and the study of religion as an academic pursuit.

The most frequent use of the terminology of the 'unique' within religious studies is in relation to Christianity; the most frequent use of this term within Christianity is in relation to the so-called 'Christ-event'. As one recent New Testament scholar (Burton Mack) has critically observed:

> The fundamental persuasion is that Christianity appeared unexpectedly in human history, that it was (is) at core a brand new vision of human existence, and that, since this is

so, only a startling moment could account for its emergence at the beginning. The code word serving as a sign for the novelty that appeared is the term unique (meaning singular, incomparable, without analogue). For the originary event the word is transformation (rupture, breakthrough, inversion, reversal, eschatological). For the cognitive effect of this moment the language of paradox is preferred (irony, parable, enigma, the irritational). It is this startling moment that seems to have mesmerized the discipline and determined the application of its critical methods.[2]

The uniqueness of the 'Christ-event', which usually encodes the death and resurrection of Jesus, is a double claim. On the ontological level, it is a statement of the absolutely alien nature of the divine protagonist (*monogenes*) and the unprecedented (and paradoxical) character of his self-disclosure; on the historical level, it is an assertion of the radical incomparability of the Christian 'proclamation' with respect to the 'environment'. For many scholars of early Christianity, the latter claim is often combined with the former, so as to transfer the (proper, though problematic) theological affirmation of absolute uniqueness to an historical statement that, standing alone, could never assert more than relative uniqueness, that is to say, a quite ordinary postulation of difference. It is this illicit transfer from the ontological to the historical that raises the question of the comparison of early Christianity and the religions of Late Antiquity.

The issue of death and resurrection will be taken up in detail in Chapters Four and Five. Here it suffices to recall some parallel instances of the same sort of assertion, for example, the notion that the gospel-genre is unique. In Bultmann's phrasing of the double ontological/historical claim, the gospels 'are a unique phenomenon in the history of literature, and at the same time are symbolic of the distinctive nature of the Christian religion as a whole'.[3]

In its most radical formulations, by K. L. Schmidt and others, the proposition of the uniqueness of the gospel-genre seems to be a variation on the Protestant model of a pristine originary

---

[2] B. Mack, *A Myth of Innocence: Mark and Christian Origins* (Philadelphia, 1988): 4.

[3] R. Bultmann, 'Evangelien', *Religion in Geschichte und Gegenwart*, 2nd ed. (1928), 2:419.

moment followed by corruption, and refers more to the gospel-behind-the-gospels than to the literary products associated with the evangelists. As Schmidt argued, 'Primitive Christianity, in general, did not enter into the World.' Its experiences and its forms of speech are, hence, by definition incomparable. This primitive community was, subsequently, subjected to change, to the 'hellenization, that is to say, the secularization, of the primitive Christian movement'.[4] From that moment on, it used common genres taken from its environment. This is an assertion of absolute originary uniqueness and relies on ontological presuppositions as to the alien nature of the object of Christian discourse. It also, if taken to extremes, would have the 'primordial gospel' fail at communication, unless through some Pentecost-like agency of the Spirit – a not unintended consequence, I fear – consonant with the general Reformers' impulse to shift the locus of inspiration from text to recipient.

Other arguments appear more 'statistical'. Scholarship has related the gospel to many forms of contemporary literature, from biography to aretalogy, but none of them seems precisely the same. However, this is a quite ordinary statement of difference which need not be raised to the language of the 'unique' except when under the influence of a nostalgia for the 'specialness' conceded to early Christianity by the ontological model. Besides, as already observed, such formulations are necessarily relative *and* reciprocal. If the Gospel of Mark is different from Iamblichus's *Life of Pythagoras*, so is Iamblichus different than Mark, so are both different from the Gospel of Matthew, and from Porphyry's *Life of Pythagoras*. Difference abounds. As James Robinson has argued, with respect to our topic, 'in view of the plurality of kerygmatic trends in primitive Christianity ... the view that one distinctive *Gattung* Gospel emerged sui generis from the uniqueness of Christianity seems hardly tenable.'[5]

---

[4] I have taken these citations of Schmidt from the important article by J. C. Meagher, 'The Implications for Theology of a Shift from the K. L. Schmidt Hypothesis of the Literary Uniqueness of the Gospels,' in B. Corley, ed., *Colloquy on New Testament Studies: A Time for Reappraisal and Fresh Approaches* (Macon, 1983): 203–33; passage quoted, p. 208. (There is also a discussion of Maher's paper, pp. 235–62, and an introduction by Ch. Talbert, 197–202.)

[5] J. M. Robinson, 'On the *Gattung* of Mark (and John),' in D. G. Buttrick and J. M. Bald, eds., *Jesus and Man's Hope* (Pittsburgh, 1970), 1:104.

The use of eschatology as a locus of uniqueness is even more revealing. In the hands of Schweitzer and others, the notion of eschatology was used as a critical tool against the liberal lives of Jesus and the 'perils of modernizing Jesus' (H. J. Cadbury's phrase). That is to say, it was a strongly marked (historical) indicator of difference between the environment of Jesus and that of our time. But, in the hands of other New Testament scholars it was transformed into an indicator of absolute (ontological) uniqueness. As Dieter Georgi has shrewdly observed:

> [Bultmann] opposes what he calls the relativism of the history-of-religions school. [In this context] I need to mention the term 'eschatological'. It works for Bultmann and for many New Testament scholars and systematic theologians ever since as a magic wand. Whereas for the history-of-religions school the term 'eschatological' described the foreignness of Jesus and of the early church – together with Jewish apocalypticism and other comparable ancient eschatologies – for Bultmann and many contemporary New Testament scholars and Christian theologians the term 'eschatological' stands for the novelty of Christianity, its incomparable superiority, the uniqueness of the victorious religion ... Wherever a comparison is ventured, wherever analogies lift their head, wherever challenges are heard from other religious options but the canonical ones, the invocation of the 'eschatological' is made, and the demons, the shadows have to disappear. Historical criticism thus turns into exorcism.[6]

To translate this into my sort of language, what was a relative statement that Jesus is 'alien' or 'strange' with respect to our time has been transformed, by later scholarship, into an absolute statement that Jesus is 'unique' in all respects for all time.

The same sort of critique could be made of the so-called 'criterion of dissimilarity' as a test for the *ipsissima verba* of Jesus.[7] As an ontological notion, it makes impossible the project of

---

[6] D. Georgi, 'Rudolf Bultmann's *Theology of the New Testament* Revisited,' in E. C. Hobbs, ed., *Bultmann: Retrospect and Prospect* (Philadelphia, 1985): 82, in the series Harvard Theological Studies, 35.

[7] N. Perrin, *The New Testament: An Introduction* (New York, 1971): 281, calls the test of dissimilarity, 'the fundamental criterion'.

communication (leading to odd theories of a parabolic mode of speech which, paradoxically, destroys speech); as an historical project, it is implausible, both practically (by what procedures could we ever hope to gather all instances of contemporary speech?), and in principle (the majority of human utterances, which are nonetheless comprehensible, have never been uttered before).

No, what is required is an end to the imposition of the extra-historical categories of uniqueness and the 'Wholly Other' upon historical data and the tasks of historical understanding. From an historian's viewpoint, to cite Toynbee, 'This word "unique" is a negative term signifying what is mentally imcomprehensible.'[8] What is required is the development of a discourse of 'difference', a complex term which invites negotiation, classification and comparison[9], and, at the same time, avoids too easy a discourse of the 'same'. It is, after all, the attempt to block the latter that gives the Christian apologetic language of the 'unique' its urgency. To offer but one example of the rhetoric of the 'same', containing themes that will preoccupy us in the next three chapters, Alfred Loisy writing on 'The Christian Mystery' in 1911:

> [Jesus] was a saviour-god, after the manner of an Osiris, an Attis, a Mithra. Like them, he belonged by his origin to the celestial world; like them, he had made his appearance on the earth; like them, he had accomplished a work of universal redemption, efficacious and typical; like Adonis, Osiris, and Attis he had died a violent death, and like them he had returned to life; like them, he had prefigured in his lot that of the human beings who should take part in his worship, and commemorate his mystic enterprise; like them, he had predetermined, prepared, and assured the salvation of those who became partners in his passion.[10]

[8] A. J. Toynbee, *A Study of History* (Oxford, 1961), 12:11.

[9] It is possible, in fact, to make the same argument for theological discourse, although that is not my purpose here. One may note the delicious expression of the difficulty with the notion of utter alterity in H. W. Turner's, *Commentary on Otto's 'Idea of the Holy'* (Aberdeen, 1974): 19, 'when Otto describes this experience of the Numen as "Wholly Other", he cannot mean *wholly* "Wholly Other,"' as well as the welcoming of the language of 'difference' as opposed to 'otherness', in D. Tracy. *Plurality and Ambiguity* (New York, 1987): 20–21, et passim.

[10] A. Loisy, 'The Christian Mystery,' *The Hibbert Journal*, 10(1911–12): 51.

From such a parataxis of 'likeness', little of value can be learned. The reiterated 'like them' has swallowed up the differences that would render such a chain of comparisons interesting.

There is more concerning the matter of 'uniqueness'. If one illicit transfer with respect to the 'unique' shifts an ontological meaning to an historical one with respect to inter-religious comparisons, there has been a second, equally illicit, transfer which centres on an intra-religious comparison. According to this view, if Christianity is 'unique' with respect to other religions, then apostolic (or Pauline) Christianity is 'unique' with respect to other (especially later) modes of Christianity. This is a modulation of the Protestant historiographic myth: a 'uniquely' pristine 'original' Christianity which suffered later 'corruptions'.

In this construction one is not, in fact, comparing early Christianity and the religions of Late Antiquity. The latter have become code-words for Roman Catholicism and it is the Protestant catalogue of the central characteristics of Catholicism, from which it dissents, which provides the categories for comparison with Late Antiquity. (See Chapter One.)

This polemic strategy is often cunningly concealed in more recent writings as if it were merely a matter of chronology. Thus a recent New Testament scholar can assert, as his starting point, in an article concerned with the methodology of comparison:

> First of all, a distinction must be made between the faith and practice of the earliest Christians and that of the Church during subsequent centuries. One cannot deny that post-Constantinian Christianity, both Eastern and Western, adopted not a few pagan rites and practices ... The real difference of opinion, however, arises with regard to the relation of nascent Christianity to its pagan rivals.[11]

Hence the reiterated insistence, by most scholars concerned with the question, on the fact that the bulk of the evidence from the so-called 'mystery' cults is of a third century date, or later. The duplicity of this chronological caution is revealed when the same

---

[11] B. M. Metzger, 'Methodology in the Study of the Mystery Religions and Early Christianity,' *Harvard Theological Review*, 48(1955): 1–20, reprinted, with revisions, in Metzger, *Historical and Literary Studies: Pagan, Jewish and Christian* (Grand Rapids, 1968): 1–24, in the series, NTTS, 8. I cite the latter version; passage quoted: pp. 4, 6.

scholars, eager to demonstrate the close relationship of early Christianity to Judaism – the latter imagined to provide an insulation against 'paganism' (see Chapter Three) – recklessly quote alleged rabbinic parallels from Jewish documents no earlier than the same third century, and frequently far later.

Earlier scholars do not trouble with such disguise and state the object of comparison far more bluntly. Take, for example, a characteristic article, from 1924, by John Alfred Faulkner, a professor of New Testament at Drew University, devoted to the question, 'Did Mystery Religions Influence Apostolic Christianity?'[12] His conclusion is the same as the more recent essay in methodology just referred to:

> It has been shown ... that apostolic Christianity did not borrow anything of importance from the mystery religions. But when we come into the third, fourth, and following centuries we are in a different world. (2:266)

But the grounds for insisting on the lack of relationship are far more explicit. It is that 'apostolic Christianity' was essentially 'Protestant', and the 'mystery' religions essentially 'Catholic'. The very first comparison gives the game away. The early Christian communities were small, being only for 'rare spirits' willing to 'wrestle with God' and not, like those with 'untutored souls', distracted by a 'love of ritual'. The 'mystery' cults, by contrast to the Christian, were popular and 'spectacular'.

> Therefore, the Society of Friends is a wee folk, but the Roman Catholic, the Greek Catholic, and the Anglican Catholic Churches are a mighty body (1:388).

Off-hand polemic comparisons abound: 'Like the Roman Catholic priests and the officers of secret orders today, priests and hierophants of the mystery religions held the keys of the kingdom of light' (1:392); 'the benefit of the initiations [in the "mysteries"] depended on male priests who alone knew the

---

[12] J. A. Faulkner, 'Did Mystery Religions Influence Apostolic Christianity?' *The Methodist Quarterly Review*, 73(1924): 387–403; Faulkner, 'Did Ancient Christianity Borrow from the Mystery Religions?' *The Methodist Quarterly Review*, 74(1925): 266–78. In citing these articles above, I have distinguished between them by designating them as '1' or '2'.

secrets of the Way, as in the Catholic Church of all schools'
(1:393); and more extended comparisons insistently reiterate the
point.

> So far as we know Christianity of the apostolic age and of
> the age immediately after, we can impute but little to this
> [pagan] influence. Christianity did not get the fact of sin
> from this source, nor her method of dealing with it by
> repentance and faith in Christ ... She had no secret meetings
> or initiations ... Nor did she play on the pride of knowledge
> in general, as did Gnosticism and some of the mysteries. Her
> first disciples were plain men and not scholastically trained,
> and she welcomed everybody into her ranks and not simply
> philosophers and the learned. Nor did Christianity deal in
> ritual or spectacular display, thus being far removed from
> the mystery religions. In apostolic times we have a full
> description of the services in Corinth, and they remind you
> of a modern prayer meeting or an old-fashioned Methodist
> class meeting [!] (1:395).

As Faulkner would have it, apostolic 'Christianity separated itself
from all ancient religions by not being magical, no *deus ex
machina*, no *ex opere operato*, no repeat-formulae-and-it-is-done,
no turn-common-things-into-sacred by-an-incantation, no
priestly-sleight-of-hand' (1:397) until the 'change' to a 'sacramental' doctrine which became characteristic from 'the fourth century to the present in all so-called Catholic Churches. In these the
mystery religions still function to-day before our very eyes'
(2:269, cf. 2:274).

One can formulate the principle of comparison that has
informed the majority of scholarship in this area as follows:
'Apostolic Christianity' and 'Protestantism' are 'unique'; the
religions of Late Antiquity, most especially the 'mysteries' and
'Catholicism', are the 'same'.

The model for this defensive strategy is as old as the recorded
history of religious comparison. It is the notion of 'autochthony'
as present in Herodotus. And this concept of self-generation, in
the Herodotean enterprise, is always conjoined to a second topos,
the notion of 'borrowing'. Thus the Egyptians are dependent on
no one for their customs and borrow no foreign practices

(*Histories* 2.79, 91); the Persians, objects of scorn for both the Greeks and the Egyptians, borrow from everyone. 'No people are so ready to adopt foreign ways as are the Persians' (1:135). For secondary cultures, such as Greece, everything depends on pedigree, on borrowing from a prestigious primary centre. Thus, taking up Egyptian propagandistic claims, Herodotus writes that the 'younger' Greeks borrowed freely from the 'older' Egyptians (e.g. 2.4, 43, 49, 50, 57, 58, 81, 82) with no suggestion that this implies a necessarily negative evaluation.[13]

In the study of the relations of early Christianity to the religions of Late Antiquity, the names have been altered from Herodotus's time, but the relations remain the same. Early Christianity is primarily to be considered as autochthonus. If there is any dependency, it is from a prestigious centre. In this model, Israel appears in the role of the Herodotean Egypt. The Catholic Church, or in more recent treatments, 'Greco-Oriental syncretism', plays the part of Persia. This requires that the enterprise of comparison focus on questions of borrowing and diffusion. The use of comparison as a hermeneutic device, or as a principle of discovery for the construction of theories or generic categories plays no role. What rules, instead, is an overwhelming concern for assigning value, rather than intellectual significance, to the results of comparison. This may be seen when, in a remarkable moment of candour, the former president of San Francisco Seminary declared in an interview in the *New York Times* (29 May 1966/E:7): 'In his own education, Dr. Gill added, the Jew as opposed to the ancient Greek, the Gnostic or the mystery religionist was the "good guy"'. (This common, and duplicitous use of Judaism as an insulating device for early Christianity will be taken up in Chapter Three.)

II

Having set aside the issue of the 'unique' in its various forms and questioned the simple discourse of the 'same', we need to think

---

[13] See, on the Herodotean enterprise, Smith, *Map Is Not Territory*: 243–49. On the question of prestigious pedigree in the cultural propaganda of the Hellenistic world, see the suggestive article by E. J. Bickerman, 'Origines Gentium,' *Classical Philology*, 47(1952): 65–81.

about the enterprise of comparison under the aspect of difference. As I have argued elsewhere:

> It is axiomatic that comparison is never a matter of identity. Comparison requires the acceptance of difference as the grounds of its being interesting, and a methodical manipulation of that difference to achieve some stated cognitive end. The questions of comparison are questions of judgement with respect to difference: What differences are to be maintained in the interests of comparative inquiry? What differences can be defensively relaxed and relativized in light of the intellectual tasks at hand?[14]

That this is *not* the working assumption of many scholars in the field may be seen by noting the poverty of conception that usually characterizes their comparative endeavours, frequently due, as has already been suggested, to apologetic reasons. It is as if the only choices the comparativist has are to assert either identity or uniqueness, and that the only possibilities for utilizing comparisons are to make assertions regarding dependence. In such an enterprise, it would appear, dissimilarity is assumed to be the norm; similarities are to be explained as either the result of the 'psychic unity' of humankind, or the result of 'borrowing'.

Within the field of study under review, these options are expressed as the choice between 'analogy' and 'genealogy' (i.e. homology), with the latter used in the sense not only of establishing direct relations (borrowing and dependency), but also prestigious origins (pedigree).[15] The thought appears to be

---

[14] Smith, *To Take Place*: 14.

[15] In the above, I appeal to the well-known biological distinction, first formulated in the nineteenth century by Richard Owen, between homology and analogy which replaced the older Aristotelian distinction between substance and accident. As reformulated, after Darwin, in the works of biologists such as E. Haeckel, C. Gegenbaur and E. R. Lankester, a homology is a similarity of form or structure between two species shared from their common ancestor; an analogy is a similarity of form or structure between two species not sharing a common ancestor. To give the textbook illustration, the human hand and the whale's flipper are homologous; the whale's flipper and the fish's fin are analogous. The task of taxonomy, since Darwin, especially in its dominant phylogenetic forms, has been to eliminate analogies (which serve, to use a linguistic term, as 'false friends'), and to construct relationships entirely on the basis of homologies.

Prior to Darwin, analogous relationships were usually explained on the basis of similarity and economy of function (i.e. the whale's flipper and the fish's fin are efficient

that, from a standpoint of protecting the privileged position of
early Christianity, it is only genealogical comparisons that are
worthy of note, if only, typically, insistently to be denied. As
'analogies' pose no apparent threat, they are most often held to be
without interest. Thus, in an article entitled, 'Methodology in the
Study of the Mystery Religions and Early Christianity,' which
contains the presupposition that 'Christianity is *sui generis*,' Bruce
M. Metzger writes that:

> Even when parallels are actual and not imaginary, their
> significance for purposes of comparison will depend on
> whether they are genealogical and not merely analogical
> parallels. That is to say, one must inquire as to whether the
> similarities have arisen from more or less equal religious

modes of locomotion); post-Darwin, analogous relations are most often explained by
convergent processes of natural selection in terms of environment (i.e. the whale's flipper
and the fish's fin are independent and parallel adaptations to an aquatic milieu). Hence,
most of the major developments in taxonomy, from the late nineteenth century interest in
embryological classification to the contemporary interest in genetic classification, have
been attempts to set aside convergent similarities and to base taxonomy entirely on
ancestry and descent. The task has been to distinguish 'kinds' (homologies) from 'sets'
(analogies), and to privilege the former. Matters are, of course, not quite this simple. The
matter of construing the relationship between taxonomic groups remains deeply controversial, most especially when there are different rates of divergence. While numerical
taxonomy would insist on a purely phenetic approach, and cladistics on a purely
phylogenetic approach, the dominant modes of evolutionary taxonomy have, in fact,
compromised the two: all things being equal, phylogenetic classification is to be preferred;
however, in cases of relatively rapid development, phenetic classifications are to be
employed.

In contradistinction to the taxonomists, contemporary morphologists continue to work
successfully with analogies, although the understanding of the phenomenon has clearly
changed from the older idealistic postulations of *Urformen* to the notion of the primacy of
the environment. Form is no longer a question of pure architecture, of intrinsic
relationships and principles of construction, rather, since the 1930s, form is seen as the
product of extrinsic environmental selection.

There is one paramount issue which appears to distinguish the biological enterprise of
phylogenetic comparison from those within the human sciences. The phylogeneticist
strives, at least in theory, for a 'natural' classification; the human scientist must always
propose an 'artificial' classification. This is because there is, arguably, nothing comparable
to genetic processes within the sphere of human culture. Even here, however, matters are
more complex than they first may seem, for in all schools of evolutionary taxonomy, it is
only at the level of species that the hereditary and reproductive link is key. Hence the
fundamental, though far from unproblematic, definition of species in terms of interbreed-
ing. Higher taxa can only be defined by similarity of form and thus represent relatively
artificial schema. That is to say, at the level of species (or at lower levels) homology
conventionally rules biological comparison; at higher levels, procedures more closely akin
to analogy govern classification.

experience, due to equality of what may be called psychic pitch and equality of outward conditions, or whether they are due to borrowing from one another.[16]

The foundation text for this distinction is that of Adolf Deissmann. About mid-point through his enormous monograph, *Licht vom Osten*, concerned with largely philological parallels, Deissmann pauses to raise a 'methodological problem which has engaged my liveliest interest since the beginning of my studies'. The question is: 'Is it analogy or is it genealogy?' Are the apparent similarities 'parallelisms of more or less equal religious experiences ... or are they dependent upon one another, demonstrable borrowings'. Deissmann's further reflections indicate that he had something more complex in mind than is usually represented in those who cite him.

> Where it is a case of inward emotions and religious experiences and the naive expression of these emotions and experiences in word, symbol, and act, I should always try first to regard the particular fact as 'analogical'. Where it is a case of formula, a professional liturgical usage, or the formulation of some doctrine, I should always try first to regard the particular fact as 'genealogical'.

Unlike later proponents of the distinction (as represented by the Metzger passage), there is no sense in Deissmann that significant parallels are genealogical ones because they threaten the uniqueness of early Christianity, and, hence, the concomitant desire to reduce all parallels to 'mere' analogies. In Deissmann, the significance and utility of both are affirmed. This is because Deissmann has a general theory of religious phenomena which governs the distinction. Whilst there are good reasons to challenge its adequacy, he presumes a dichotomy between spontane-

---

[16] Metzger, 'Methodology in the Study of the Mystery Religions': 18 and 9. The second sentence of the second citation is an unacknowledged direct quotation from Deissmann, see below, n. 17. The lengths to which Metzger carries this distinction may be illustrated by a characteristic sentence: 'the resemblance between the Lord's Supper and certain Mithraic ceremonies ... may be regarded as either fortuitous or as the result of adaptation by Mithraic priests of an impressive rite in the Christian cultus' (16, n. 2). What an odd choice! For Metzger, the 'resemblance' is either to be classified as analogical, understood as a matter of chance, or it is genealogical and asserted to be of Christian pedigree.

ous expressions which reflect 'emotions and experiences', and
stereotyped second-order expressions, assuming that the generality
of the former leads, as an initial hypothesis, to explaining similarities as 'analogical', whilst the specificity of the latter leads, as an
initial hypothesis, to explaining similarities as 'genealogical'. He
further demonstrates an awareness of the politics of such explanations. 'The apologist, if he ever acknowledges anything, acknowledges as a rule only analogy, and prefers to erect walls and fences
around his own little precinct' – an apt description of Metzger!
The 'amateur in these subjects thinks only of genealogy.'[17]

Nevertheless, one cannot help but be struck by the paucity of
imagination present in even a sophisticated formulation of this
apparently self-evident duality. If one opens any dictionary of
synonyms, one gains an immediate sense, by contrast, of the rich
vocabulary of similarity and difference. While there are terms
which suggest the sort of kinship implied by the notion of the
'genealogical' – for example, 'affinity', 'homology', and
'divergent' – the majority of the terms presume *intellectual
operations* on the part of the individual making the comparison, as
well as the notion that we are comparing *relations and aspects* not
things. This observation is reinforced by looking at other
comparative endeavours within the field of religion, when the
subject is remote from that of early Christianity. One will find,
alongside of terms such as 'homology' and 'analogy', 'identity'
and 'difference,' a vocabulary of 'transformation,' 'inversion,'
'reversal,' 'opposition,' 'contrast,' 'correspondence,' 'congru-
ence,' 'isomorphic,' 'conjunction,' 'disjunction,' and so forth,[18] as
well as a more polythetic notion of classification (in opposition to
a monothetic one) that employs phrases such as 'family resem-
blances,' 'connotative features,' 'fuzzy sets,' 'cluster concepts,'
among others.[19]

What this terminology reminds us of is that, like the effort of

---

[17] A. Deissmann, *Licht vom Osten*, 4th ed. (Tübingen, 1923): 226–27; I cite the English
translation, *Light from the Ancient East: The New Testament Illustrated by Recently Discovered
Texts of the Greco-Roman World*, (New York, 1927): 265–66.

[18] While, perhaps, an extreme example, all of these terms can be found in the 'Table of
Symbols' in C. Lévi-Strauss, *The Raw and The Cooked* (New York, 1969): xiii.

[19] See the fuller list in the seminal article by F. J. P. Poole, 'Metaphors and Maps:
Towards Comparison in the Anthropology of Religion,' *Journal of the American Academy
of Religion*, 54(1986): 428. The entire article (pp. 411–57) will well repay careful study.

taxonomy which forms its presupposition, there is nothing 'natural' about the enterprise of comparison. Similarity and difference are not 'given'. They are the result of mental operations. In this sense, *all comparisons are properly analogical*, and fall under J. S. Mill's dictum, 'if we have the slightest reason to suppose any real connection between ... A and B, the argument is no longer one of analogy.'[20]

In the case of the study of religion, as in any disciplined inquiry, comparison, in its strongest form, brings differences together within the space of the scholar's mind for the scholar's own intellectual reasons. It is the scholar who makes their cohabitation – their 'sameness' – possible, not 'natural' affinities or processes of history. Taken in this sense, 'genealogy' disguises and obscures the scholar's interests and activities allowing the illusion of passive observation (what Nietzsche has termed [*Zarathustra* 2.15], the 'myth of the immaculate perception').

Without engaging in the intricacies of resemblance theory, it can usefully help us at this point.[21] It is agreed that the statement '*x* resembles *y*' is logically incomplete, for what is being asserted is not a question of the classification of species *x* and *y* as instances of a common genus, but rather a suppressed multi-term statement of analogy and difference capable of being properly expressed in formulations such as:

'*x* resembles *y* more than *z* with respect to ...;'

or,

'*x* resembles *y* more than *w* resembles *z* with respect to ...'.

That is to say, the statement of comparison is never dyadic, but always triadic; there is always an implicit 'more than', and there is always a 'with respect to'. In the case of an academic comparison, the 'with respect to' is most frequently the scholar's interest, be this expressed in a question, a theory, or a model – recalling, in the case of the latter, that a model is useful precisely when it is different from that to which it is being applied.

---

[20] J. S. Mill, *A System of Logic*, 10th ed. (London, 1879), 2:371

[21] See, among others, D. J. O'Connor, 'On Resemblance,' *Proceedings of the Aristotelian Society*, 46(1945–46): 47–77 and P. Butchvarov, *Resemblance and Identity* (Bloomington, 1966) which include the essential bibliography.

This is to say, comparison does not necessarily tell us how things 'are' (the far from latent presupposition that lies behind the notion of the 'genealogical' with its quest for 'real' historical connections); like models and metaphors, comparison tells us how things might be conceived, how they might be 'redescribed', in Max Black's useful term.[22] A comparison is a disciplined exaggeration in the service of knowledge. It lifts out and strongly marks certain features within difference as being of possible intellectual significance, expressed in the rhetoric of their being 'like' in some stipulated fashion. Comparison provides the means by which *we* 're-vision' phenomena as *our* data in order to solve *our* theoretical problems.

The 'political' implications of this 're-visioning' must be faced as they go to the heart of a widely shared set of assumptions within religious scholarship, nowhere more so than in the study of early Christianity.

In his seminal essay on the sociology of knowledge, Karl Mannheim introduced a valuable distinction which bears directly on the question of the ideological dimension of comparison. Mannheim distinguished between 'right-wing' and 'left-wing' methodologies:

> Early nineteenth century German conservatism ... and contemporary conservatism, too, for that matter, tend to use morphological categories which do not break up the concrete totality of the data of experience, but seek rather to preserve it in all its uniqueness. As opposed to the morphological approach, the analytical approach characteristic of the parties of the left, broke down every concrete totality in order to arrive at smaller, more general, units which might then be recombined ...[23]

Religious studies, with its bias towards the 'unique' and the 'total', expressed methodologically through its deep involvement in morphology, phenomenology and, more recently, in a morality of regard for local interpretations, has been a discipline profoundly and not unsurprisingly of the 'right'. The compara-

---

[22] M. Black, *Models and Metaphors* (Ithaca, 1962):236–38; cf. M. B. Hesse, *Models and Analogies in Science* (Notre Dame, 1966): 164–65.

[23] K. Mannheim, *Ideology and Utopia* (New York, n.d.; reprint): 274.

tive endeavour herein described is relentlessly an affair of the 'left'. To quote the anthropologist, F. J. P. Poole:

> Comparison does not deal with phenomena *in toto* or in the round, but only with an aspectual characteristic of them. Analytical control over the framework of comparison involves theoretically focused selection of significant aspects of the phenomena and a bracketing of the endeavor by strategic *ceteris paribus* assumptions ... The comparability of phenomena always depends both on the purpose of comparison and on a theoretically informed analysis. Neither phenomenologically whole entities nor their local meanings are preserved in comparison. What matters in comparison are certain variables that are posited by and cohere in theories and that are aligned with aspects of the phenomena to be compared through some set of correspondence rules.[24]

Comparison, as seen from such a view, is an active, at times even a playful, enterprise of deconstruction and reconstitution which, kaleidoscope-like, gives the scholar a shifting set of characteristics with which to negotiate the relations between his or her theoretical interests and data stipulated as exemplary. The comparative enterprise provides a set of perspectives which 'serve different analytic purposes by emphasizing varied aspects' of the object of study.[25]

It is the scholar's intellectual purpose – whether explanatory or interpretative, whether generic or specific – which highlights that principled postulation of similarity which is the ground of the methical comparison of difference being interesting. Lacking a clear articulation of purpose, one may derive arresting anecdotal juxtapositions or self-serving differentiations, but the disciplined constructive work of the academy will not have been advanced, nor will the study of religion have come of age.

---

[24] Poole, 'Metaphors and Maps': 414–15.
[25] Poole, 'Metaphors and Maps': 432.

III

On Comparing Words

I

Words are notoriously difficult and slippery affairs, yet, in recent years, we have seen them impeached, by individuals within the field of religious studies, for their clarity and fixity. There is a body of sentiment impatient with the scholar's preoccupation with texts, a preoccupation scorned, in some recent literature, with such distaste as to be reminiscent of the old polemics against 'bibliolatry'.[1] 'The letter killeth; but the spirit giveth life,' we are insistently reminded – a dualism escaped by the old rabbinic pun on the tablets of the Law being *ḥrt* (Ex 32.16), a syllabic formation capable of being pointed as either, *ḥarut*, 'engraved', or, *ḥerut*, 'free' (*Pirke Avot* 6.2). These same scholars of religion charge us to be at least equally attentive to a range of non-verbal phenomena, from performance to iconography, or, failing this, to focus on the polysemy of terms and symbols, a focus that at times seems to verge on pan-symbolism.[2]

Often, it would appear, lying behind such calls is a nostalgia for the fabled experience of direct, non-mediated communication, a nostalgia at least as old in western tradition as Plato's seventh epistle with its language of a lengthy 'companionship' during which, 'suddenly, a spark leaps', (7.341d) and its concommitant mistrust of words (7.341c, 343a, 344c), a process elsewhere expressed in the *Dialogues* as the characteristic Platonic erotics of vision. It is a yearning for the power to convert a 'talking-about' to a 'talking-with' through essentially non-linguistic means, whether expressed in the old mystical ideals of silence and 'non-symbolic' communication or in the newer emphases of Barth on the 'Word of God' or Eliade on 'hierophanies', 'epiphanies',

---

[1] See, A. Dorner, 'Bibliolatry,' in J. Hastings, ed., *Encyclopedia of Religion and Ethics*, (New York, 1917), 2:615–18.

[2] See on this, H. Penner, 'Bedeutung und Probleme der religiösen Symbolik bei Tillich und Eliade,' *Antaios*, 9(1967): 127–43.

'kratophanies', and all his other neologisms constructed on the root *phaino* as non-verbal self-display. It is, above all, a modulation of one of the regnant Protestant *topoi* in which the category of inspiration has been transposed from the text to the experience of the interpreter, the one who is being directly addressed *through* the text. This *topos* continues to supply the fundamental presuppositions for much contemporary hermeneutic theory. As employed by some scholars in religious studies, it must be judged a fantastic attempt to transform interpretation into revelation. It expresses a refusal to concede that all speech is mediated and necessarily indirect, and that, therefore, all speech requires translation, whether we are treating with interpersonal, intracultural or intercultural communication.

For the students of antique religions, such hermeneutical proposals, often combined with some dialogic theory of religious research as being an encounter with an 'other', whether the latter is understood as an ontological or anthropological category, have seemed largely irrelevant. Trained exquisitely in philological procedures, they protest that their data are largely embedded in written documents, and that the interpretation of non-literary materials, severed from the 'control' of texts, often appear to have no more validity than a Rorschach test, illuminating the investigator's mind-set, but casting little light on archaic intentions.[3] If words stand at the heart of our enterprise, then it is with the question of words and their comparisons that we must begin.

The first scholar to concern himself directly with the question of the relationship of 'mystery-terminology' within early Christian literature to the wider use of the same terminology within archaic and Late Antique documents was that superb philologian, Isaac Casaubon.[4] The context is not unimportant. Casaubon, in *De rebus sacris et ecclesiasticis exercitationes XVI* (1614), had undertaken to write a detailed critical (and Protestant) commentary on the vast Roman Catholic historiographical work of Cardinal Baronius, *Annales Ecclesiastici* (1588–1607), itself a Cath-

---

[3] For a characteristic example, see this issue in the work of E. R. Goodenough as described in Smith, *Imagining Religion*: 32.

[4] For Casaubon's philological expertise, see M. Pattison, *Isaac Casaubon: 1559–1614*, 2nd ed. (Oxford, 1892): 314–17, 332, 455–60, et passim.

olic rejoinder to the *Magdeburg Centuries*.[5] Due to its nature as a
commentary on another's work, much of Casaubon's treatise has
a disjointed quality. Fortunately, the best organized section is also
the one most relevant to our topic, his essay, *De sacrosancta
eucharistia*,[6] in which his commentary on *mystērion* (477–99) plays
a pivotal role.

As the setting for the discussion, Casaubon raises the question
of the 'novelty' of Christianity. If the Christian religion was not
to be dismissed as an *opinio novitatis*, then, as Paul had done in the
Areopagus speech, connection had to be made to the religious
traditions of the 'pagans' (477, 480). In part, this was accomplished through terminology, in particular, that of the mysteries
(481–84), which occur not only in the writings of the Church
fathers (485–99), but in the Pauline epistles and the Gospels as
well (478–80).

By way of introduction to his essay, after noting the derivation
of *mystērion*, meaning, 'secret doctrine', from *muein*, Casaubon
indulges in an odd bit of etymologizing. *Mystērion*, he writes, was
'originally' the Hebrew *str*, meaning 'to hide', as revealed in
formations such as *master*, *mistār*, and *mistôr* (478). While such a
derivation must be rejected as fanciful,[7] although no more
fantastic than some playful old Greek etymologies,[8] it established

---

[5] On the *Magdeburg Centuries*, see above, p. 14. Baronius's *Annales* carried its
narrative to 1198. It was, posthumously, extended by other editors. See the major edition
by Mainsi, (Lucca, 1738–59), 1–38. Note that, at the time of Casaubon's commentary,
criticism of Baronius was forbidden by papal decree (Pattison, *Casaubon*: 196, 216).

[6] I. Casaubon, *De rebus sacris et ecclesiasticis exercitationes XVI. Ad Cardinalis Baronii
Prolegomena in Annales*, 1st ed. (London, 1614): 500–86. I cite, throughout, the more
accessible 4th edition published in Geneva, 1663, where the essay occurs on pp. 441–512.

[7] For the Semitic etymology of *str*, see *Theologisches Wörterbuch zum Alten Testament*
(Stuttgart, 1970–), 5:967, s.v. *sātar*, and compare the useful semasiological study by
S. E. Balentine, 'A Description of the Semantic Field of Hebrew Words for "Hide,"'
Vetus Testamentum 30(1980): 137–53. In rabbinic Hebrew, *misṭerîn* is a loan-word from the
Greek, *mystērion*. (M. Jastrow, *A Dictionary of the Targumim, the Talmud Babli and
Yerushalmi, and the Midrashic Literature* [London, 1903], 2:806). In contrast to Casaubon's
Semitic derivation, the Greek, *mystērion/muein*, appears to depend on an Indo-European
derivation, perhaps from *mu* (see J. Pokorny, *Indogermanisches etymologisches Wörterbuch*
[Bern, 1959–60]: 751, s.v. *mū*), although, as G. Bornkamm wittily reminds us, 'the
etymology of the word is itself a mystery' (*TDNT* 4:803, s.v. *mystērion*).

[8] E.g. Aristotle, *Rhetoric* 2.24.1401a, which attributes to Polycrates a joke relating *mus*,
'mouse' and *mystērion*, and Athenaios, *Deipnosophists* 3.98d, which attributes to Dionysius
the Tyrant the pun, *mystērion = mus tērein*, 'mouseholes'. I leave to the imagination of my
readers the question as to whether the expressions 'quiet as a [church] mouse' or 'to be as
mute [or, to mumble] as a mouse in a cheese' continue this playful notion.

a pattern of argumentation that would persist to our own time: the insistence that *mystērion*, especially as found in early Christian literature, was to find its meaning in relation to Hebrew terminology and usage rather than Greek.

The pioneering work of Casaubon had two other implications which were to be significant for future research. First, by collecting the mystery-words used in patristic sources (480, 485–99) he reduced the question to a matter of terminology. For nearly three centuries, scholarship would be devoted to conceiving the relationship between early Christianity and other antique religions primarily as a linguistic affair. His catalogue, but little expanded, would be determinative: *mystērion, muēseis, teletas, teleiōseis, epopteias, mystagogiam*, et al.

Second, despite his knowledge that the 'mysteries' focused on rituals, his definition of *mystērion* as *arcanum doctrinam* (478) gave rise to the notion that the 'mysteries' were essentially concerned with secret teachings, with *dogmata*.[9] This definition, in turn, led to the Protestant polemic preoccupation with the alleged Roman Catholic practice of the *disciplina arcani*, a term first put forth by John Daillé, in 1666, and often used, in the early Protestant literature, with explicit reference to Casaubon.[10] This argument was double-edged. On the one hand, as the evidence for this practice was post-apostolic, it became another element in the Protestant reconstruction of Catholic history, evidence for the later 'corruption' of 'pristine' Christianity – from public proclamation to private teaching, from an affair of the common to one of the elite. On the other hand, Catholic apologists attempted to account for those items which the Protestants termed 'innovations' by arguing that doctrines such as transubstantiation were

[9] I refer, here, to the distinction, in some patristic texts, between *kērygmata* as doctrine proclaimed openly and *dogmata* as guarded doctrine proclaimed secretly to the Christian initiate. See, among others, G. W. Lampe, *A Patristic Greek Lexicon* (Oxford, 1961–68), 2:377, s.v. *dogma*, sect. B.5.d.ii, who cites Basil, *Liber de Spiritu sancto* 25 et passim.

[10] J. Daillé (= Dallaeus), *De Scriptus quae sub Dionysii Areopagitae nomine circumferuntur* (Geneva, 1666): 140–45, esp. 142; cf. 490–91. Daillé frequently cites Casaubon (e.g., pp. 168–73), although not on this topic. For the influence of Casaubon on the notion of the *disciplina arcani*, see esp. G. N. Bontwetsch, 'Wesen, Entstehung und Fortgang der Arkandisciplin,' *Zeitschrift für die historische Theologie*, 43(1873): 203–13; P. Battifol, 'Arcane,' *Dictionnaire de théologie catholique* (Paris, 1909–), 1:1740; O. Perler, 'Arkandisziplin,' *Reallexikon für Antike und Christentum* (Stuttgart, 1950–), 1:667–78.

58 DRUDGERY DIVINE

present from the beginning, but were held secret.[11] The rhetorical heat generated by this controversy may be gauged from a citation from Joseph Bingham's, *Antiquities of the Christian Church* (1708–22), perhaps the only work, despite its fulminations, worthy of being termed a history of Christianity as a religion. Bingham writes of the:

> vain pretences of the Romanists concerning the original and the reasons of this discipline ... This is an artifice that would justify as many errors and vanities as any church could be guilty of: it is but working a little with this admirable discipline and tool, called *disciplina arcani*, and then all the seeming contradictions between the ancient doctrines and practices of the church universal, and the novel corruptions of the modern church of Rome will presently vanish and disappear. So that we need not wonder, why men, whose interest it serves so much, should magnify this as a noble invention. [The 'discipline of silence' has] no relation to such doctrines as that of transubstantiation, or the number of the seven sacraments, or such superstitious practices as the worship of images, or saints and angels, which are mere novelties, and the modern inventions of the Romish church.[12]

It is a mark of Casaubon's enduring influence on the subject of early Christianity and the 'mysteries', that the first modern scholarly treatments of the topic are essentially concerned with comparing vocabulary (largely, Casaubon's list of mystery-words) and devote considerable space to the question of the *disciplina arcani*. This is the case with the four foundation studies in the field: the works of Edwin Hatch (1890), Gustav Anrich (1894), Georg Wobbermin (1896), and Samuel Cheetham (1897).[13]

[11] See the dispute between E. von Schelstrate, *Dissertatio apologetica de disciplini arcani*, contra ... *Tentzelii* (Rome, 1685) and W. E. Tentzel, 'Dissertatio de disciplina arcani,' in Tentzel, *Excercitationes selectae* (Leipzig, 1692), 2:9–2:31. See the useful review of this dispute in V. Huyskens, *Zur Frage über die sogennante Arkandisziplin* (Münster, 1891): 16–22.

[12] J. Bingham, *Origines ecclesiasticae: The Antiquities of the Christian Church*, 1st ed. (1708–22); I cite a later edition (London, 1875), 1:467, 472.

[13] E. Hatch, *The Influence of Greek Ideas on Christianity* (London, 1890; rp. New York, 1957) makes the *disciplina arcani* and shared vocabulary the heart of his chapter on 'The

The Casaubon-tradition, through the end of the nineteenth century,[14] makes three central assumptions: 1) both features, the vocabulary and the *disciplina arcani*, can be traced to an "accommodation", whether apologetic or paedagogic, to 'pagan' converts and thus 2) indicate a direct transmission of both mystery terminology and notions from the 'gentile background' to the early Christian texts; 3) what is transmitted is essentially doctrinal formulations. The influential work of Hatch can serve as a typical example.

Hatch's 1888 Hibbert Lectures, *The Influence of Greek Ideas on Christianity*, both as posthumously published in English (edited by A. M. Fairburn) and in its rapid German translation, set a standard for an enlarged view of the matter which has rarely been attained in subsequent scholarship. 'Greek ideas' were understood in an expansive fashion – hence his introduction of the topics 'education' (ch. 1), 'exegesis' (ch. 2), 'rhetoric' (ch. 3), 'philosophy' (ch. 4), and 'ethics' (ch. 5), before turning to the explicitly religious issues of 'theology' (chs. 7–9) and 'the influence of the mysteries upon Christian usages' (ch. 10). 'Christianity' included, not only early Christian literature, but also later Roman and Byzantine Christian materials up to the fifteenth century. (See the methodological statement on p. 14.) He claims not to be interested in questions of isolated parallels or influences, but rather in

Influence on the Mysteries upon Christian Usage' (283–309, esp. 292–93, 296). G. Anrich, *Das antike Mysterienwesen in seinem Einfluss auf das Christentum* (Göttingen, 1894) begins by listing Casaubon as the 'originator' of research into the relations of early Christianity and the 'mysteries' (1) and goes on to discuss the question of the *disciplina arcani* (2–4), a subject which preoccupies him throughout his study (67–68, 126–29, 150–54, et passim), and to which he returns towards the conclusion in a chapter whose title sums up Casaubon's influence, 'Mysterienterminologie und Arcan-Disciplin' (155–67). G. Wobbermin, *Religionsgeschichtliche Studien zur Frage der Beeinflussung des Urchristentums durch das antike Mysterienwesen* (Berlin, 1896) is far less concerned with the issue of the *disciplina arcani*, raising it only at the conclusion of his work (177–78), but focuses heavily on matters of shared vocabulary. S. Cheetham, *The Mysteries, Pagan and Christian* (London, 1897), like Anrich, begins with an extended discussion of the *disciplina arcani*, giving pride of place to Casaubon, and indicating that it was upon reading a set of more recent studies on the subject 'that I was first attracted to the comparison of Christian and pagan mysteries' (ix–xii). He returns to the subject at length (78–90). Much of his labour, especially in the central chapters (III–IV) focuses on matters of vocabulary (see esp. the long note, 135–38, n. 15).

[14] For purposes of this argument, I have made no attempt to trace the genealogy of the Casaubon tradition beyond indicating its origins, and its effects in the four works cited above (n. 13).

'the whole mental attitude of the Greek world in the first three centuries of our era' (3).

Hatch's opening move is worthy of attention, as it signals a viewpoint that will recur throughout his work. He begins by contrasting the Sermon on the Mount to the Nicene Creed, observing that the former 'belongs to a world of Syrian peasants, the other to a world of Greek philosophers' (1), that the former is concerned with 'ethics', the latter with 'doctrine', and that the 'change in the centre of gravity from conduct to belief is coincident with a transference of Christianity from a Semitic to a Greek soil' (2). Thus, Hatch's question is that of the rapid hellenization of Christianity from its 'primitive' simplicity to the complexity of its later 'Catholic' forms. While he maintains that this essentially Protestant model is but one of two interpretative choices (351), it is, in fact, the one which he employs throughout, nowhere more so than in the section which deals with the topic with which we are primarily concerned, the relation of the 'mysteries' to early Christianity.

Hatch's discussion of the influence of the 'mysteries' needs to be seen in the context of his (Protestant) portrait of early Christian community organization. There is, he argues:

> no adequate evidence that, in the first age of Christianity, association was other than voluntary. It was profoundly individual[15] ... There was not necessarily any organization ... When once [Christian organizations] began to be formed, they were formed on a basis which was less intellectual than moral and spiritual ... The associations, like the primitive clusters which were not yet crystallized into associations, were held together by faith and love and hope, and fused, as it were, by a common enthusiasm. (334-45)

It is with respect to this formation of Christian organizations that Hatch introduces the subject of the 'mysteries', arguing that 'it was inevitable' that the new organizations, existing side by side

[15] That this is a theological rather than an historical or sociological judgement is made plain by the next sentences, omitted above, 'It assumed for the first time in human history the infinite worth of the individual soul. The ground of that infinite worth was a divine sonship' (334). If the Pauline letters are not too late to offer evidence for Hatch's, undefined, 'first age of Christianity', they would be sufficient evidence that there was, by no means, a lack of organization.

with older religious associations, 'should tend to assimilate, with the assimilation of their members, some of the elements of these existing groups' (292). In each case, this 'assimilation' was a move from 'original simplicity' to 'later complexity'. Thus,

> Up to a certain time there is no evidence that Christianity had any secrets. It was preached openly to the world ... its rites were simple and its teaching was public. After a certain time all is changed: mysteries have arisen in the once open and easily accessible faith, and there are doctrines which must not be declared in the hearing of the uninitiated (293).

Along with this change – Hatch is distressingly vague as to its chronology – are two further fundamental transformations, the one of 'name', the other of 'character'.

> The term *mystērion*; is applied to baptism, and with it comes a whole series of technical terms [Hatch provides what is, essentially the Casaubon list] unknown to the Apostolic Church, but well known to the mysteries, and explicable only through the ideas and usages peculiar to them. (296)

And, as a concomitant, a sharp distinction is made between the initiated and the uninitiated.

> I dwell upon these broad features, and especially on the transference of names, because it is necessary to show that the relation of the mysteries to the sacrament was not merely a curious coincidence; and what I have said as to the change of name and the change of conception, might largely be supplemented by evidence of parallelism in the benefits conceived to attach to the one and the other. (297–98)

The transfer of terminology and distinction was direct; the result of Christianity's accommodation to new converts, and the indigenous understandings and vocabularies of these converts. For this reason, the initial duality between the original world of 'Syrian peasants' and the subsequent environment of 'Greek philosophers' (1) persists throughout the work. The one is, by nature, simple; the other complex. The transition from the one to the other – from 'peasant' to 'philosopher' – is necessarily abrupt and drastic. Nowhere in Hatch's lectures, for all of his pioneering work on the Septuagint,[16] is the latter quoted, nor is there any sense of hellenistic Judaism as possibly supplying an intermediary link between 'Greek' and 'Christian' usage. When 'Greco-Judaism' (69) is spoken of in this work, it is always in the context of what Hatch terms 'philosophical Judaism' (128) and means Philo and the other Alexandrians adopting Greek philosophical conceptions and modes of reading texts (65–69, 128–29, 177 n. 1, 182, 199–200), an adoption Hatch relates more frequently to modes of Gnosticism (esp. 129–34) than to other forms of Christian tradition.[17]

II

With the enormous increase in research, in the late nineteenth and early twentieth centuries, both into the Septuagint and *koine* Greek, particularly as represented in the papyri and epigraphical materials, the Casaubon tradition was replaced, on the one hand by a strong revaluation of the Septuagint as a source for the vocabulary of early Christianity, and, on the other, by a reevaluation of the Greek documentation on the basis of 'non-

---

[16] In his *Essays in Biblical Greek* (Oxford, 1889), Hatch takes a somewhat ambivalent view towards what he conceives of as an independent Biblical Greek (11). While this work is best known for its first canon: 'A word which is used uniformly, or with few and intelligible exceptions, as a translation of the same Hebrew word, must be held to have in Biblical Greek the same meaning as that Hebrew word' (35), Hatch, nevertheless, cautions against 'too great a stress on the meaning of individual words', characterizing the Septuagint as a 'targum or paraphrase' rather than a strict translation (15). His essay on *mystērion* (57–62) stresses continuity. In Daniel and the Apocrypha, *mystērion*, in the majority of the passages, refers to 'secrets of state, or the plan which the king kept in his own mind. This was a strictly Oriental conception ... It was natural to extend the conception to the secret plans of God.' This extended meaning carries over in the New Testament writings (58). Hatch devotes most space, however, to the question of the Apostolic use of *mystērion* as all but interchangeable with *typos, symbolon* and *parabolē*, having in mind the even later connection of *mystērion* with *sacramentum* and attempting to capture this under his rubric of a 'natural' extended meaning. 'The secret purpose or counsel was intimated enigmatically by a symbolical representation in words, or in pictures, or in action ... It was by a natural process that the sign and the thing signified came to be identified, and that the word which was used for the one came also to be used for the other' (61).

[17] See, on this latter point, the shrewd observations of A. Momigliano, 'Hellenismus und Gnosis: Randbemerkungen zu Droysens Geschichte des Hellenismus,' *Saeculum* 21(1970): 185–88, incorporated into his longer article on Droysen, 'J. G. Droysen, Between Greeks and Jews,' *History and Theory* 9(1970): 139–53, as reprinted in Momigliano, *Essays in Ancient and Modern Historiography* (Middletown, 1977): 307–23, esp. 315–16.

literary' rather than literary remains. In the work of some scholars (e.g. Deissmann), this double expansion of data was held together in a mutually informing fashion; in other scholars (e.g. H. A. A. Kennedy), the one, the Septuagint, was used largely to displace the perceived centrality of the other. It is this latter strategem that will be our chief concern.

What made this repositioning possible was that remarkable space of two decades which saw the rapid publication of the essential tools for Septuagint study, the manual edition of Vaticanus edited by Swete (1887–94), the Hatch-Redpath *Concordance* (1892–1906), the first volume of the Cambridge Septuagint edited by Brooke and McLean (1906), and the grammar of Helbing (1907), among others.[18] These could allow Swete to assert, in 1900, that:

> The Greek terminology of Christian Doctrine is largely indebted to the Alexandrian translators ... The influence of Greek philosophy and of Gnostic speculation must also be borne in mind by the student of the language of dogma. But it is perhaps even more important that he should trace it back to its source in the Greek Old Testament, which was far more familiar to Christian teachers of the first three centuries than the writings of Plato or the schools of Basileides and Valentinus.[19]

and Deissmann to declare, in his Uppsala lectures of 1909, that:

[18] H. B. Swete, *The Old Testament in Greek according to the Septuagint*, 1st ed. (Cambridge, 1887–94), 1–3; E. Hatch and H. A. Redpath, *Concordance to the Septuagint* (Oxford, 1892–1906), 1–3; A. E. Brooke and N. McLean, *The Old Testament in Greek according to the Text of Codex Vaticanus* (Cambridge, 1906), 1, *Genesis*; R. Helbing, *Grammatik der Septuaginta Laut- und Wortlehre* (Göttingen, 1907). For an early attempt to use the new linguistic data, both the *koine* materials from the papyri and inscriptions, and the LXX, see, Th. Nägeli, *Der Wortschatz des Apostel Paulus: Beitrag zur sprachgeschichtliche Erforschung des Neuen Testaments* (Göttingen, 1905), who gives approximately equal treatment to Paul's classical (12–37), hellenistic (28–58) and Septuagintal (59–75) vocabularies.

A useful overview of the history of LXX-scholarship can be gleaned from S. Brock, C. T. Fritsch and S. Jellicoe, *A Classified Bibliography of the Septuagint* (Leiden, 1973) in conjunction with S. Jellicoe's magisterial work, *The Septuagint and Modern Study* (Oxford, 1968). I regret that I have been unable to obtain J. Ros, *De studie van het bijbelgrieksch van Hugo Grotius tot Adolf Deissmann* (Nijmegen, 1940).

[19] H. B. Swete, *Introduction to the Old Testament in Greek* (Cambridge, 1900); I cite the 2nd ed. (Cambridge, 1902): 473.

Paul, the Christian, never withdrew from the divine world of the Hellenistic Old Testament. To understand the whole Paul from the point of view of the history of religion one must know the spirit of the Septuagint.[20]

The consequences of this position, for our theme, were taken up in a pioneering fashion by H. A. A. Kennedy and, later, by A. D. Nock in a series of essays that have become all but canonical in the literature on the relation of early Christianity to the religions of Late Antiquity. Focus on their treatment of the single term, *mystērion*, will be sufficient to display both the achievements and the problems inherent in their work.

In his earlier study of the Septuagint in relation to the New Testament, published in 1895, Kennedy had argued that, while the Septuagint plays a major role in 'moulding the *religious* vocabulary of the New Testament', this has been, at times, 'overestimated', and that, overall, the influence of the Septuagint is 'surprisingly' small.[21] When one turns to his better known study of 1912–13, *St. Paul and the Mystery Religions*, a quite different picture emerges.[22] 'The religious history of Judaism [is]

[20] The first printed version of Deissmann's lectures, 'Paul, a Study in Cultural and Religious History,' was a Swedish translation, *Paulus: En kultur- och religionshistorisk skiss* (Stockholm, 1910), followed by the German edition, *Paulus: Eine kultur- und religionsgeschichtliche Skizze* (Tübingen, 1911). I cite the 2nd ed. of the English translation, A. Deissmann, *Paul: A Study in Social and Religious History* (New York, 1927; rp. New York, 1957): 99, cf. 87, 90, 99–104, 145–47, 188, 190. Cf. Deissmann's 1907 Cambridge lectures, *The Philology of the Greek Bible: Its Present and Future* (London, 1907): 8, 9, 12.

[21] H. A. A. Kennedy, *Sources of New Testament Greek, or The Influence of the Septuagint on the Vocabulary of the New Testament* (Edinburgh, 1895): 45, 109, 135, 142–45, 164–65. Note Deissmann's strictures on Kennedy's statistics in *Licht vom Östen*; I cite the English translation of the 4th German edition (Tübingen, 1923), *Light from the Ancient East*: 76–77.

[22] H. A. A. Kennedy, *St. Paul and the Mystery Religions* (London, 1913) which pagination I cite above. The bulk of the text originally appeared as a multi-part article, 'St. Paul and the Mystery Religions,' in *The Expositor*, ser. 8, 3(1912): 289–305, 420–41; 4(1912): 60–88, 212–37, 306–27, 434–51, 539–54; 5(1913): 62–75, 115–26. Cf. Kennedy, 'St. Paul's Conception of the Knowledge of God,' *The Expositor*, ser. 8, 16(1918): 241–69 and Kennedy, 'A New Interpretation of Paulinism,' *The Expositor*, ser. 8, 14(1917): 81–97, 175–94, esp. 86, 193. The latter citation reads: 'There is no necessity to look for the origin of any important religious conception of the Pauline theology in the Hellenistic *milieu* ... If we are keen to detect the influence of the environment, we must have recourse to the paramount authority in Paul's religious training, the Scriptures of the Old Testament, and these especially in their Greek dress. A clamant task, which as yet has been barely touched, is that of examining Paul's theological vocabulary in the light of the terms used in the Septuagint to translate the language of Hebrew religion.' See further, Kennedy, 'Mysteries, Christian,' in J. Hastings, ed., *Encyclopedia of Religion and Ethics*, 9:72–74.

sufficient' to account for the 'mystery' elements in Paul. There-fore, 'no explanation from his Hellenistic environment' is re-quired (x). Such an explanation, given Paul's grounding in the Greek Old Testament, would be 'wholly superfluous' (198).

It is important to note that Kennedy's arguments do not chiefly rest on his philological demonstrations. He asserts the conviction that Dobschutz is correct in asserting that 'the unique sacramental conception of the Early Church, which has no analogy in the history of religion because it belongs essentially to the Christian religion, has its origin solely in Christian faith and Christian experience' (279). For Paul, the 'centrality of faith' must serve as the 'criterion' of any theory as to his 'ideas', and, for this, 'there is no corresponding feature in the framework of the Mystery-Religions' (284, cf. 223, 243). Furthermore, while Paul was 'too sensitive ... to disparage the simple rites which he found existing in the nascent Church ... the essential characteristic of his thought was detachment from ceremonial' (282–83). All is to be sub-sumed to the category of faith and 'sacramental grace'. There could be no comparison with the mysteries, for their view of ritual was confined to its 'working *ex opere operato*' (254–55).

When he turns, in his fourth chapter, to the specific topic of 'St. Paul's Relation to the Terminology of the Mystery Reli-gions' several theses, each relatively undeveloped, are put forth. 1) There can be no essential relation; 'every leading conception' in Paul has 'its roots definitely laid' in the 'soil' of the Greek Old Testament (154–55). 2) If there is a relation it is accidental – and certainly not genealogical. They both 'spring directly from that strain of Mysticism which seems to be everywhere latent in humanity ... Here Christianity and Pagan religion were bound to manifest affinities' (120). 3) The genius of Paul precludes any suggestion of passive appropriation. 'An individuality like Paul could not borrow without transforming' (122). And finally, 4) his most extended argument, when he does employ mystery-termi-nology 'the interesting question arises: How far does the use of mystic terminology involve the adoption of the ideas it ex-presses?' (121). The terms may occur, but they have been shorn of their meaning. They have become 'mere' words 'signifying nothing', perhaps employed, rhetorically, as 'little else than convenient channels of appeal to the popular interest' (122).

Consistent with these theses, when he turns to the specific topic of the word, *mystērion*, he notes:

> There are, roughly speaking, about a dozen instances of *mystērion* in the LXX, and with the exception of two ... it seems invariably to mean 'secrets' or 'secret plans', once or twice of God, usually of men ... When we turn to the Pauline Epistles, we at once discover that some of the instances directly tally with the LXX and Synoptics ... Let us briefly collect the implications of Paul's use of *mysterion*. It is remarkable that it is found, paradoxically, in close connection with verbs of revelation (*apokaluptein, phaneroun, gnōrizein*). That wholly accords with Paul's favourite idea of his own function of *kerussein*. (123–24, 128; cf. Kennedy, 'Mysteries, Christian', J. Hastings, ed., *Encyclopedia of Religion and Ethics*, 9:72).

Thus, there is no contact with the notion of 'mystery' in the 'mystery cults'. It is not secret teachings or cult practices which are being preserved, but rather a 'prophetic' notion of divine plans, hitherto hidden from men, but meant to be revealed in Christian preaching (171, et passim).[23]

Fifteen years later, the same enterprise was taken up by Arthur Darby Nock in a setting not innocent of apologetic concerns.[24]

---

[23] Note that this contrast between *mystērion* in the mystery cults as matters meant to be kept secret and *mystērion* in Christian (i.e. Pauline) discourse as matters meant to be proclaimed was commonplace in nineteenth century exegetical literature which made *no* reference to alleged Septuagintal usage or influence, and which conceded some relationship between the Pauline usage and that of the mystery cults. See, among others, J. B. Lightfoot, *Saint Paul's Epistles to the Colossians and to Philemon* (London, 1886): 165–66, '*to mystērion*. This is not the only term borrowed from the ancient mysteries, which Paul employs to describe the teaching of the Gospel ... There is this difference, however; that, whereas the heathen mysteries were strictly confined to a narrow circle, the Christian mysteries are freely confided to all ... Thus the very idea of *secrecy* or *reserve* disappears when *mystērion* is adopted into the Christian vocabulary by Saint Paul: and the word signifies simply "a truth which was once hidden but now is revealed" ... Hence *mystērion* is almost universally found [in Paul] in connection with words denoting revelation or publication.'

[24] The editor of the volume in which Nock's first essay originally appeared takes considerable pains to disassociate Nock from the theological interests of his fellow essayists. 'It is to be understood, however, that the essay in question [by Nock] stands somewhat apart from the rest ... Mr. Nock would not, I think, wish to disclaim general sympathy with the point of view of the book as a whole. He desires, however, that it should be made clear that he does not himself write either as a philosopher or as a

theologian, but purely and simply as an historian of religion. He has attempted (so far as that may be possible) to give a purely objective account of the religious facts of the period with which his essay is concerned. He is not of necessity to be taken as being in agreement with the presuppositions, whether of a philosophical or theological kind, which may be supposed to have been in the minds of his colleagues' (A. E. J. Rawlinson, 'Preface,' *Essays on the Trinity and the Incarnation by Members of the Anglican Communion* [London, 1928]: vii). Yet, when Nock himself reprinted this article, he chose to begin his prefatory note by relating Rawlinson's volume to previous collective volumes from Oxford, 'each in its own way a landmark in the theological thinking of the English-speaking world': *Essays and Reviews* (1860), *Lux Mundi* (1889) and *Foundations* (1912) (Nock, 'Introduction to the Torchbook Edition,' *Early Gentile Christianity and Its Hellenistic Background* [New York, 1964]: vii). That is to say, this volume by 'Members of the Anglican Communion,' including Nock's essay, needs to be read in the context of late nineteenth century and early twentieth century Church of England 'modernist' theological debates.

There is more. Once one is sensitive to the context, the Nock essay raises fundamental questions as to intent. Why an essay on Christianity prior to 80 AD which makes no reference to the two governing themes of the volume, incarnation and the trinity? The editor clearly considered this article a necessity, first asking Edwyn Bevan, and, after he declined, Nock (Nock, 'Introduction': viii), even though another essay in the volume, that by K. E. Kirk, 'The Evolution of the Doctrine of the Trinity' (159–237), dealt with both topics within the New Testament literature (see his summary statement, p. 208) and furiously rejected any notions of borrowing, hyperbolically suggesting that such claims painted 'Paul as the arch-criminal of a successful band of plunderers' (162, cf. 164). I would speculate that the interest was not the *religionsgeschichtliche* scholarship of the Germans with whom Nock is in constant dialogue, but rather a more parochial British issue. The essays in the Rawlinson volume were commissioned in 1924 (Nock, 'Introduction': vii), hard on the heels of the 'famous or infamous' Girton 'Modern Churchman's Conference' of 1921 which had as its prime impetus the rejection of the reconstruction of 'early Gentile Christianity' proposed by Kirsopp Lake. (See, among others, A. M. G. Stephenson, *The Rise and Decline of English Modernism* [London, 1984]: 109–22.) The addresses at the conference were reprinted in the September, 1921 issue of *The Modern Churchman* in which references of Lake abound. (*Modern Churchman*, 11[1921–22]: 194, 215–16, 218, 220, 228–36, 258, 264, 268–69; cf. the counter-Lake reading list proposed for the conference, 'Books for the Girton Conference,' *Modern Churchman*, 10[1921–22]: 181–82). Nock's essay, while never explicitly referring to Lake, can be understood as a systematic refutation of Lake.

Lake's thesis succinctly stated is that 'Christianity became sacramental – or a Mystery religion – on passing from Jewish to Greco-Oriental surroundings' (*Modern Churchman*, 11[1921–22]: 235). He had first proposed this understanding in Lake, *The Earlier Epistles of St. Paul: Their Motive and Origin* (London, 1911) – references to which make up the polemic spine of H. A. A. Kennedy's *St. Paul and the Mystery Religions*, e.g. x, 2, 212, 232–36, 244, 247, 264–65 – in a form particularly offensive to the Protestant consensus concerning Christian ritual and its difference from the 'sacraments' of both the 'mystery cults' and Roman Catholicism (see above, Chapter One, n. 58). The first generation gentile convert, drawn from the ranks of the 'god-fearers' – in recent scholarship, a more dubious category than in Lake's time – 'saw every reason for equating the Lord [Jesus] with the Redeemer-God of the Mystery Religions ... and to consider Baptism as an *opus operatum* which secured his admission to the Kingdom apart from the character of his future behaviour' (44, 46, cf. 233). 'Baptism is, for St. Paul and his readers, universally and unquestioningly accepted as a "mystery" or sacrament which works *ex opere operato* ... this sacramental teaching is central in the primitive Christianity to which the Roman Empire began to be converted' (385). Even the question of 'borrowing' was put, by Lake,

Nock's original article, along with his subsequent restatements, continue to be cited as the definitive treatment of the topic of the negative relationship of mystery terminology to early Christianity.[25]

Nock's original 1927 article is a comprehensive survey of 'Gentile Christianity' prior to 'A.D. 80' (1:50 n. 1) which seeks to establish that each of its constitutive elements may be traced to a background in Judaism and that no postulation of influence from the 'mysteries' is, therefore, required. The argument from terminology is but one step in the development of this thesis. In contrast to the Casaubon-tradition, *mystērion* is here defined in cultic terms.

> [It] is a secret rite, in which the individual participates of his own free choice, and by which he is put into a closer relation

in a form calculated to offend with specific reference to the Protestant consensus alluded to above: 'It is impossible to ignore the fact that much of the controversy between Catholic and Protestant theologians has found its centre in the doctrine of the Eucharist, and the latter [the Protestants] have appealed to primitive Christianity to support their views. From their point of view the appeal fails: the Catholic doctrine is much more nearly primitive than the Protestant. But the Catholic advocate in winning his case has proved still more: the type of doctrine which he defends is not only primitive, but pre-Christian. Or, to put the matter in terms of another controversy, Christianity has not borrowed from the Mystery Religions, because it was always, at least in Europe, a Mystery Religion itself' (215)!

Lake's later works, which led to the Girton conference – Lake, *The Stewardship of Faith: Our Heritage from Early Christianity* (New York, 1915) as well as his contributions to F. J. Foakes Jackson and K. Lake, eds., *The Beginnings of Christianity* (London, 1920), vol. 1, *Prolegomena 1: The Jewish, Gentile and Christian Backgrounds*; and Lake, *Landmarks in the History of Early Christianity* (London, 1920) – continue this approach (e.g., *Stewardship*: 81–95, 116–17 et passim; *Landmarks*: 74), although *Beginnings* is more muted. Their major new statement is the notion that while Judaism was the only religion in Late Antiquity to resist 'being absorbed' into the new 'Oriental synthesis' of the mystery religions, early Christianity filled this role. 'Christianity became the Jewish contribution to the Oriental cults, offering, as the Synagogue never did, private salvation by supernatural means to all who were willing to accept it' (*Landmarks*: 8, cf. *Beginnings*, 1:265–66, et passim). See Lake's final statement on the subject in Lake, *Paul: His Heritage and Legacy* (New York, 1934): 78–79, 105, et passim.

[25] A. D. Nock, 'Early Gentile Christianity and its Hellenistic Background,' in A. E. J. Rawlinson, ed., *Essays on the Trinity and the Incarnation by Members of the Anglican Communion* (London, 1928): 53–156, reprinted in Nock, *Early Gentile Christianity and Its Hellenistic Background* (New York, 1964): 1–104 and in Z. Stewart, ed., *Arthur Darby Nock: Essays on Religion and the Ancient World* (Cambridge, MA., 1972), 1:49–133 – which latter pagination I cite; Nock, 'The Vocabulary of the New Testament,' *Journal of Biblical Literature*, 52(1933): 131–39, rp. in Stewart, *Essays* 1:341–47 which I cite; Nock, 'Mysterion,' *Harvard Studies in Classical Philology*, 60(1951): 201–204; Nock, 'Hellenistic Mysteries and Christian Sacraments,' *Mnemosyne*, 5(1952): 177–213, rp. in Nock, *Early Gentile Christianity*: 109–45 and Stewart, *Essays*, 2:791–820, which latter pagination I cite.

with the deity honoured; normally he must undergo ceremonies of initiation (not usually capable of repetition)
conferring a new and indelible spiritual condition and
commonly giving the assurance of happiness hereafter ...
These rites were, in spite of their differences, fundamentally
akin ... At the time which we are studying they share the
notes of universality, of conversion, in part of moral basis;
further, they all involve a joining in the sorrows and in the
joys of the god. We know them best from sources in the
second century A.D. and later, and it is fairly clear that they
rose in importance in the second century, but there can be
little doubt that much of what is then characteristic of them
had taken shape earlier. (1:53–54)

This 'second century or later' dating is consistently used by Nock,
despite the qualification in this passage, to render implausible the
notion of 'influence' on first century Christianity (1:57, 72, 96, et
passim).

Nock goes on to argue (eschewing much of the critical
scholarship on the New Testament [e.g. 1:68–72, 86, 97, nn. 200,
202]) that there is no evidence for a sharp cleavage between the
teachings of Paul and of the Jerusalem community. This alone
leads one to 'in the main reject the hypothesis' of hellenistic rather
than Jewish influence. 'This conclusion', he claims, 'is confirmed
by an examination of certain linguistic points of contact'
(1:72–73). The first term considered is *mystērion*.

The term *mystērion* is used fairly freely, but not of the
sacraments – a clear point of distinction between New
Testament and later [Christian] usage, which freely applies
mystery-terminology to them; St. Paul applies it chiefly to
God's purpose, previously concealed but now revealed, of
calling the Gentiles. This use is to be connected with its
employment in *Daniel*, *Wisdom*, and *Sirach* to represent the
Aramaic *rāz*, 'secret', and not in the first instance with the
Greek religious use. [After considering several other terms,
Nock concludes that all these parallels] are superficial; it is
difficult to resist the impression that the religious content of
many of them had disappeared in popular use. Figurative
language of this kind was applied to philosophy, to poetry,

to rhetoric, to love, not to mention magic ... The importance of these points of contact is that they remind us that the
Christian missionary had to use the language of the time,
that this language often had religious connotations that were
more or less living, and that a stray hearer might well regard
the new teaching as something not different in kind from the
other religions of the time (1:73–74).

Nock continues this sort of argumentation through a series of
Christological titles, maintaining in each case that they are
dependent on Jewish and Septuagintal usage rather than on
'Hellenistic beliefs' (1:74–86). The same, he insists, is the case with
the ritual activities of eucharist and baptism (1:95–119). In each
case, 'the evidence as we have reviewed it does not seem to justify
the supposition of substantial borrowing by Christianity' (1:119);
'the key to the Christian doctrine is given to us by Jewish
conceptions alone' (1:84); what is important is 'the linguistic
usage of the Septuagint; for the study of the New Testament in
general and of St. Paul in particular it can hardly be over-
emphasized' (1:84).

In his later articles, Nock insistently returns to these themes.
Both the terms employed by Paul (as well as the terms *not*
employed) reveal no close connections with the Hellenistic
'mysteries'. Paul 'saw life around in terms of the Septuagint and
of Jewish apologetics' (1:347). 'Mystērion in Paul's letters and in
Mark 4.11 has no relation to its familiar use to denote either
pagan initiatory ceremonials (and their symbols or concomitants)
or other experiences metaphorically so described. What lies
behind it is the meaning "secret" (whether natural or supernatural), found in the Greek versions of the Old Testament' ('Mystērion': 201; cf. 2:801). 'Any idea that what we call the Christian
sacraments were in their origin indebted to pagan mysteries or
even to the metaphorical concepts based upon them shatters on
the rock of linguistic evidence' (2:809). Finally, in a stunning
paragraph, Nock undertakes what none of his predecessors had
concerned themselves with, a brief description (and acceptance)
of the sociological consequences of his position:

> When we open the Septuagint and the New Testament we
> find at once a strange vocabulary ... Such usages are the

product of *an enclosed world living its own life, a ghetto* culturally and linguistically if not geographically; they belong to a literature written entirely for the initiated ... (1:344, emphasis added.)

Nock's essays provide a bench-mark in the assessment of the relationship of early Christianity to the 'mysteries'. They continue to be quoted in any number of articles devoted to the state of the question in a manner that suggests the conviction that the issue has been closed with respect to the linguistic aspects.[26] For this reason, it is imperative that they be subjected to scrutiny in a manner not innocent of larger methodological and theoretical implications.

1) *Chronologies.* Beginning with the narrowest questions and moving out to the broadest, the first matter that needs to be pressed is that of chronology with respect to the Septuagint. Two presuppositions appear to govern the appeal to its data. The first is that the Septuagint brings one to a stage of hellenistic Judaism sufficiently prior to early Christianity to guarantee that its Greek is the source of early Christian vocabulary. Oddly, neither Kennedy in *St. Paul and the Mystery Religions* nor Nock in his various essays date the Septuagint or specify what layer of its complex history they have in mind when they cite its usage. The intended inference would appear to be one of associating the evidence quoted with the traditional third century BC date of the Pentateuch-translation. To cite the only relative chronology I have found in the scholarly tradition we have been considering, Kennedy's earlier study of 1895: 'Roughly speaking, an interval of about two hundred years separates the New Testament from the Septuagint.'[27] The second presupposition, building on the first, takes it for granted that, as the Septuagint is an authoritative

[26] See especially, B. M. Metzger, 'Methodology in the Study of the Mystery Religions and Early Christianity,' *Harvard Theological Review*, 48(1955), 1–20 as reprinted in Metzger, *Historical and Literary Studies: Pagan, Jewish and Christian* (Grand Rapids, 1968): 1–24, esp. 12, in the series, NTTS, 8; D. H. Wiens, 'Mystery Concepts in Primitive Christianity and in its Environment,' *ANRW* 2.23.2:1259–60; A. J. M. Wedderburn, 'Hellenistic Christian Traditions in Romans 6?' *New Testament Studies*, 29(1983): 337. See further the discussion (and rich bibliography) in G. Wagner, *Pauline Baptism and the Pagan Mysteries* (Edinburgh and London, 1967): 43–57. (This latter work is discussed in some detail below, Chapter 4.)

[27] Kennedy, *Sources*: 46.

translation-document, recovery of the Hebrew terminology lying behind the Greek is both determinative of the meaning of the Greek and, therefore, enables the scholar to recover an archaic, pre-hellenistic, indigenous 'Jewish' (or, 'Semitic') understanding of the terminology in question. While I doubt the adequacy of either of these assumptions in their most general form, neither can be sustained in the particular case at hand.

That *mystērion* is a relatively rare term in the Septuagint is well-known. What has not been sufficiently reflected on is the limited range of the six documents in which it occurs – Daniel, Judith, Tobit, Sirach, Wisdom, and 2 Maccabees. None are from archaic Israel; each was composed, at the earliest, during the hellenistic period and thus reflect a Late Antique situation from their origin, not just in their translation. Indeed, their status as translation-documents is scarcely homogenous. In only two cases can a late Hebrew original be persuasively presumed: Sirach, where the Hebrew has been recovered, and Judith, where the arguments for a Hebrew original are compelling although not unanimous. In the case of Daniel, what Hebrew survives is most likely itself a translation from an Aramaic original subsequently translated into Greek. The case of Tobit, even with the new Qumran materials (the previously known late Hebrew and Aramaic versions have all been translated from the Greek) is unsettled. There is the possibility of an Aramaic original, although there is strong argument for a Greek original with two subsequent Greek expansions before translation into Aramaic and Hebrew. In the remaining two instances, Wisdom and 2 Maccabees, the original language was undoubtedly Greek. In no case are we treating with an archaic indigenous Israelitic document later clothed in hellenistic form. We are reading six documents representative, in their very composition, of differing modes of hellenized Judaisms.

There is more. As a careful reading of Kennedy and Nock clearly displays, the full semantic range of *mystērion* even within these six documents is not under consideration. To repeat Nock's conclusion, 'This use [of *mystērion* in Paul] is to be connected with its employment in Daniel, Wisdom and Sirach to represent the Aramaic *rāz*, "secret"' (Nock, 1:73–74). The conjunction of *mystērion* and *rāz* makes plain that, in fact, only one document is being considered as determinative of the meaning of *mystērion*, its usage in Daniel. This limitation is methodologically unjustified; it also compounds the chronological difficulties inherent in the appeal to the Septuagint.

The question of the Greek translations of Daniel is a particularly thorny one, symbolized by the Christian preservation of two major translation traditions. Without undertaking a review of the various hypotheses concerning the 'LXX-Daniel', the so-called '*kaige*-recension' or 'Proto-Theodotian' (Barthélemy), 'Theodotian-Daniel' (Schmidt), 'Ur-Theodotian' (Montgomery, Gwynn), et al., two issues become clear. First, the text of Daniel (as is the case with other texts lumped together by scholars such as Kennedy and Nock under the artificial umbrella term, 'Septuagint') was an on-going and complex historical process with a number of parallel, intersecting and revised versions. Second, regardless of the particular theory adopted with respect to the Greek Daniel, a relatively late date must be presumed for its translation, no earlier than the first century BC, quite possibly as late as the first century AD.[28] Either way, when we compare the use of *mystērion* in Paul to that of Greek Daniel, we are comparing roughly contemporary usages, not comparing the authoritative usage of an ancestor or a teacher to his pupil. (In this latter I strain the schoolroom and genealogical metaphors of Kennedy and Nock with respect to the relation of Greek Daniel and Paul. In fact, Paul neither cites Daniel nor betrays any knowledge of it.)

2) *Semantic Range.* There is no doubt that both of the surviving Greek translation-traditions of Daniel employ, in chapter two, the Greek *mystērion* eight times to translate the Aramaic *rāz* (2.18, 19, 27, 28, 29, 30, 47 [twice]; Theodotian adds an additional instance in 4.9). But it is straining the point, I think, to find in this

---

[28] See, among others, D. Barthélemy, *Les Devanciers d'Aquila* (Leiden, 1963): 44, 46–47 148–56, in the series, SVT, 10; P. Grelot, 'Les versions grecques de Daniel,' *Revue biblique*, 47(1966): 381–402; A. Schmitt, *Stammt der sogenannte Θ -Text bei Daniel wirklich von Theodotian?* (Göttingen, 1966), in the series, MSU, 9; S. Jellicoe, *The Septuagint and Modern Study* (Oxford, 1968): 83–94, cf. Jellicoe, 'Some Reflections on the KAIGE Recension,' *Vetus Testamentum*, 23(1973): 15–24, esp. 23–24. K. Koch's attempt to demonstrate a Syro-Mesopotamian provenance is tempting, but unconvincing. See Koch, 'Die Herkunft der Proto-Theodotian-Übersetzung des Danielbuches,' *Vetus Testamentum*, 23(1973): 362–65.

use of *mystērion* 'for the first time a sense which is important for
the further development of the word, namely, that of an
eschatological mystery'.[29] Setting aside the dubious developmental presuppositions lying behind such a statement, the term has a
quite specific contextual sense. Recall the second chapter of
Daniel. King Nebuchadnezzar has proposed a 'double-bind' test.
He challenges the wise men to interpret a dream which he does
not tell them. They must first recount the dream and, then, offer
a plausible interpretation of it. The dream is a secret, and this fact
appears to be the referent of *rāz* throughout the chapter. If one
places chapter two within the wider context of such royal
wisdom contests, the most adequate substitution for the 'secret'
represented by *rāz* or *mystērion* in Daniel would be something like
'puzzle'. (Cf. the wise man's ability to formulate or decipher the
krypta of proverbs and the *ainigmata* of parables in Sirach 39.3 and
47.15–17.) The interpretation of the dream (that is to say, the
decoding of the puzzle after it has been made known by the wise
man) most certainly concerns the future of Nebuchadnezzar's
rule and empire. Knowing the later chapters of Daniel, and the
use of Daniel in subsequent Jewish and Christian apocalyptic
traditions, it is tempting to read an eschatological connotation in
chapter two, but such a sense is not required. The language of
rāz/mystērion does not recur in the more explicitly apocalyptic
chapters. For this reason, I doubt the cogency of the comparison
of the usage in Daniel to that in Paul which is based upon such an
eschatological understanding. (There is a slight overlap in the
relationship of 'parable' and 'mystery', of privileged insiders
and outsiders, in the sole Synoptic use of the term in Mark 4.11
and parallels, but this appears to occur in an eschatological
context.)

Having thus denied the adequacy of the privileged comparison, we may turn and examine those usages which have been
allowed to recede into the background by the scholarly tradition
under consideration. A group, almost as large as that in Daniel,
has been removed from view, because, I presume, in the words of

[29] G. Bornkamm, '*Mystērion*,' *TDNT*, 4:814; cf. G. Finkenrath, '*Mystērion*,' in L. Coe-
nen, E. Beyreuther and H. Bietenhard, eds., *Theologisches Begriffslexikon zum Neuen
Testament* (Wuppertal, 1969–), 2:1100.

later scholars on the question, their sense is perceived to be 'purely secular'.[30] Such usages include *mystērion* in the sense of keeping a royal secret (Tobit 12.7, 11; Judith 2.2, the latter a notoriously difficult verse in Greek), a military or tactical secret (2 Maccabees 13.21) or respecting the privacy or secrets of a friend (Sirach 22.22; 27.16–17, 21; cf. Symmachus-Proverbs 11.13; Theodotian-Proverbs 20.19). To eliminate instances of usage on the grounds that they are judged to be (by unknown criteria) 'secular' is dubious linguistic methodology; it is also exceedingly odd reading. To take but the first two instances, Tobit 12.7, 11, they occur in the revelation-discourse of the angel Raphael and twice compare the proverbial wisdom of keeping a king's secret with the imperative of revealing 'the works of God'. The reference of the word *mystērion* is to a king; the referent of the sentence in which it occurs is to divine revelation.

The only other set of occurrences of *mystērion* within the Septuagint is in the Wisdom of Solomon. While there are exceptions (2.22 and most probably 6.22), the majority of the instances unambiguously refer, in a polemic fashion, to contemporary hellenistic 'mystery' cults (8.4; 12.5; 14.15, 23).

Examination of the rather limited number of occurrences of *mystērion* in the Septuagint reveals a fairly wide semantic range which partially overlaps with aspects of the equally limited number of occurrences in the New Testament. The notion of a singular biblical meaning of the term – indigenous to the Hebrew and translated into Greek – is wholly implausible in light of the evidence.

Of course, one might press the semantic argument further, conscious of the theological presuppositions that limited the range of data considered only to the Septuagint, for example looking at *rāz* in other Jewish Aramaic documents ranging from its use in the Ein Gedi synagogue inscription[31] to 1 Enoch[32] and

---

[30] R. E. Brown, 'The Pre-Christian Semitic Concept,' *Catholic Biblical Quarterly*, 20(1958): 422; Bornkamm *TDNT*, 4:814. Compare the quotation from H. Rahner below (XXXX)!

[31] See the text, translation and commentary in J. A. Fitzmeyer and D. J. Harrington, *A Manual of Palestinian Aramaic Texts*, (Rome, 1978): 260–61, 288–89.

[32] Compare, for example, the quite different usages and contexts of *rāz* in 4Q Enoch Giants[a] 9; 4Q Enoch[c] 5.ii.26 and 4Q Enoch[a] 1.iv.20 in J. T. Milik, *The Books of Enoch: Aramaic Fragments of Qumran Cave Four* (Oxford, 1976): 316–17, 209, 216, 158, 161.

other manuscripts from Qumran[33]. One might explore the use of *mystērion* in other texts from Hellenistic Judaism[34] or in Greek translations of the Hebrew Bible other than the Septuagint. One might go further, and undertake a consideration of the total 'semantic field' in both Hebrew and Greek, examining the family of 'mystery/secrecy' terminology (including, among others, *sôd, nistārôt, krypta, aporrētos*). But such enterprises, if carried on in the same manner as those we have passed in review, would necessarily fail, for they are flawed in other respects than those of data.

3) *Linguistic Theory.* The scholarly tradition with which we have been concerned has primarily focused on the matter of words. As such, it has an implicit linguistic theory and its individual philological studies can only gain validity in light of a judgement on the relative adequacy of this wider enterprise.[35] As judged from its practice, its theory must be judged inadequate.

[33] See, among others, E. Vogt, 'Mysteria in textibus Qumran,' *Biblica,* 37(1956): 247–57; A. Mertens, *Des Buch Daniel im Lichte der Texte vom Toten Meer,* (Stuttgart, 1971): esp. 124–30, in the series, SBM, 12; R. E. Brown, 'The Pre-Christian Semitic Concept of "Mystery,"' *Catholic Biblical Quarterly,* 20(1958): 417–43; cf. Brown, 'The Semitic Background of the New Testament *Mystērion,*' *Biblica* 39(1958): 426–48, 40(1959): 70–87.

[34] For a particularly interesting example, see W. C. van Unnik, 'Flavius Josephus and the Mysteries,' in M. J. Vermasaren, ed., *Studies in Hellenistic Religions* (Leiden, 1979): 244–79, in the series, EPRO, 78.

[35] What is at stake may be gauged by comparing this tradition with a rival one, the sort of study represented by R. Reitzenstein in his *Die hellenistischen Mysterienreligionen,* 3rd ed. (Stuttgart, 1926). I cite the English translation, Reitzenstein, *Hellenistic Mystery-Religions: Their Basic Ideas and Significance* (Philadelphia, 1978). From one perspective, Reitzenstein's complex and ill-formed work may be viewed (especially in its 'Elucidations' which make up the bulk of the book) as a protracted series of word studies; but what a difference from the tradition we have been considering! The Septuagint rarely appears – indeed Reitzenstein speaks of 'Paul's relative independence of any influence from the Septuagint' (396) and heaps scorn on the theological 'overstressing' of the 'Jewish components' (73). But these differences, as significant (and problematic) as they may be, are not the heart of the disagreement. Reitzenstein has a richer general theory of religion, of language, and of their interrelationship. (Cf., R. Reitzenstein, 'Religionsgeschichte und Eschatologie,' *Zeitschrift für die neutestamentlichen Wissenschaft,* 13(1912): 1–28.) Procedurally, these theoretical concerns lead in several directions which affect our topic. The most pressing of these is Reitzenstein's insistence that one cannot compare isolated words, but rather he insists on the comparison of groups of words in their 'connections' and 'combinations' (68. 357, 458, et passim). 'It [the question of borrowing] will depend in considerable measure on the number of words and figures that Paul has in common with the mystery religions. It is easy, but utterly pointless constantly to refer back to one single individual case ...' (259). 'In such investigations, everything hinges on the contexts of the passages involved ...' (330, cf. 325–30, 368, 381, 434, 458). While, in part, this stems from Reitzenstein's notion of the philological enterprise (cf. 87, 148–49, 166–67 n. 77, 360), it stems as well from his conviction that the designation 'hellenistic' refers to a 'system' (he

What makes all the difference to our assessment of these earlier works is the awareness, in contemporary linguistics, that matters of semantics must be joined with issues of syntax, pragmatics and stylistics. In terms of the sort of studies represented by Kennedy and Nock, two central features of their procedures and implicit theories may be questioned: the priority of words over sentences as the bearers of meaning; and the lack of a theory of translation.

Following the pioneering work of James Barr, all recent studies of biblical semantics have agreed that 'syntactical relations ... and groupings of words ... [are] just as important for the bearing of significance as the more purely lexicographical aspects of the single word'.[36] It is, after all, the sentence, rather than the individual word which makes translation possible. The implications of this for the tradition we have been studying have been spelled out in some detail by Barr:

> Let us now return to the main point here being made, namely that the linguistic bearer of the theological statement is usually the sentence and the still larger literary complex and not the word or the morphological and syntactical mechanisms. The most important consequence of this arises

also uses the more unfortunate language of 'essence' [e.g. 154, n. 77]) which provides both the 'thought-world' for early Christianity and an occasion for its 'individual reshaping' in the context of a particular instance, such as a Pauline paragraph (see, 495, 517, 540). Whether or not this latter be accepted, Reitzenstein's insistence on 'groups' and 'context' rather than isolated words is of major importance. It may be illustrated by the rule designed by Archibald Hill with respect to poetic discourse: 'the likelihood of the parallel being significant is approximately doubled with each additional item which is added to form or extend a cluster.' (A. H. Hill, 'Principles Governing Semantic Parallels,' in E. M. Jennings, ed., *Science and Literature* [Garden City, 1970]: 72–82, passage quoted, p. 75.) Judged from this perspective, Paul scores highly. In almost no case, among the genuine epistles, is a single item of so-called 'mystery-terminology' found in isolation. 1 Corinthians exhibits this most clearly, from 1 Corinthians 2.6–16 which is densest, to 1 Corinthians 14.2 which has the sparsest cluster. (Compare, in order of decreasing density, 1 Corinthians 13.1–2; 15.51–57; 4.1–5.) To his credit, this is recognized by Kennedy, *St. Paul and the Mystery Religions*: 121, 'In certain contexts, as *e.g.* 1 Corinthians ii.6ff, we light upon *groups* of conceptions which have associations with the Mystery-Religions. This cannot be accidental.' Although, on the whole, Kennedy is more responsive to linguistic issues than Nock, he vitiates this observation by paralleling Paul's usage to that of contemporary religious writers who 'are fond of using analogies and illustrations from the field of biology ... as channels of appeal to the popular interest.'

[36] J. Barr, *The Semantics of Biblical Language* (Oxford, 1961): 222. Cf. 233–34, 264, 269–72, et passim. Barr's statement remains the presupposition of more recent treatments, e.g. A. Gibson, *Biblical Semantic Logic: A Preliminary Analysis* (New York, 1981) and J. P. Louw, *Semantics of Biblical Greek* (Philadelphia, 1982).

because the sentence unlike the word is unique and non-recurrent. A language has a vocabulary ... but it does not have a stock of sentences ... The question of distinctiveness of biblical thinking has to be settled at this level and not at the lexical level ... The distinctiveness of biblical thought and language has to be settled at sentence level, and not by the words they say them with. (269–70)

The new content of the Jewish-Christian tradition and of the Christian gospel was expressed linguistically *in sentence form* ... the content of these sentences was something largely foreign to the Hellenistic ethos (precisely *how* largely foreign, it is beyond my purpose to discuss); but that for the formation of these sentences Greek words could often be employed in the same semantic function as they normally had in the usage of Hellenistic speakers ... I suggest that the impress of the Jewish tradition in the Pauline letters and speeches was borne mainly by the things he said, his sentences, his complex word-combinations, his themes and subject matter; and that this impress remained even where the individual semantic value of many words was not changed from the average Hellenistic ... (249–50)

The quest for linguistic distinctiveness in Paul (a distinctiveness shared by Paul with *every* other speaker) is a legitimate undertaking. It will not be settled by the study of particular words, nor by the attempt to carve out essentially non-linguistic domains such as 'Judaism' or 'Hellenism'.

These same general considerations affect the argument with respect to the centrality of the Septuagint. While there is little doubt that the Septuagint contributed sentences (largely in the form of citations) and word-clusters (largely in the form of allusions and free paraphrases) to the Pauline corpus, there is no cause to argue that the corpus is deeply influenced, at the level of morphology or syntax, by either Hebraic-Aramaic usage or the Septuagint. (I set aside the undeniable presence of so-called 'Semiticisms' – although their presence, in some strata of the New Testament, has been much exaggerated.) But, regardless of how this matter be adjudicated, the mere citation of parallels, regardless of linguistic level, is insufficient. As Barr insists, one must 'attempt to discover the method by which translators read Hebrew texts and decided on a rendering' as well as making 'the obvious and necessary distinction between two sets of mental processes, those of the translators themselves, whose decisions about meaning were reached from the Hebrew text, and those of later readers, most of whom did not know the original'.[37] It is only in the absence of such an attempt to articulate a translation theory that one can continue the notion of direct translation (both linguistic and cultural), itself but a variant of the fantasy of direct, unmediated speech.

While other elements may be singled out for criticism from the perspective of linguistic theory[38], such matters need not be further pursued. For the tradition under review was not, in the final analysis, concerned with linguistic matters. Philology has served as a stratagem. The central task has been the protection of the uniqueness of early Christianity, its *sui generis*, or non-derivative nature.[39] For some, the appeal to lexicographical

[37] J. Barr, 'Common Sense and Biblical Language,' *Biblica*, 49(1968): 379.

[38] I would single out three further aspects. 1) The claim that Paul used 'mystery-terminology' without 'meaning it'. It is difficult to assess just what this claim means. The phenomenon of linguistic change is ubiquitous. One common feature is the shift as between specialization/generalization or restriction/extension. There is no doubt that *mystērion*, as is the case with the majority of the lexical units, undergoes these processes. But this does not correspond to a shift from a 'religious' to a 'secular' meaning, or from the notion of 'real' mysteries to a 'figurative' one. The term *mystērion* has a shifting semantic field, but one which retains, to a considerable degree in the texts cited as evidential, its associative field. Again, this matter cannot be settled on the level of words. 2) Citing a list of 'mystery-terminology' which does *not* occur in the New Testament (or in the Septuagint) has no probative value. (See the satire on this mode of argumentation in Barr, *Semantics*: 154–55, 282–87.) 3) Indeed, the whole question of 'mystery-terminology' needs reexamination. It is striking that the majority of texts cited as illustrative of this 'terminology' are secondary or tertiary texts *about* this or that 'mystery'. We have very few primary documents from the mysteries themselves. With the newer corpus of inscriptional materials (largely made available in the series, *EPRO*), it should be possible to reevaluate this question.

[39] While an extreme example, of neither philological nor historical merit, see the oft-cited article by H. Rahner, 'Das christliche Mysterium und die heidnischen Mysterien,' *Eranos-Jahrbuch*, 11(1944): 347–449; I cite the English translation, 'Christian Mysteries and Pagan Mysteries,' in Rahner, *Greek Myths and Christian Mystery* (New York, 1963; reprint, New York, 1971): 3–45. Rahner claims, 'Christianity is a thing that is wholly *sui generis*. It is something unique and not derivative from any cult or other human institution, nor has its essential character been changed or touched by any such influence' (28). Nevertheless, he notes in the next paragraph, the term 'mystery' is used in the New Testament, especially by Paul. But, 'St. Paul has in mind something radically different from the Hellenistic conception of *mysteria*. The difference is further accentuated if we see

studies of the presumed Semitic background of the notion of 'mystery' has simply enabled them to sweep from view the spectre of Hellenistic influence to such a degree that it disappears entirely from the scene. Thus R. E. Brown (in a set of more sophisticated linguistic investigations than those treated above) declares that:

> Parallels in thought and vocabulary in the OT, the pseudepigrapha ... and the Qumran literature ... [demonstrate] that the NT writers, particularly Paul, had all the raw material they needed for the use of 'mystery' in this background, without venturing into the pagan religions.
>
> We have been able to draw from the Semitic world good parallels in thought and word for virtually every facet of the NT use of mystery ... We believe it no exaggeration to say that, considering the variety and currency of the concept of divine mysteries in Jewish thought, Paul and the NT writers could have written everything they did about *mystērion* if there had never been pagan mystery religions. 'Mystery' was part of the native theological equipment of the Jews who came to Christ.[40]

the matter in the context of semantic development. From where did St. Paul get his terminology? ... It is clear that before Paul's day the word "mystery" and related terms were already in common use [in Christian discourse(?)] with a fairly wide penumbra of significance. Christ himself brought the message of the "mysteries of the kingdom of heaven" (Mat. 13.11, Mk. 4.11, Luke 8.10) and even if we cannot identify the exact term used in the original Aramaic, the fact remains that Mark and Matthew record the use of the word which they render as *mysterion* before it was employed by Paul.[!] And what is the sense in which Christ uses it? The mysteries of the kingdom are Jesus' "hidden revelation", his royal and sovereign communications which are nevertheless concealed within the cloak of the parables ... To attribute such a meaning to the word carries us back even further, right into the ideology of the Old Testament in fact, and particularly into that of the so-called deutero-canonical books. [Note that this is one of only two references to Judaism in the whole of Rahner's article; the other being an offhand reference to 'Jewish monotheism' and its influence on later 'pagan' mysteries (44).] Here the concept akin to 'mystery' is the *sacramentum regis* (Tobit 12.7), the secret decision of the king communicated only to those who are in his confidence, the plan of campaign which the supreme ruler has devised in his heart and which he deigns to communicate to his council (Judith 2.2) ... This is the meaning which the translators of the Septuagint associated with the word *mysterion*. Jesus, and after him Paul, applied this meaning to the divine decision, which was also a hidden one but 'now is manifested to his saints' (Col 1.26). How far removed is this from the meaning which the Hellenistic mind attached to the word *mysteria* ...' (29–30).

[40] R. E. Brown, 'The Semitic Background of the New Testament *Mystērion* (I),' *Biblica*, 39(1958): 427; Brown, 'The Semitic Background of the New Testament *Mystērion*

Others use the image of an insular and insulated Judaism in relation to its larger environment to claim that early Christianity, as an originally inner-Jewish phenomenon, fell, likewise, within Judaism's *cordon sanitaire.* Recall Nock's sociological conclusion to his philological studies:

> When we open the Septuagint and the New Testament we find at once a strange vocabulary ... Such usages are the product of *an enclosed world living its own life, a ghetto* culturally and linguistically if not geographically (Nock, 1:344, emphasis added).

Two generations of scholarly labour on both 'Palestinian' and 'Hellenistic' Judaisms as well as on early Christianities have rendered such a 'ghetto' portrait impossible.

More frequently, the notion of the centrality of the Septuagint in relation to early Christian discourse has had a double-thrust. On the one hand, it asserts the antiquity and purity of the generative language of early Christianities: on the other, it can be used to distance early Christianities from contemporary Judaisms. When the former is emphasized, the inclusive nomenclature will be one of 'Hebrew', 'Israel', the 'Old Testament', or, as in Brown, 'Semitic'. When the latter is to the fore, the contrast terms are 'Pharisaism', 'rabbinism' — both reformulations of the old polemic distinction between 'law' and 'gospel' — or, simply, 'Judaism'. This can be illustrated by the most recent monograph devoted to the topic of comparing words, one which escapes none of the theoretical strictures indicated above, David Hill's *Greek Words and Hebrew Meanings.*[41] He claims that the language of the New Testament reveals 'a strong Semitic cast, due in large measure to the Jewish biblical Greek of the Septuagint' and, further, that 'Greek *words* changed their meaning, or added a new meaning, in Jewish and Christian usage, and the change was due to the influence of the Greek version of the Old Testament scriptures' (18). Thus his discussion of *dikaiosynē* and cognate

---

(II),' *Biblica,* 40(1959): 87. This is quite similar to H. A. A. Kennedy's position as cited above. Brown quotes Kennedy consistently in his footnotes.

[41] D. Hill, *Greek Words and Hebrew Meanings: Studies in the Semantics of Soteriological Terms* (Cambridge, 1967), in the series SNTSM, 5. See the extended review by J. Barr, 'Common Sense and Biblical Language,' *Biblica,* 49 (1968): 377–87.

words begins with the pre-Israelitic use of *ṣdḳ* (82–83), continues through the Old Testament usages (84–98), and culminates in Deutero-Isaiah's 'fundamentally soteriological' (and Protestant) view of 'salvation which is unmerited … a new beginning in grace' (91, 95. Note that this 'conclusion' with Deutero-Isaiah is clearly not a chronological terminus, but a theological 'peak' as Hill's christianized vocabulary indicates). After reviewing Greek usage (98–102), Hill contrasts 'the Greek *dikaios*-words with the Hebrew *ṣdḳ*-words' with the major difference being the presence, in the latter of 'the covenant relation' and, therefore, the notion of 'conformity to the divine will' (102–103). Within the Septuagint (104–109), the Greek terminology 'underwent considerable expansion and change of meaning through being consistently used to render the Hebrew root *ṣdḳ*' (108), and this continues through the apocrypha and pseudepigrapha (109–110). Within the Qumran literature (110–15) there is a return to the understanding expressed by Deutero-Isaiah, an 'evangelical piety', and 'awareness of the weakness of unaided human nature [which] forms the background for the assertion of trust in the mercy of God' (112). At this point in his exposition, Hill breaks his pseudo-chronological schema and treats 'the rabbinic literature'[42] with a strong emphasis on the notion of 'intention' (115–20). With this as 'background', Hill turns to the '*dikaios*-words' in the New Testament, first in the Synoptics (120–39), then in Paul (139–62). It is here that the inclusion/contrast noted above becomes most pressing. Within the Synoptics, *dikaios* and related words 'must be interpreted within the framework of thought of the Old Testament, the witness of Israel's religious faith' as transferred through the Septuagint (139). In the case of Paul, the agendum abruptly becomes more complex. 'How far does the Old Testament idea … as channelled through the LXX usage explain his usage of the term? To what extent are the expressions of "evangelical piety" in the [Qumran] Scrolls the clue to his

---

[42] See Hill, *Greek Words*: 20. 'Extreme caution is required in postulating rabbinic influence upon the New Testament because of the uncertainty which prevails in the dating of the various traditions' – in this section, the majority of *documents* he cites are fourth century or later – 'but, in these studies, we have not tried to show precise areas of dependence; rather we have sought to suggest the state of Jewish thinking, or (more correctly) the directions in which it was moving in relation to the themes we discuss, which directions the New Testament writers might share or reject.'

understanding of "righteousness"? How far, if at all, has he introduced new elements from secular Greek thought and usage or through his own Christian conceptions?' (139). We need not tarry on his answers, except to observe that a note of urgent distinction enters Hill's exposition.

> In opposition to Jewish teaching, Paul asserts that 'to be righteous (in the right) before God' depends not upon a man's achievement through obedience to the Law, but solely on his trust in Christ (141).

> What is a matter of hope for the Jew becomes for Paul a present possibility and reality (141).

> In the teachings of the Old Testament and pre-Christian sectarian Judaism we see the framework of Paul's doctrine and the background of his thought *as he faced a degenerating and legalistic religion*, but the special content of his doctrine was his own (162, emphasis added).

Thus the issue of comparing words, as we have traced out its history, has never been primarily a philological issue, but always an apologetic one. In the earlier Casaubon-tradition, the effort at distinction was between Roman Catholicism and a Protestant portrait of Christian origins. The later studies have shifted focus to Jewish 'backgrounds'. In this latter endeavour, Judaism has served a double (or, a duplicitous) function. On the one hand it has provided apologetic scholars with an insulation for early Christianity, guarding it against 'influence' from its 'environment'. On the other hand, it has been presented by the very same scholars as an object to be transcended by early Christianity. These two apologetic enterprises are joined in a recent statement which may serve as the epitaph of this chapter:

> The Christianity of the New Testament is a creative combination of Jewish and Hellenistic traditions transformed into a *tertium quid* ('a third something'): that is, a reality related to two known things but transcending them both.[43]

---

[43] D. Aune, *The New Testament in its Literary Environment* (Philadelphia, 1987): 12.

In the next chapter, we turn from the question of words to more syntagmatic matters, to the comparing of myths and stories, and to figures to whom the Pythagorean notion of the *triton genos* or the *tertium quid* can be more correctly applied: the 'dying and rising gods' or 'god-men' of the Mediterranean world.

IV

On Comparing Stories

I

The notion of comparing stories, of constructing *vitae parallelae* is not, of course, foreign to early Christianity. What is largely unknown is any sense of parity with the non-Christian materials. Within the New Testament literature, such parallelism is most often expressed by asserting typological correspondences between details in the lives of figures from Israelitic narratives and details in the traditions of Jesus's life. While most of these comparisons are exceedingly economical, a few have been highly developed, such as the contrast of Moses and the Son in John 6, or of Moses and Christ throughout Hebrews. Beyond such instances of typology, there is a striking example of subordinate comparison within an extended narrative in the double infancy stories of John the Baptist and Jesus in Luke 1–2, a duality later elaborated in Mesopotamian Christian accounts of Jesus's twin brother.

Outside the New Testament corpus, the most persistent, positive Christian parallel has been that of Jesus and Socrates. Already developed in the earliest apologetic tradition, it was reiterated by Renaissance savants concerned with 'perennial philosophy', and reevaluated in both Free Thought and Romantic works from the eighteenth century to the present.[1]

---

[1] For the comparison in the early apologists, beginning with Justin Martyr, see A. Harnack, *Sokrates und die alte Kirche* (Giessen, 1901), rp. Harnack, *Reden und Aufsätze*, 2nd ed. (Giessen, 1906), 1:27–48; J. Geffcken, *Sokrates und das alte Christentum* (Heidelberg, 1908); J. M. Pfättisch, 'Christus und Sokrates bei Justin,' *Theologisches Quartalschrift* 90(1908): 503–23; G. Natali, *Socrate nel giudizio dei Padri apologisti* (Ascoli, 1912); Th. Deman, *Socrate et Jésus* (Paris, 1944), esp. 9–16; E. Benz, 'Christus und Sokrates in der alten Kirche,' *Zeitschrift für die neutestamentliche Wissenschaft* 43(1950–1): 195–224; A. M. Malingrey, 'Le personnage de Socrate chez quelques auteurs chrétiens du IVe siecle,' *Festschrift M. Pellegrino* (Turin, 1975): 159–78; D. Jackson, 'Socrates and Christianity,' *Classical Folia*, 31(1977): 189–206 [the most superficial treatment here cited]; I. Opelt, 'Das Bild des Sokrates in der christlichen Literatur,' *Jahrbuch für Antike und Christentum*, Erganzungsband, 10(1983): 192–207. There is a convenient collection of translated testimonia in G. Giannantoni, ed., *Socrate: Tutte le testimonianze da Aristofane e Senofonte ai padri cristiani* (Bari, 1971): 501–52.

I know of no good treatment of the interpretation of Socrates in the Renaissance. A

One need only recall that the Adams-Jefferson exchanges on Christianity with which we began chapter one were triggered by Joseph Priestley's *Socrates and Jesus Compared* (see above, pp. 4–5). It is impossible, however, in examining a representative sample of these Jesus/Socrates comparisons to escape the sense that they are largely rhetorical. That is to say, the parallels are seldom carried out systematically, and they yield no major conclusions: Socrates did not write, just as Jesus did not write; Socrates was a good man (or a man with a divine spirit) who consented to being put to death for his teachings, just as Jesus was a good man (or a man with a divine spirit) who consented to being put to death for his teachings.[2] It will not be until early twentieth century scholarship begins to compare both Socrates and Jesus with respect to a more general category such as 'divine man' or martyr that the parallelism becomes theoretically interesting.[3]

What is lacking, in addition to a superordinate category for

most striking comparison occurs in Marsilio Ficino's letter to Paolo Ferrobanti (Ficino, *Opera omnia* [Basel, 1562]: 868).

For the later comparisons, and omitting the large literature devoted to Socrates in the writings of Nietzsche or Kierkegaard, see, among others, E. Brenning, 'Die Gestalt des Sokrates in der Litteratur des vorigen Jahrhunderts,' *Festschrift der 45 Versammlung deutscher Philologen und Schülmanner* (Bremen, 1899): 421–81; W. Hertel, *Sokrates in der deutschen Dichtung der Aufklärung* (Münich, 1921); B. Bohm, *Sokrates im achtzehnten Jahrhundert* (1929, rp. Neumünster, 1966), in the series, Kieler Studien zur deutschen Literaturgeschichte, 4; H. G. Seebeck, *Das Sokratesbild vom 19 Jahrhundert bis zur Gegenwart* (Göttingen, 1947); E. Abma, *Sokrates in der deutschen Literatur* (Utrecht, 1949); R. Marcel, "Saint Socrate," Patron de l'humanisme,' *Revue internationale de philosophie*, 5(1951): 135–43; F. Kellerman, 'Montaigne's Socrates,' *Romanic Review* 45 (1954): 170–77; J. Seznec, 'Le Socrate imaginaire,' in *Essais sur Diderot et l'antiquité* (Oxford, 1957): 1–22; R. Trousson, *Socrate devant Voltaire, Diderot et Rousseau: La conscience en face du mythe* (Paris, 1967); M. A. Raschini, *Interpretazioni socratiche* (Mailand, 1970); K. Carson, 'Socrates Observed: Three 18th Century Views,' *Diderot Studies* 14(1971): 273–81; L. O. Lundgren, *Sokratesbilden: Från Aristofanes till Nietzsche* (Stockholm, 1978), esp. 99–142, in the series, Acta Universitatis Stockholmiensis: Studies in the History of Literature, 20. There is a convenient anthology of representative passages in H. Spiegelberg, ed., *The Socratic Enigma: A Collection of Testimonies Through Twenty-Four Centuries* (Indianapolis, 1964).

[2] Aquinas, *Summa theologica* IIa.3a.42.4 is a well-known commonplace instance of the comparison that neither Jesus nor Socrates wrote. For the earliest comparison of Socrates and Jesus's death, see Justin, *2 Apology* 10; Origen, *Contra Celsum* 6.56. John Chrysostom, *Hom. ad 1 Cor.* 4.7 is an early attack on the parallel.

[3] The earliest fully developed proposal of this comparison in the scholarly literature occurs in H. Windisch, *Paulus und Christus: Ein biblisch-religionsgeschichtlicher Vergleich* (Leipzig, 1934), esp. 34–38, in the series, UNT, 24.

comparison is, above all, a rich notion of *myth*. For the acceptance of the category 'myth', however defined, as applicable to the Christ stories, thereby establishing parity with non-Christian materials, is a prerequisite for comparative research. Any attempt to escape this requirement, and its consequences, will render the enterprise necessarily vain. (I call attention to the most frequent contemporary dodge, that of substituting 'the Christ of faith' for the expression 'the mythical Christ'.)

Having declared this, I must go on to recognize that, casting one's eyes upon the spectacle of New Testament scholarship in the first decade of this century when the term 'myth' became commonplace in research on 'Christian origins', it would be understandable if an observer concluded that, as in Hesse's *Steppenwolf* formula, the price of entry was the loss of one's mind. What a mad farrago of notions confronts the observer's gaze! Each lays claim to the legitimation of the notion of 'myth' brought first to critical attention, albeit in a most inadequate understanding, by D. F. Strauss.[4] Works with titles such as: *The Legend of Jesus the Solar Deity, The Astral Myth of Jesus,*[5] *Did Jesus*

[4] D. F. Strauss, *Das Leben Jesu kritisch bearbeitet*, 1st ed. (Tübingen, 1835). Here the definition of myth seems to be chiefly the rationalist one of a narrative of events beyond empirical verification (pp. 28–30, et passim). In later editions – I cite the 2nd ed. of the English translation of the 4th German edition, *The Life of Jesus Critically Examined* (London, 1892) – far more attention is given to the notion of myth being generated in a condition of 'religious enthusiasm' (p. 75) in relationship to an 'idea' rather than to a '*Faktum*' (p. 86), leading to the formulation that 'the historical mythus has for its groundwork a definite individual fact which has been seized upon by religious enthusiasm, and twined around with mythical enthusiasm culled from the idea of the Christ' (p. 87). Despite this romantic Idealism, Strauss (as is the case with most New Testament scholars until the present) remains too wedded to the dichotomy, myth/history, with 'legend' as a mediating term. See further the general survey by Ch. Hartlich and W. Sachs, *Der Ursprung des Mythosbegriffes in der modernen Bibelwissenschaft* (Tübingen, 1952), in the series, SSEA, 2.

In the light of the importance of Dupuis for my argument, both above, in Chapter One, and in this chapter, it is of interest to note that the German translation of Dupuis, by C. G. Rhe, *Ueber den Ursprung des Kultus* (Stuttgart, 1839), in addition to being supplied with an expanded title, *Geschichtlich Parallelismus zwischen der Glaubenslehre und den Religionsgebrauchen der Heiden und der Christen* is provided with a new sub-title as well, *Geschichtliche Entwicklung des Aberglaubens und der Priesterherrschaft zu allen Zeiten bei allen Völkern. Seitenstuck zum 'Leben Jesu' von Dr. D. F. Strauss*. It is difficult to see the sense in which Dupuis's work could be considered a *Seitenstuck* to the work of Strauss, but the fact that the two were associated is significant (see below, n. 8).

[5] P. Koch, *Die Sage von Jesus dem Sonnengott* (Berlin, 1910); C. F. Fuhrmann, *Der Astralmythen von Christus: Die Lösung der Christussage durch Astrologie* (Leipzig, 1912). Cf. A. Niemojewski, *Gott Jesus im Lichte fremder und eigener Forschungen samt Darstellung der*

88 DRUDGERY DIVINE

Live 100 B.C.?, *The Prechristian Jesus*, *The Christ Myth*, *Pagan Christs: Studies in Comparative Hierology*,[6] and, most odd-sounding of all, *Moses, Jesus, Paul: Three Variants of the Babylonian Divine-Man Gilgamesh.*[7]

While little, if anything, of the historical proposals of these works has survived scrutiny, there was one additional formula-

evangelischer Astralstoffe, Astralszenen und Astralsysteme (Munich, 1910); Niemojewski, *Astrale Geheimnisse des Christentums* (Frankfurt am Main, 1913). From a methodological perspective, the fantastic astrological proposals of W. Erbt are most interesting. Rather than comparing isolated motifs, he seeks to demonstrate that the gospel of Mark is arranged on a solar scheme of 28 incidents, beginning with the winter solstice of December 22, each incident picturing Jesus in terms of the characteristic of the appropriate Babylonian month. Jesus, as a solar figure thus understood, appears primarily in the form of a 'renewer' of the cosmos. See W. Erbt, *Die Markusevangelien: Eine Untersuchung über die Form der Petruserinnerungen und die Geschichte der Urgemeinde* (Leipzig, 1911): 1–51, in the series, MVAG, 16.1; cf. Erbt, *Von Jerusalem nach Rom: Untersuchung zur Geschichte und Geschichtsdarstellung des Urchristentums* (Leipzig, 1912): 12–15, in MVAG, 17.2.

[6] G. R. S. Mead, *Did Jesus Live 100 B.C.?* (London-Benares, 1903); W. B. Smith, *Der vorchristliche Jesus: Nebst weiteren Vorstudien zur Entstehungsgeschichte des Urchristentums* (Giessen, 1906), cf. Smith, *Ecce Deus: Studies of Primitive Christianity* (Chicago, 1912); A. Drews, *Die Christusmythe* (Jena, 1909–11), 1–2; J. M. Robertson, *Pagan Christs: Studies in Comparative Hierology*, 2nd ed. (London, 1911). With the exception of Mead (who relies on the historicity of Jewish anti-Christian traditions), the other authors lay great stress on a pre-Christian Palestinian Joshua-deity and the testimony of Epiphanius concerning a pre-Christian 'Nazorean' cult (*Haer*, XXIX.6). Of these authors, Robertson is the most interesting. He attempts to place his theories within a rich contemporary theoretical context (Jevons, Frazer, et al.).

[7] P. Jensen, *Moses, Jesus, Paulus: Drei Varianten des babylonischen Gottmenschen Gilgamesch*, 2nd ed. (Frankfurt am Main, 1909). The section on Jesus/Gilgamesh (esp. 26–37) is a convenient condensation of the treatment in Jensen's enormous monograph, *Das Gilgamesh-Epos in der Weltliteratur* (Strassburg-Marburg, 1906–28), 1:811–1030. It should be recalled that Jensen was responsible for the major, early edition of the Gilgamesh epic in the *Keilschriftliche Bibliothek* (Berlin, 1889–1915), 6:116–265. While Jensen is frequently treated as the reduction to absurdity of 'Pan-Babylonianism' (on which see Smith, *Imagining Religion: From Babylon to Jonestown*: 26–29 and Smith, 'Mythos und Geschichte,' in H.-P. Duerr, *Alcheringa oder die beginnende Zeit* [Frankfurt am Main]: 35–42), his methodological – as opposed to his historical – proposals deserve serious attention. He insists that, to guard against accidental parallels, comparisons need to be of entire systems, by which he means, in narratives, the *parallel sequence* of incidents and events (1–10, and the important note on p. 10). While his comparative table (27–30) shows a disturbing tendency to alter the sequence in a few instances (in a 'structural analysis', the alteration of names is less open to criticism), I honour the methodological advance. However, this does not render his genetic proposals more likely. The two most searching reviews of Jensen's methodology that I am familiar with – H. Gunkel, 'Jensens Gilgamesh-Epos in der Weltliteratur,' *Deutsche Literaturzeitung* 30 (1909): 901–11 (conveniently reprinted in K. Oberhuber, *Das Gilgamesch-Epos* [Darmstadt, 1977]: 74–84), and W. Anderson, *Über P. Jensens Methode der vergleichenden Sagenforschung* (Dorpat, 1930), in the series, Acta et commentationes Universitatis Tartuensis, ser. B, 21.2 – unaccountably fail to comment on this insistence on 'parallel sequence'.

tion of the 'mythic Christ' which was to prove both influential and theoretically interesting. It was the comparison between Christ (largely as understood by Paul in Romans 6) and the so-called Mediterranean 'dying and rising gods'. This comparison, as we have seen in the first chapter, may be traced back to Dupuis.[8] Although most highly developed by the members of the *Religionsgeschichtliche Schüle*, to the best of my knowledge the first New Testament scholar to introduce this comparison in any extended form was Otto Pfleiderer in 1902–1903.[9] Pfleiderer's

[8] I intend the reference to Dupuis in a positive manner. As noted above, in Chapter One, Frazer nowhere cites Dupuis in his development of the 'seasonal pattern'. He is aware, however, of the work of Ch. Vellay, *Le culte et les fêtes d'Adônis-Thammouz dans l'orient antique* (Paris, 1901), in the series, Annales du Musée Guimet, 16, which develops a solar interpretation of Adonis (73–105) with strong reliance on Dupuis (esp. 94–96).

It is clear that in the polemic literature against the 'mythical Christ' the name of Dupuis has become a sign of 'rationalistic atheism'. See the reference to 'the notorious work of Charles François Dupuis' in Th. J. Thoburn, *The Mythical Interpretation of the Gospels* (Edinburgh, 1916): xiii–xiv. See the same charge in Case, *The Historicity of Jesus*: 45; H. M. van Ness, *Historie, Mythe, en Geloof: Jezus Christus en de hedendaagsche Wetenschap* (Leiden, 1912): 74; M. Goguel, *Jesus the Nazarene, Myth or History?* (New York, 1926; French original edition, Paris 1925): 6–8; G. Bertram, 'Christentum, Entstehung des Christentums,' *Die Religion in Geschichte und Gegenwart*, 2nd ed. (Tübingen, 1927–32), 1:1533, among others. It is by no means clear to me that the authors of these polemic works have, in fact, read Dupuis.

[9] Two other works, also published in 1903, hint at the presence of the pattern. 1) A. Dieterich, *Eine Mithrasliturgie*, 1st ed. (Leipzig, 1903):159–61 focuses on the pattern of the initiant's experience of death and rebirth, rather than the deity's, and does so in a passage framed by references to Frazer). 2) H. Gunkel, *Zum religionsgeschichtlichen Verständnis des Neuen Testaments*, 1st ed. (Göttingen, 1903), in the series, FRLANT, 1.1, presents a more complex picture. He writes of the resurrection and enthronement of Christ that it is based on 'the myth of the sun-god, who, rising from the depths, forces his way to heaven and founds there his new celestial kingdom' (72); likewise Christ's descent into Hell is paralleled by Osiris, Nergal, Marduk, Tammuz, Ishtar, Gilgamesh, Odysseus and Orpheus (72 and n. 9). The fixing of Sunday depends on an already existing, pre-Christian notion of the 'dying and rising' of a god fixed on 'this day' (79). His general thesis concerns a general 'oriental' pattern: 'To one who comes to the study of the New Testament from the Old, [such Pauline doctrines as] the mystical union with Christ, the interpretation of baptism as drowning ... must occasion surprise [for] they have no analogies in the Old Testament. These did not organically arise from the practice of baptism, but were added on ... Comparisons have been made to the Greek mysteries ... but the Orient has not been taken into consideration. Here, for thousands of years, such notions existed, especially in Egypt in the Osiris mysteries. Osiris too was slain and then came back to life ...' (83–4). 'In the Orient, the belief that gods die and are resurrected is well-known. We know it from Egypt ... Babylonia, Syria, Phonecia. In Greece, they even show Zeus's grave, empty of course. The resurrection of these gods was originally nature-worship ... the gods of sun and vegetation die in the winter and rise in the spring as if new' (77). This 'pre-Christian belief in death and resurrection' was passed on to early Christianity from 'Jewish-syncretistic circles' (82). With the exception of the emphasis on

comparison is entirely dependent upon the pattern of 'dying and rising' first proposed, in fully articulated form, in J. G. Frazer's, *The Golden Bough*.[10]

In the first edition of *The Golden Bough* (1890), Frazer asserts that 'the central idea' of his work is 'the conception of the slain god' (1:xiii), and devotes his longest chapter, the third, to the topic, 'Killing the God' (1:213–409 and 2:1–222). The logic of the overall argument is as follows. The putative question Frazer set out to answer, that of the slaying of the 'King of the Wood' at Nemi,[11] led Frazer first to demonstrate the wide-spread occurrence of a 'vegetation spirit', often represented as incarnate in kings, who was responsible for fertility (chapter I). Because of this power, the king's life had to be protected by 'taboos' (chapter II). But there is a 'problem'. When the king aged, his powers of fertility 'naturally' waned, and a dramatic 'solution' was thereby required.

> The danger is a formidable one; for if the course of nature is dependent on the man-god's life, what catastrophes may not be expected from the gradual enfeeblement of his powers and their gradual extinction at death? There is only one way of averting these dangers. The man-god must be killed as soon as he shows symptoms that his powers are beginning to fail, and his [incarnate vegetative] soul must be transferred to a vigorous successor before it has been seriously impaired by the threatened decay. (1:215)

It is in the context of this issue, 'the death of the god-man – the divine king or priest' (1:217), that Frazer introduces the pattern of 'dying and rising' gods, having first presented European folk-materials, largely following Mannhardt, on the battle between summer and winter, the custom of appointing mock kings and ceremonies of the 'carrying out of death' (1:241–78), where the

---

'Jewish syncretism', for which Gunkel's chief evidence is the notion of the 'death of the Christ' in 4 Ezra 7.29 (78), it is difficult not to suppose that the pattern in Gunkel is ultimately derived from Frazer, probably through Pfleiderer, whom he cites at crucial junctures (92, 96), the whole essay being framed by citations to Pfleiderer (6, 96).

[10] J. G. Frazer, *The Golden Bough: A Study in Comparative Religion*, 1st ed. (London, 1890), 1–2.

[11] On the overall argument of *The Golden Bough*, see J. Z. Smith, 'When the Bough Breaks,' *History of Religions*, 12(1973):342–71, rp. Smith, *Map Is Not Territory*:208–239.

'death and revival of vegetation' (1:275), that which is represented in the vicissitudes of the incarnate 'vegetative spirit', is ritually expressed.

> But it is in Egypt and Western Asia that the death and resurrection of vegetation appear to have been most widely celebrated with ceremonies like those of modern Europe. Under the names of Osiris, Adonis, Thammuz, Attis and Dionysus, the Egyptians, Syrians, Babylonians, Phrygians, and Greeks represented the decay and revival of vegetation with rites which, as the ancients themselves recognized, were substantially the same, and which find their parallels in the spring and midsummer customs of our European peasantry. (1:278–79)

This paragraph, with but minor revisions, will persist as the introduction to Frazer's treatment of the pattern in all three editions of *The Golden Bough*.

In the first edition of *The Golden Bough*, this treatment is relatively brief (1:278–332, 359–63) with most space being devoted to Adonis (1:278–96) and Osiris (1:301–20). Each is understood in a similar manner: 'the ceremony of the death and resurrection' of the deity, 'must also have been a representation of the decay and revival of vegetation' (1:281, cf. 1:282, 284, 296, 301, 330–1, et passim). The second edition (1900) is virtually unchanged;[12] the third edition (1907–1915), able to take advantage of a number of specialized monographs and the increased knowledge of ancient Near Eastern texts, dramatically increases the data while maintaining the thesis intact.[13]

---

[12] J. G. Frazer, *The Golden Bough: A Study in Magic and Religion*, 2nd ed. (London, 1900), 1–3. In the second edition, while the treatment of the introductory matters, chiefly on magic, has more than doubled (278 pages in the first edition; 582 pages in the second edition), the section on 'dying and rising' gods is virtually unchanged. With the exception of a sentence or two, the treatments of Adonis, Dionysus and Demeter-Persephone are unaltered. There is a slight expansion in the treatment of Attis (2:134–37), adding material on Hyacinth. The section on Osiris has been somewhat more revised: a few pages have been added (2:139–40, 152–60) and an argument with previous scholars has been abbreviated and chiefly reduced to a footnote (2:150 and 151 n. 1; cf. the 1st ed. 1:316–17). None of these revisions alters the interpretation in any way. It is this edition which is relied on by Pfleiderer, Dieterich and the other New Testament scholars who assert the relevance of the pattern in the first decade of the twentieth century.

[13] J. G. Frazer, *The Golden Bough: A Study in Magic and Religion*, 3rd ed. (London, 1907–15, rep. 1935), 1–12. The history of the relevant volumes is more complicated. *Attis,*

What is most interesting, from our perspective, is that Frazer, during his entire discussion of 'dying and rising' gods, rarely entertains any explicit comparisons to the myth of the dying and rising Christ. Those few parallels to Christianity which occur are largely variants of the old 'Pagano-papist' apologetics.[14] But the implicit comparisons are relentless. As one literary critic has noted:

Adonis, Osiris: Studies in the History of Oriental Religions (London, 1906), 1–2 originally appeared as a separate work. After the publication of the 2nd ed. (London, 1907), Frazer decided to incorporate the volumes into *The Golden Bough*. All bound volumes of this 2nd ed. have a pasted half-page title indicating that the volumes are Part IV of *The Golden Bough*. In some copies, Frazer's three-page prospectus for the 3d ed. of *The Golden Bough* is bound in. As Part I of the 3d ed. of *The Golden Bough* did not appear until 1911, rather than 1908 as Frazer had announced in his prospectus, it is the 3d ed. of *Attis, Adonis, Osiris* which becomes Part IV of *The Golden Bough* rather than this 2nd ed. There are no significant changes between the various editions of *Attis, Adonis, Osiris*. Despite this, I have retained the usual dating for the 3d ed. of *The Golden Bough* as 1907–15 rather than the more accurate dating of 1911–15.

The major changes from the first and second editions are in bulk. The 59 pages devoted to the subject in the first edition, have grown to 535 pages in two volumes of the third edition, Attis and Adonis in the first volume, Osiris in the second. The materials on Dionysus and Demeter have been transferred to a new volume, *Spirits of the Corn and Wild*, 1:1–91. The only new theoretical point is the unfortunate suggestion that Osiris might once have been an historical figure (*Attis, Adonis, Osiris*, 1:vii and 2:158–200).

[14] For explicit parallels, see, among others, *The Golden Bough*, 3d ed., 5:254, 256–67, 306 (Adonis); 5:306, 308 (Attis); 5:302 (Mithras). Note that these are all framed with reference to Catholic ceremonial. Frazer explains these, not primarily by parallels at the level of myth and pattern, but by a version of an accommodation theory with respect to ritual: 'Taken together, the coincidences of the Christian with the heathen festivals are too close and too numerous to be accidental. They mark the compromise which the Church in the hour of its triumph was compelled to make with its vanquished yet still dangerous rivals. The *inflexible Protestantism* of the primitive missionaries, with their fiery denunciations of heathendom, had been exchanged for the supple policy, the easy tolerance, the comprehensive charity of shrewd ecclesiastics ...' (5:310, emphasis added). In the case of Osiris, Frazer introduces a more functional comparison. 'In the faith of the Egyptians the cruel death and resurrection of Osiris occupied the same place as the death and resurrection of Christ hold in the faith of Christians' (6:159). But this is undertaken in order to introduce his euhemeristic interpretation of Osiris. 'If Christ lived the life and died the death of a man on earth, may not Osiris have done so likewise?' (ibid.)

Frazer's most controversial thesis regarding Jesus was his suggestion, in the 2nd ed. of *The Golden Bough*, 3:186–98 that Jesus was crucified as part of a Purim-ritual, based on an older Babylonian ritual of the killing of a temporary king. 'A chain of causes which ... might ... be called an accident, determined that the part of the dying god in this annual play should be thrust upon Jesus of Nazareth' (*The Golden Bough*, 2nd ed. 3:197. Cf. P. Wendland, 'Jesus als Saturnalien- König,' *Hermes*, 33 [1898]: 175–79). In the 3d ed., this passage has been reduced to an additional note (9:412–23) with a prefatory note (9:412, n. 1) insisting that this thesis in no way impugns the 'historical reality of Jesus of Nazareth'.

However wide we wander, however deep we delve into the records of the past, we are always coming up against one being, the Vegetable God, who as decapitated Tescatlipoca or the dismembered Osiris is strange, but who is not strange at all, once our astonished gaze has recognized the likeness, as Jesus. Christianity is seldom mentioned; there is no need that it should be, for Sir James naturally assumes that the main articles of the Christian faith are known to his readers ... With Attis, Adonis or Thammuz, we begin to close about the Christian altar. Behind them, as behind the slave who was King of the Wood, there looms, scarcely named, the shadow of that other God, who as Son of Man ... died on the tree. And inescapably we are brought to conclude that Jesus the Christ acquired divinity by assuming the attributes of another deity. [Christ's birth, death and resurrection] conform to the pattern of the Vegetable God.[15]

What is implicit in Frazer, is made explicit in Pfleiderer's writings. Pfleiderer's earliest publications on the New Testament (1873–87) situate Paul entirely within the circle of Judaism. The most extended comparison concerns Paul's conversion, an ecstatic visionary experience for which 'there are many analogous cases,' 'the desert being especially favourable' for provoking the same.[16] In a tentative footnote, the notion of 'new birth' in Pauline baptism is briefly compared to the Eleusinian mysteries as is the Lord's Supper to 'pagan sacrificial meals'.[17] Yet, when not

[15] J. P. Bishop, 'The Golden Bough,' *Virginia Quarterly Review*, 12(1936): 430–47; passages quoted, 432–3. Frazer does not appear to have known the curious work by M. Kulischer, *Das Leben Jesu, Eine Sage von dem Schicksale und Erlebnissen der Bodenfrucht, inbesondere der sogenannten palästinischen Erstlingsgarbe, die am Passahfeste im Tempel dargebracht Wurde* (Leipzig, 1876), which develops the interpretation of Jesus as a 'mythical [vegetative] spirit of fertility' (47, 49, 59, 61, 74, 77, 101, 110), a 'personification' of the 'seasonal pattern' (16–17), a 'representation of the fate of vegetation' (32) conceived of as an 'analogy' to the cult-personifications of Demeter-Persephone, Dionysus, Osiris and Attis (64–65, 105–108). Using arguments such as Bethlehem, Jesus's birthplace, meaning 'house of bread' (12), Kulischer interprets the birth-narrative: 'the savior was, thus, born in Bethlehem – the Fruit of the Earth, the Fertility [deity] first appeared in [Bethlehem] the House of Bread' (26).

[16] O. Pfleiderer, *Das Urchristenthum, seine Schriften und Lehren* (Berlin, 1887):40. The Jewish setting for Paul is likewise emphasized in Pfleiderer, *Paulinismus: Ein Beitrag zur Geschichte der Urchristlichen Theologie*, 1st ed. (Leipzig, 1873) which constitutes a virtul first draft of the Pauline sections in *Urchristentum*.

[17] *Urchristentum*: 259n.: 'In this connection [Romans 6] it may be remembered that reception into the Eleusinian mysteries was also regarded as a sort of new rebirth and in

writing on specifically Christian topics, Pfleiderer shows less caution. In his *Philosophy of Religion* (1878),[18] he freely adopts a position of 'nature mythology'.

> The earliest action in the way of worship in the primitive history of mankind, was nothing but a dramatic repetition of the divine life seen in the processes of nature, with a view to taking part in it in a mutual intercourse of gods and men. The usages connected with the spring and autumn festivals in nature-religions everywhere show very plainly an effort to represent the coming and the departure of the deity of life and light, in such a manner that the changing fortunes of the deity may be repeated and experienced afresh in the imitative acts and emotions of their worshippers. Thus in Egypt was celebrated the complaint of Isis for Osiris, in Syria the marriage and the death of the sun-god Melcarth or Adonis, in Eleusis the search and lament for her daughter Core ... in Athens the death and resurrection of Dionysus. (4:185–86)

In this context, Pfleiderer repeats his parallelism of Paul's notion of baptism 'as a symbolic and dramatic repetition of Christ's death and resurrection' with rebirth in the Eleusinian mysteries (4:189) and goes on to make a more generic, if tortured, comparison:

> [Worship is] always a transaction moving through a series of connected acts, *i.e.* a drama ... The contents of the dramatic representation may be of the most varied nature; from the epic nature-mythology of the earliest heathenism, which turned on the course of the sun and of nature, to the most ideal processes of man's emotional life as they are set forth in

particular that the hierophant appointed to the temple service had to take a sacramental bath, from which he emerged as a "new man" with a new name, whereupon the "first was forgotten," i.e. the old man was put off together with the old name.' This note does not reappear in the second edition of *Urchristentum* (1902).

[18] O. Pfleiderer, *Religionsphilosophie auf geschichtliche Grundlage*, 1st ed. (Berlin, 1878). I cite the English translation, *The Philosophy of Religion on the Basis of its History* (London, 1886–88), 1–4, of the 2nd German edition (Berlin, 1883–84). A 3d German edition was published in two volumes with separate titles: *Die Geschichte der Religionsphilosophie von Spinoza bis auf die Gegenwart* (Berlin, 1893) and *Religionsphilosophie aud geschichtliche Grundlage* (Berlin, 1896). On Pfleiderer's philosophy of religion, see P. Gastrow, *Pfleiderer als Religionsphilosoph* (Berlin-Schöneberg, 1913) and R. Leuze, *Theologie und Religionsgeschichte: Der Weg Otto Pfleiderers* (München, 1980).

Christian worship. There is no intention to underestimate the immense difference between these two, or to deny in any way whatever the specific superiority or uniqueness of Christian worship [in making this statement]. (4:185)

Yet, the whole discussion is set forth only to conclude with a (now familiar) Protestant polemic against the automaticity of Catholic ritual where 'a true and profound idea ... was most fatally distorted' in the 'magical idea' of the Mass (4:193), a distortion traced back to the Church Fathers being 'led away by the similarity' between Christian praxis and the 'solemnities of the [Greek] mysteries' (4:189). This 'cardinal error of Catholicism ... [was] unanimously and with perfect justice' protested against by 'the Reformers' (4:194).

The second edition of *Das Urchristentum* (1902) finds Pfleiderer wrestling, in a far more provocative manner, with these issues in a work designed for scholars of early Christianity.[19] In stark contrast to the first edition, comparative matters abound, especially with respect to Mithraism to which he devotes a separate chapter (3:101–12), drawing largely on the recently published work of Cumont.[20] His first lengthy comparison displays his persistent intellectual dilemma. He observes that the Mithraists, besides the 'expiatory blood-baptism' (*Taurobolium*) which they 'took over' from the rituals of Attis and Cybele, had a 'sacred meal ... in the form of consecrated bread and a cup (of water or wine)'. The Mithraists, in their cult representations, he continues, show the initiants 'in animal masks' standing by the table. He interprets the masks as showing that 'they have "put on" their god in order to place themselves in closest fellowship with him'. Pfleiderer goes on to make the Pauline comparison, but in a bizarre fashion, appealing to a double unconsciousness, that of the contemporary scholar and that of Paul!

Involuntarily [*unwillkürlich*] we remember the words of Paul, that all who are baptized into Christ have 'put on'

[19] O. Pfleiderer, *Das Urchristentum, seine Schriften und Lehren*, 2nd ed. (Berlin, 1902), 1–2. While I occasionally quote a phrase from the German, I cite the English translation of the 2nd ed., *Primitive Christianity: Its Writings and Teachings in their Historical Connections* (New York-London, 1906–11), 1–4, throughout.

[20] F. Cumont, *Textes et monuments figurés relatifs aux mystères de Mithra* (Brussels, 1896–99), 1–2.

Christ, and that the consecrated cup and bread that we break in the Lord's Supper are the 'fellowship of the blood and body of Christ'. I do not of course mean to assert that Paul borrowed these thoughts and words direct from the mysteries of Mithras. But the possibility cannot, I think, be denied that Paul ... had some slight knowledge of the heathen cults practiced [in Tarsus] ... and that the pictures and representations of this kind so impressed themselves upon his memory that, later, when they were called forth by natural association of ideas from the background of his consciousness [*Ideenassoziationen aus dem Hintergrund des Bewusstseins hervorgerofen*], they became the prepared material for the combinations formed by the genius of the Apostle. (1:62–63)

Similar statements, and a similar ambivalence as to genealogy and parity, recur throughout.[21] And while the Reformation polemics against 'heathenising error' (1:471) are continued, they are modified in significant ways such as to call into question the myth of 'pristine origins', and to exhibit an uncharacteristic appreciation, in the thought of a liberal Protestant theologian, for ritual. The 'animistic' notion of the sacraments, he boldly proclaims, 'did not first make its way into Christianity in the post-apostolic time, but pervades the whole Pauline theology' (1:414). What Paul accomplished was to 'ethicize' the 'original enthusiasm' of the early Christians 'which in its original form was closely related to the orgiasm of Mysteries' (1:101). In so doing, Paul 'created for the growing Christian Church the elements of its ceremonial, without which no Church religion could arise or maintain itself' (1:101).[22]

---

[21] For example, *Primitive Christianity*, 1:101, 103, 331, 372, 376, 414, 417, 420 n. 1.

[22] This more complex view persists in Pfleiderer's later writings, reaching its fullest expression in his last published book, *Die Entwicklung des Christentums* (Munich, 1907). I cite the English translation, *The Development of Christianity* (New York, 1910). There, in a chapter devoted to 'Ceremonial and Establishment' (83–99), Pfleiderer positively interprets such well-known Protestant polemic *topoi* as the worship of saints and relics (83–86) as well as the Mass. 'Now, we Protestants are accustomed to condemn the Mass as something repugnant because of its magical and hierarchical relations, but even here we ought not to be unjust towards the old Church.' He offers three arguments: accommodation to the 'stream of heathen that poured into the Church'; the requirement that ideal relations be represented, that the 'spiritual be thought of in connection with the sense symbol'; and that the ceremonials awaken 'real religious ideas and Christian emotions ... [which find] completion and correction in the sensuously tangible sacrifice of the Mass' (90–91).

Just one year later, in a lecture on *The Conception of Christ in Early Christian Belief*,[23] delivered before the International Congress of Theologians meeting in Amsterdam (September, 1903), and published, later that year, in expanded form, Pfleiderer, for the first time citing Frazer as his 'authority' for both the comparative religions materials and his 'remarks upon the mysteries' (92n.1), details the full pattern. After presenting a composite portrait (84–86), drawn from New Testament sources, of 'Christ as the conqueror of death', Pfleiderer announces his central thesis, 'in the history of religion, many parallels are found to all these traits of Christ as the Saviour of the world' (86–87). His chief example: 'the idea of the dying and reviving god which lies as the root of the mysteries'(90). Employing characteristic Frazerian language, he writes:

> In its original form this idea belongs to the most ancient elements of the religious legends and customs which arose from man's yearly experience of the withering of vegetation in autumn and its revival in spring ... Relics of this primitive belief have been almost everywhere preserved in popular customs ... personifications of the Cornspirit, and so forth. However, among the peoples of Asia Minor, Egypt and Greece these universal customs ... have given rise to definite myths of the death and return of a god whose former history is realised and represented in the rites of the yearly festivals.
> (91–93)

He continues, 'essentially the same myth lies at the origin of the mysteries' of Osiris, Adonis, Demeter and Persephone, and Dionysus, while 'nearly allied to these legends of the violent death of a god are those which tell of the voluntary descent of a god or hero into the underworld and his fortunate return', such as Tammuz (93–99).

In his last work devoted to the topic and published in 1905,[24] Pfleiderer more strongly insists on the parallels between Paul and

[23] O. Pfleiderer, *Das Christusbild des urchristlichen Glaubens in religionsgeschichtlicher Beleuchtung* (Berlin, 1903). I cite the English translation, *The Early Christian Conception of Christ: Its Significance and Value in the History of Religion* (London-New York, 1905).

[24] O. Pfleiderer, *Die Entstehung des Christentums*, 1st ed. (Münich, 1905), I cite the English translation, *Christian Origins* (London, 1906).

the mysteries of the dying and rising gods,[25] as well as Paul's creative genius in transforming them into an 'ethical' system (e.g. 176–77), and makes an additional set of arguments. The use of these 'borrowings' was necessary to distinguish Christianity from Judaism (183, 189). Its 'orgiastic' enthusiasm, now domesticated by Paul, is what freed early Christianity from the rigidities of 'national-legal' Judaism. When this domestication later failed, the 'dangerous one-sidedness' of Gnosticism resulted (244–45).

To complete the Pfleiderer dossier, the first book that I am aware of, devoted to scholarship into Christian origins to bear the title, 'Dying and Rising Gods' – Martin Brückner's, *Der sterbende und auferstehende Gottheiland in den orientalischen Religionen und ihr Verhältnis zum Christentum* (Tübingen, 1908, RVV, 1.16) – is dedicated 'to the memory of Otto Pfleiderer'.

From Pfleiderer's initial publications, although never without challenge, the interpretation, especially, of Pauline myth and ritual as being intrinsically related to the pattern of dying and rising gods, has persisted in some circles of New Testament scholarship. Thus R. Bultmann could continue to declare, in 1965, that Paul's understanding of baptism was grounded in the theology of the Hellenistic-Christian community:

> which understood this traditional initiation-sacrament on analogy with the initiation-sacraments of the mystery religions. The meaning of the latter is to impart to the initiates a share in the fate of the cult-deity who has suffered death and reawakened to life – such as Attis, Adonis, or Osiris[26]

[25] As these are Pfleiderer's strongest statements of dependence, I quote a representative sample. After citing Dieterich's *Eine Mithrasliturgie*, which Pfleiderer understood, with Dieterich, (incorrectly) to be 'the initiatory service by which proselytes were admitted into the Mithra religion,' he writes, 'so striking is the connection of these ideas with Paul's teaching of Christian baptisim [in Romans 6] ... that the thought of historical relation between the two cannot be evaded' (158). 'Perhaps Paul was influenced by the popular idea of the god who dies and returns to life, dominant at that time in the Adonis, Attis and Osiris cults of Hither Asia ... The relation of these ideas and customs to Paul's mystical theory of the death and resurrection of Christ and the participation of the baptized therein is too striking to avert the thought of influence by the former on the latter' (175–76). 'This analogy to heathen acts of worship, which Paul himself drew [1 Cor 10.16–22] is an analogy which holds throughout the Pauline teachings of the sacraments; and the analogy is not mere chance but rests on more or less direct influence' (182).

[26] R. Bultmann, *Theologie des neuen Testaments*, 5th ed. (Tübingen, 1965): 142. I cite the English translation of the 3d German edition (1958), *Theology of the New Testament* (London, 1959), 1:140 which is the same.

Despite the current opinion in other quarters that the matter is closed, that the comparisons have proved false, the most careful recent student of the motif of 'dying and rising with Christ' in Paul has insisted, 'the question of the relation of this motif to the mysteries, then, is not yet settled.'[27]

From our comparativist perspective, regardless of the judgments, yet to be made, as to the genealogical validity of the 'dying and rising' myth with respect to early Christianity, the observation brought forth in the first chapter, with respect to Dupuis, must, now, be repeated here. The work of Frazer and Pfleiderer, as well as their intellectual descendents, are significant because they introduced a *third term* to the comparative project. At their best, what these scholars proposed was not a comparison between early Christianity and some other Late Antique religion with respect to this or that detail or word, a comparison which invites conclusions as to borrowing or dependence, but rather the comparison of both with respect to a more generic (in this case, a seasonal) pattern, a comparison which resists conclusions as to borrowing or dependence.[28] Although carried out in a far from consistent manner, for this methodological advance, we owe these predecessors a debt of gratitude.

II

While our primary interest is in matters of method and theory, in thinking critically about the comparisons proposed in terms of the 'dying and rising' pattern, it is necessary to turn first to issues

[27] R. C. Tannehill, *Dying and Rising with Christ: A Study in Pauline Theology* (Berlin, 1967): 2, in the series, BZNTW, 32.

[28] While I regret his awkward platonic language (1:4, et passim), the most striking instance of this sort of generic comparison with respect to a third term I know of in the scholarly literature on Late Antique religions is that of L. Bieler, *Theios Anēr: Das Bild der 'göttlichen Menschen' in Spätantike und Frühchristentum* (Vienna, 1935–36, rp. Darmstadt, 1967), 1–2. The first volume is devoted to describing the generic category (the *Gesamttypus*); the second volume, to comparing this category to a series of individual cases. While justifiable criticisms can be brought against both Bieler's theoretical presuppositions and his methodological procedures, it is sadly revealing and utterly characteristic that most scholars of early Christianity have fundamentally misunderstood his enterprise, in that they have historicized the *Typus* and viewed the second comparative step as genealogical. E. V. Gallagher, *Divine Man or Magician? Celsus and Origen on Jesus* (Chico, 1982): 10–18, in the series, SBLD, 64, offers a sophisticated account of Bieler's enterprise, and usefully compares his work to Max Weber's notion of the 'ideal type'.

of data, for these are not innocent of more general concerns. Since the pioneering researches of P. Lambrechts[29] and the synthesis of the state-of-the-question by Günter Wagner[30], it has become commonplace to assume that the category of Mediterranean 'dying and rising' gods has been exploded; in the succinct formulation of one (apologetic) scholar, 'the description "dying and rising gods" is a product of the modern imagination'.[31] To

[29] P. Lambrechts, 'Cybèle, divinité étrangère ou nationale?,' *Bulletin de la Société Belge d'Anthropologie et d'histoire*, 62(1951): 44–60; 'Livie-Cybèle,' *Nouvelle Clio*, 4(1952): 251–59; 'Les Fêtes "phrygiennes" de Cybèle et Attis,' *Bulletin de l'Institut Historique Belge de Rom*, 27(1952): 141–70; 'La "résurrection" d'Adonis,' *Annuaire de l'Institut de philologie et d'histoire orientales et slaves*, 13(1953): 207–40; *Over Griekse en oosterse mysteriegodsdiensten: De zogenannte Adonismysteries* (Brussels, 1954), in the series, MVAW, Letteren en Schone Kunst, 16.1; *Op de grens van Heidendom en Christendom: Het Grabschrift van Vettius Agorius Praetextatus en Febias Aconia Paulina* (Brussels, 1955), in the series, MVAW, 17.3; 'Aspecten van het onsterfelijkeidsgeloof in de Oudheid,' *Handlingen der Zuidnederlandse Maatschappij voor Taal- en Letterkunde en Geschniedenis*, 10(1956): 13–49; *Attis: Van herdersknaap tot god* (Brussels, 1962), in the series, VVAW, Klasse der Letteren, 24.46; *Attis en het feest der Hilärien* (Amsterdam, 1967); 'De Kybele-eeredienst te Athene in de Hellenistische tijd,' *Acta Classica*, 13 (1970): 73–78. Lambrechts's methodological work, *De fenomenologische Methode in de Godsdienst- wetenschap* (Brussels, 1964), in the series, VVAW, 26.6, focuses on the motif of 'dying and rising' deities and a treatment of the major theories on the topic, beginning with Frazer, and provides a full bibliography of Lambrechts's publications on the subject. The most thorough-going critiques of Lambrechts have been by M. J. Vermaseren, *Cybele and Attis: The Myth and the Cult* (London, 1977): 119–24, 206 n. 713, et passim – although the implications he draws from the figure of *Attis hilaris* fall short of being persuasive – and F. L. Bastet in two reviews, one of Lambrechts's *Attis: Van herdersknaap tot god* in *Bibliotheca Orientalis*, 22(1965): 201–203; the other, of Lambrechts's *Attis en het feest der Hilärien* in *Bulletin van de Vereeniging tot Bevordering der Kennis van de Antieke Beschaving*, 45(1970): 159–61. See also, G. Sfameni Gasparro, *Soteriology and Mystic Aspects in the Cult of Cybele and Attis* (Leiden, 1985): 30–31, 58–59, n. 137, in the series, EPRO, 103.

[30] G. Wagner, *Das religionsgeschichtliche Problem von Römer 6, 1–11* (Zürich, 1962), in the series, ATANT, 39. I cite the English translation, *Pauline Baptism and The Pagan Mysteries: The Problem of the Pauline Doctrine of Baptism in Romans VI, 1–11, in the Light of its Religio-Historical 'Parallels'* (Edinburgh-London, 1967). See also the recent brief survey of the data in J. Z. Smith, 'Dying and Rising Gods.' in M. Eliade, ed., *The Encyclopedia of Religion* (New York, 1987), 4:521–27. For a critique of Wagner, see A. M. Wedderburn, 'Paul and the Hellenistic Mystery-Cults: On Posing the Right Questions,' in U. Bianchi and M. J. Vermaseren, eds., *La soteriologia dei culti orientali nell'impero romano* (Leiden, 1982):817–33, in the series, EPRO, 92. In the light of the programme announced in this article (see esp. the summary set of propositions, p. 829), Wedderburn's more recent treatment of the subject, 'The Soteriology of the Mysteries and Pauline Baptismal Theology,' *Novum Testamentum*, 29(1987): 53–72 must, unfortunately, be considered a retrograde step.

[31] K. Prümm, 'Mystery', in J. B. Bauer, ed., *Sacramentum Verbi: An Encyclopedia of Biblical Theology* (New York, 1970), 2:606, and compare the opening pages of Prümm's important synoptic article, 'Die Endgestalt des orientalischen Vegetationsheros in der hellenistisch-römischen Zeit,' *Zeitschrift für katholische Theologie*, 58(1934): 463–502, as

put this new, critical perspective over-simply, it is now held that the majority of the gods so denoted appear to have died but not returned; there is death but no rebirth or resurrection. What evidence was relied on by previous scholarship for the putative resurrection can be shown, it is claimed, to be based on a misinterpretation of the documents, or on late texts from the Christian era (frequently by Christians) which reveal an *interpretatio Christiana* of another religion's myths and rituals, or a borrowing of the Christian motif, at a late stage, by the religions themselves. Thus, there has never been a claim for the 'rising' of Mithras in any Late Antique document. The notion of the 'dying and rising' of Marduk is based on a misreading of the ancient Near Eastern sources. The alternation of Tammuz and Kore (as well as Adonis in some traditions) between the underworld and the land of the living does not conform to the usual stipulation of the 'dying and rising' pattern. The same may be said for Osiris's continued royal existence in the realm of the dead. In the case of Adonis, the myths and early rituals emphasize his death and the mourning for him. It is Christian authors (Origin and Jerome commenting on Ezekiel 8.14 [Turchi, nos. 298–99]; Cyril of Alexandria [Turchi, no. 300] and Procopius of Gaza [*MPG* 87.2:2140] commenting on Isaiah 18.1) who mention a joyous celebration, on the 'third day', commemorating the resurrection of Adonis (identified with Tammuz) as analogous to that of Christ. The 'gardens of Adonis' (the *kēpoi*), to which Frazer devoted so much attention, were proverbial illustrations of the brief and transitory nature of life, and contain no hint of rebirth. The point is that the young vegetative shoots rapidly wither and die, not that the seeds have been 'reborn' when they sprout. In the case of Attis, the mythology gives no comfort. The traditions contain no unambiguous claims of a rebirth until two late interpretations of the myth: the complex allegory in the *Naassene Sermon* (Turchi, no. 265), and the euhemerist account in Firmacus Maternus (Turchi, no. 252). The majority of the arguments in the

well as Prümm, 'I cosidetti "dei morti e risorti" nell'Ellenismo,' *Gregorianum*, 39(1958):411–39. Cf. Smith, 'Dying and Rising Gods,' 4:526, 'The category of dying and rising deities is exceedingly dubious. It has been based largely on Christian interest and tenuous evidence. As such, the category is of more interest to the history of scholarship than to the history of religions.'

scholarly literature concerned with Attis have depended, rather, on a reconstructed Cybele-ritual which can be shown to be mistaken. Scholars, intrigued by the calendaric relationship between the Day of Blood (24 March) and the Day of Joy (25 March) employed the analogy of the Christian relationship of Good Friday to Easter Sunday to reason that, if the Day of Blood included, among other activities, mourning for Attis – it did not – then the 'joy' on the following day must be in celebration of his resurrection. There is no evidence for this hypothesis. The Day of Joy is a late addition to what was a three-day ritual in honour of the goddess, in which the Day of Blood was followed by a purificatory ritual and the return of the statue of the goddess to the temple. The new feast of the Day of Joy celebrates this cleansing and return of Cybele. Attis appears to play no role. The sole text that unambiguously connects the Day of Joy with Attis is a fifth century biography of Isidore the Dialectician by the neo-Platonic philosopher, Damascius, who writes that Isidore once had a dream in which he became Attis and the Day of Joy was celebrated in his honour, thus demonstrating that he was saved from Hades (Turchi, no. 275)! While its mythical connections to the cult of *Magna Mater* remain obscure, the same sort of developmental history has been argued for the bloody ritual of the *Taurobolium*: a sacrifice has been transformed into a ritual of purification, and finally, in the fourth century, into a 'baptism by blood'.[32]

[32] This summary is based on the works cited above, nn. 29–31. See further, W. von Soden, 'Auferstehung (I), Sterbende und auferstehende Götter,' *Die Religion in die Geschichte und Gegenwart*, 3d ed. (Tübingen, 1957–60), 1:688–89, and, especially, the important synoptic study by C. Colpe, 'Zur mythologischen Struktur der Adonis-, Attis-, und Osiris-Überlieferungen,' *Festschrift W. von Soden* (Neukirchen, 1969): 23–44, in the series, AOAT, 1, which is most important at the level of theory in denying the naturist interpretation. Colpe argues that many of the Late Antique texts adduced in support of this thesis are examples of common-place physicalist allegories. Compare Colpe's positive review of Wagner, *Das religionsgeschichtliche Problem*, in *Gnomon*, 38(1966): 47–51.

The special topic of the *Taurobolium* has been treated by J. R. Rutter, 'The Three Phases of the Taurobolium,' *Phoenix* 22(1968): 226–49 and R. Duthoy, *The Taurobolium: Its Evolution and Terminology* (Leiden, 1969), in the series, EPRO, 10. While they differ somewhat in their reconstruction, both studies are important in using the large corpus of inscriptional evidence to criticize the scanty literary record. It is a scandal to note that, by and large, scholars focusing on early Christianity continue to use the same literary evidence available to a Dupuis or a Frazer, when discussing the 'mysteries', while ignoring the newer inscriptional and archaeological data. It is with reference to the *Taurobolium* that

While these negative conclusions have not been without challenge by scholars of Late Antiquity, from the standpoint of the history of ideas, their importance cannot be underestimated. They represent a genuine reversal in scholarly thought. That which was posited as most 'primitive' – a myth and ritual pattern of 'dying and rising' deities ultimately based on human sacrifice or ritual murder in relation to the fertility of vegetation[33] – has turned out to be an exceedingly late third or fourth century development in the myths and rituals of these deities. But this is

scholars have been boldest in proclaiming Christian influence, e.g.Duthoy, 'It is obvious that this alteration in the *taurobolium* must have been due to Christianity, when we consider that by A.D. 300 it had become the great competitor of the heathen religions and was known to everyone. The complete submersion that purified the aspirant Christian of all his sins may quite possibly have inspired in the worshippers of Cybele the desire to be sprinkled all over with purifying blood' (121). While abstaining from comment on the hyperbolic 'known to everyone', I would note the easy elision from 'it is obvious that this alteration ... must have been due to Christianity' to 'may quite possibly have inspired'. Despite their polemics against speculative and reconstructive history, many scholars concerned with Christian 'origins' have eagerly seized upon Duthoy's work as demonstrating conclusively not only the lack of dependence of early Christian traditions on the 'mysteries', but also the dependence of the latter on the former with respect to elements associated with the motif of 'dying and rising', a suggestion already tentatively raised by H. Hepding in a note in his classic monograph, *Attis: Seine Mythen und sein Kult* (Giessen, 1903): 200, n. 7, cf. 179, in the series, RGVV, 1. Even as cautious a scholar on the question of Christian influence as Mircea Eliade, *Histoire des croyances et des idées religieuses*, (Paris, 1976-), 2:278–79, concedes the probability in the case of this ritual. See further, among others, D. H. Wiens, 'Mystery Concepts in Primitive Christianity and in its Environment,' *ANRW* 2.22.2 (1980): 1267 who terms Duthoy's monograph 'a complete turning-of-the-tables' on the question of 'influence'. See the critiques of Duthoy's work in the review of Duthoy by T. D. Barnes, *Gnomon*, 43(1971): 523–24; R. Turcan, *Les religions de l'Asie dans la Vallée du Rhône* (Leiden, 1972):83–88, esp. 85, n. 1, in the series, EPRO, 30, and Vermaseren, *Attis*: 107.

[33] In addition to the passages from Frazer cited above (pp. 90–91), see, *The Golden Bough*, 3d ed., 4:212; 7:iv–vi, 138–39, et passim. The charge, that the Mediterranean 'dying and rising' gods and, therefore, the Christian myth of death and resurrection, as well as the eucharist, depend on 'primitive' notions of ritual murder and human sacrifice, is a staple of 'Free Thought' polemic literature. See, J. M. Robertson, *Pagan Christs*: 99–213. Robertson maintains, 'There is an arguable case for the theory that the belief in a dying and re-arising Saviour-God, seen anciently in the cults of Adonis, Attis, Herakles, Osiris, and Dionysos, originated obscurely in the totem-sacraments of savages ... There is, however, a much stronger case for the simpler theory that the belief in question originated on another line in the practice of sacrificing ... a victim' (99). For a more savagely polemic version, see the curious work by Preserved Smith, *A Short History of Christian Theophagy* (Chicago, 1922): 23–42. The evidence for human sacrifice in the Mediterranean region (and India) is reviewed by A. R. W. Green, *The Role of Human Sacrifice in the Ancient Near East* (Missoula, 1975), in the series, ASORD, 1, in a manner that will give no comfort to 'vegetative' theories. 'This investigation encountered no evidence of a fertility ritual which involves human sacrifice' (202).

not the aspect dwelt on by most scholars concerned with Christian origins. Instead, ignoring their own reiterated insistence, when the myth and ritual complex appeared archaic, that analogies do not yield genealogies, they now eagerly assert what they hitherto denied, that the similarities demonstrate that the Mediterranean cults borrowed from the Christian.[34] In no work familiar to me, has this abrupt about-face been given a methodological justification.

Nor is this all. Far more serious, and utterly unaddressed by the literature, is the implication of this revised understanding of the 'dying and rising' deities for the usual sorts of distinctions between these myths and rituals and the Christian. Chief among these has been the insistence on the fact that figures such as Adonis or Attis are 'nature gods' representing the cyclical drama of the waxing and waning of vegetation (or, in older interpretations, of the sun) in contradistinction to the figure of Jesus who has been held to have been 'historical'.[35] As Wagner argues:

> The death of Jesus is further distinguished from the fate of all the mystery-deities by the fact that it happened once and for all (*ephapax* Rm 6.10), and is incapable of being repeated

[34] See above, n. 32. For an all too characteristic assertion, see the crudely polemic work of M. Hengel, *Der Sohn Gottes: Die Entstehung der Christologie und die jüdisch-hellenistische Religionsgeschichte* (Tübingen, 1975), in English translation, *The Son of God* (Philadelphia, 1976): 28, 'There is no indication that they [the mysteries] were particularly widespread in this early period or that they had strong religious influence. On the contrary, we should reckon rather that there is strong Christian influence on the later evidence of mysteries from the third and fourth centuries AD.'

[35] For a particularly blunt set of formulations of this characteristic distinction, see J. Prussner, *Sterben und Auferstehen im Hellenismus und Urchristentum* (Greifswald, 1930): 21–22, 38–39, 72–73, 83–84. See further, among others narrowly concerned with our theme, Brückner, *Der sterbende und auferstehende Gottheiland*: 9–10, 35, 48; A. Jacoby, *Die antiken Mysterienreligionen und das Christentum* (Tübingen, 1910): 24, in the series RV 3.12; G. Kittel, *Die Religionsgeschichte und das Urchristentum* (Gütersloh, 1931): 290. For a more recent, equally blunt, example of this truism in a wider context, see M. Simon, 'Remarques sur la sotériologie du Nouveau Testament,' *Festschrift E. O. James* (Manchester, 1963): 145, rp. in M. Simon, *Le Christianisme antique et son contexte religieux: Scripta varia* (Tübingen, 1981), 1:261, in the series, WUNT, 23.1: 'If one compares early Christianity with the mysteries, the most striking difference, that which is most immediately apparent, resides in the fact that the Christian saviour is an historical person, while the pagan saviours are mythical figures.' For the theological gymnastics caused by the problems of relating this emphasis on the 'historicity' of Jesus's death/resurrection with the notion of continued participation in 'dying and rising' with Christ, see the tortured monograph by W. T. Hahn, *Das Mitsterben und Mitauferstehen mit Christus* (Gütersloh, 1937).

cultically; here we have an historical event, there is a mythical drama[36]

This distinction collapses in the face of Wagner's own argument: in the case of the so-called 'dying and rising' gods, understood in their myths to have lived in 'historical' times, their death occurred but once; it was not repeated in the mysteries.

The issue, here, is not the truth and validation of myth, often expressed in simplicistic distinctions between myth/legend/history. It is rather in the commonplace uncritical acceptance of a contrast first developed by the Pan-Babylonian School at the turn of the century between myth as essentially cyclical, associated with what they termed the 'astronomical Babylonian pattern' or the 'seasonal Canaanite pattern', and biblical 'history' as essentially a linear pattern, merged with long-standing notions of history as concerned with the unique and myth (and ritual) as concerned with the repetitive.[37] That such an understanding is inadequate may be shown from a favourite text of the Pan-Babylonians in comparison with the Gospel-narratives: the Gilgamesh traditions.[38] The whole point, after all, of the insertion of the Flood-account in the eleventh tablet of the late recension of *Gilgamesh* is to insist that the Flood was a 'once for all' event and, therefore, the immortalizing of Utnapishtim would *not* be repeated in the case of Gilgamesh (XI.197–98).

If the distinction of cyclical myth *vs.* linear history cannot be sustained as a necessary (indeed, in some authors, as a sufficient) differentiating criterion — most usually as between the religions of Israel and other Mediterranean and Near Eastern traditions and extended to the difference between Christianity and the other religions of Late Antiquity, and if, in the words of one scholar who represents a growing consensus on the usual comparison:

> No matter how often it is repeated, a reference to the entanglement of the ancient Near East in an a-historical nature-myth of the eternal cycle of all events is meaningless

[36] Wagner, *Pauline Baptism and the Pagan Mysteries*: 284.

[37] See B. S. Childs, *Myth and Reality in the Old Testament* (London, 1960): 74–75, in the series, SBT, 1.27 and Smith, *Imagining Religion*: 26–29, cf. Smith, 'Mythos und Geschichte,' in H.-P. Duerr, ed., *Alcheringa oder die beginnende Zeit* (Frankfurt am Main, 1983): 29–48, esp. 35–41.

[38] See above, n. 7.

in light of the fact that such a mythology simply does not
exist in the historiographic documents of the ancient, i.e.
pre-Persian, Near East.[39]

then this has consequence for the manner in which these
documents are treated. It must lead us to insist on an important
element of method and theory with regard to comparison: *the
recognition and role of historical development and change.* This is a
necessary principle of parity. The work of comparison, within
and without the area of Late Antiquity, requires acceptance of the

---

[39] H. Gese, 'Geschichtliches Denken im Alten Orient und in Alten Testament,'
Zeitschrift für Theologie und Kirche, 55(1950): 127–45; I cite the English translation, 'The
Idea of History in the Ancient Near East and in the Old Testament,' *Journal for Theology
and the Church*, 1(1965): 45–64, esp. 45. For other influential, early statements see
B. Albrektson, *History and the Gods: An Essay on the Idea of Historical Events as Divine
Manifestations in the Ancient Near East and in Israel* (Lund, 1967), in the series, CB-OTS, 1
and J. J. M. Roberts, 'Myth versus History: Relaying the Comparative Foundations,'
Catholic Biblical Quarterly, 38(1976): 1–13. See further the useful comments of
H. W. F. Saggs, *The Encounter with the Divine in Mesopotamia and Israel* (London, 1978):
64–92, especially his rejoinder, with respect to reviews of Albrektson, that: 'It is this
hardly a relevant criticism of Albrektson's work that he "had merely selected similar
aspects as between the Hebrews and other nations, and not investigated the differences";
he selected similar aspects because the predominant view of Israelite religion assumed the
absence of such similarities' (70).
    The close relationship of these conventional pictures of the historicity of Israel, in
contrast to the cyclical-nature myth of the ancient Near East, to the argument over early
Christianity and the 'mysteries' may be illustrated in the characteristic comment by
B. M. Metzger, 'Methodology in the Study of the Mystery Religions and Early
Christianity,' *Harvard Theological Review*, 48(1955): 1–20, as reprinted in Metzger,
Historical and Literary Studies: Pagan, Christian, Jewish: 1–24, 'It is generally acknowledged
that the rites of the Mysteries, which commemorate a dying and rising deity, represent the
cyclical recurrence of the seasons. In other words, such myths are the expression of ancient
nature-symbolism; the spirit of vegetation dies every year and rises every year. According
to popular expectation, the world process will be indefinitely repeated, being a circular
movement leading nowhere. For the Christian, on the other hand, *as heir to the Hebraic
view of history,* the time-process comprises a series of unique events, and the most
significant of these events was the death and resurrection of Jesus Christ. Unlike the
recurrent death and reanimation of the cultic deities symbolizing the cycle of nature, for
the Christians the importance of Jesus' work was related just to this "once-for-all"
character of his death and resurrection' (23, emphasis added). In a curious note to this
passage, Metzger adds: 'It must not be supposed that the recurring annual festival of Easter
belies what has just been said regarding the particularity of the Christian message. It has
been proved that the celebration of Easter did not arise at once out of belief in the
Resurrection, but developed later by gradual stages out of the Jewish Passover' (23, n. 1).
While the argument appears as something of a *non sequitur*, it is important for illustrating
the lengths to which the notion of Israelitic/Jewish 'origins' has been used to insulate
Christian phenomena automatically from their Late Antique environment. This is a
matter already treated in Chapter 3.

notion that, regardless of whether we are studying myths from literate or non-literate cultures, we are dealing with *historical processes of reinterpretation*, with tradition. That, for a given group at a given time to choose this or that mode of interpreting their tradition is to opt for a particular way of relating themselves to their historical past and social present. This is most especially the case in the study of the religions of Late Antiquity. While usually considered as 'background' for the emergence of Christianity, such a perspective radically and illegitimately foreshortens the phenomena and, thus, radically distorts what is most interesting. In almost no case, when treating this period, do we study a new religion. Rather, almost every religious tradition that forms the object of our research has had a centuries-old history. We study archaic Mediterranean religions in their Late Antique phases. To be able to trace the Eleusinian mysteries from their origin as a fourteenth century BC family cult to the gnosticization of their central myth in the *Naassene Sermon* in the third century AD is to do justice to our data, to the traditions we seek to understand, in contradistinction to the usual static comparison of isolated items such as the putative 'raising' of this or that deity with the resurrection of Jesus.[40]

[40] This paragraph reprints, in revised form, Smith, *Map Is Not Territory*: xi. While the point of the lengthy and complex history of these deities and their cults is to be insisted on, Eliade probably goes too far in giving them 'un histoire multimillénaire' (Eliade, *Histoire des croyances* 2:274).

For a complex view of internal tradition-history with respect to the cults of Late Antiquity, see Ugo Bianchi who, in a series of articles that have proved provocative of further research, has proposed a four-fold typology of cults in the Mediterranean world. Bianchi, first, *redescribes* the category, shifting attention away from the Christological interests highlighted by the terminology of 'dying and rising' to a more properly generic category of gods who undergo a variety of 'vicissitudes'. The comparative principle of classification is the different soteriological structures and implications experienced by the cult members in relation to these vicissitudes. Bianchi distinguishes between:

Fertility cults, which serve as his base, where these vicissitudes are identified with a seasonal pattern, celebrated in a collective cult drama, which expresses confidence in the continued presence of the deity despite death or danger, in the affirmation that the 'danger will be surmounted ... and order reestablished'.

Mystery cults in which the vicissitudes of the seasonal pattern are reinterpreted in an individual manner from a 'soteriological' perspective, most frequently as good fortune for the cult participant in their post-mortem existence.

Mysteriosophic traditions in which the salvation becomes more limited, in which the vicissitudes are 'applied to the divine element in man, or to his divine soul' in a dualistic myth and ritual complex.

Gnostic traditions, in which the lingering 'seasonal' elements are wholly absent. Rather,

It is, to put matters bluntly, poor method to compare and contrast a richly nuanced and historically complex understanding of Pauline christology with a conglomerate of 'mystery texts' treated as if they were historically and ideologically simple and interchangeable; to treat the former as developmental and the latter as frozen.[41] As long as we identify recognizable humanity with historical consciousness and openness to change with critical thought – as we do – the usual treatment of the religions of Late

through a 'fresh' reinterpretation, the vicissitudes are applied to the fate of the divinity, whether expressed in the notion of a world-soul or the *salvator salvandus*.

For this typology, the fundamental article is U. Bianchi, 'Initiations, Mystères, Gnose: Pour l'histoire de la mystique dans le paganisme greco-oriental,' in C. J. Bleeker, ed., *Initiation* (Leiden, 1965): 154–71, in the series, SHR, 10. I have based my summary and taken all quotations from this. See also, Bianchi, 'Le problème des origines du gnosticisme et l'histoire des religions,' *Numen*, 12(1965): 161–78; Bianchi, 'Le problème des origines du gnosticisme,' in Bianchi, ed., *Le origini dello Gnosticismo* (Leiden, 1967): 1–27, esp. 10–13, in the series, SHR, 12; Bianchi, 'Psyche and Destiny,' in E. J. Sharpe and J. R. Hinnells, eds., *Man and his Salvation: Studies in Memory of S. G. F. Brandon* (Manchester, 1973), esp. 53–57; Bianchi, *The Greek Mysteries* (Leiden, 1976): 1–8. The conference volume, edited by U. Bianchi and M. J. Vermaseren, *La soteriologia dei culti orientali nell'impero romano: Atti del Colloquio internazionale su la soteriologia dei culti orientali nell'impero romano, Roma 24–28 Settembre, 1979* (Leiden, 1982), in the series, EPRO 92, was largely devoted to testing the utility of Bianchi's terminology for the religions of Late Antiquity. In the discussion during the course of this symposium, Bianchi offered a terminological clarification: he defines as 'mystic,' 'all cults implying a god experiencing a vicissitude – even fertility cults', and as 'mysterical', those which introduce a soteriological element, in particular, that concerned with afterlife (*La soteriologia dei culti orientali*: 469, n. 1).

While Bianchi is ambiguous, in a manner characteristic of the majority of European historians of religion, as to whether he is proposing an historical development or a morphological taxonomy of increased complexity (see, Bianchi, 'Psyche and Destiny': 56 and the criticisms noted, 56 n. 15), and while I doubt that the phenomenon of 'gnosticism' can be so readily harmonized with the preceding three elements, although it is, in fact, 'gnosticism' which is Bianchi's prime concern, this proposal is of major assistance in emphasizing that the same mythologoumenon is capable of complex generic processes of reinterpretation and reconfiguration which may be studied in both their intra-cultic and inter-cultic developments by the comparativist.

[41] On the latter point, see the 'document final' of the Colloquio internazionale su la soteriologia dei culti orientali nell'impero romano (1979), 'The traditional [scholarly] schemas are not well adapted to the diversity of the oriental cults', in Bianchi-Vermaseren, *La soteriologia*: xvii. On the former, see, for example, Tannehill, *Dying and Rising with Christ*, who distinguishes between 1) a pre-Pauline association between baptism and dying with Christ (7–14); 2) a use of the formula, in Paul, to refer to a past association of dying and rising as a contrast betwen the two 'aeons' (14–74); 3) the use of the formula, in Paul, to express a present association of the Christian, in suffering, with Christ's dying and rising (74–129); and 4) the use of the formula, in Paul, with special reference to the Christian's future rising with Christ (130–34). Without arguing for the probity of this particular classification, this is to accept an order of complexity within a single author not granted to the entire corpus of the so-called 'mystery' texts.

Antiquity, as well as the bulk of the other mythic traditions of humankind, is inhumane. (The latter is, I fear, not an unintended consequence.) The claimed ahistorical character of myth is a product of the scholar's gaze and not of some native world-view, be it of a literate or non-literate culture. It robs the 'other', whether understood as 'primitive' or 'oriental', of indigenous capacity for thought with respect to the hard work of cultural creation. In the question under review, the complex internal history of those traditions, as put forth by recent scholarship, hitherto labelled as possessing 'dying and rising' deities forever shatters this presumption.

We can go further, for the principle of parity is always and necessarily double-edged. From a comparativist point of view, if the possibility of freezing a particular instance of this or that Late Antique tradition is methodologically foreclosed, the same must obtain for the varieties of early Christianities as well. Neither Paul − indeed, a single passage in Paul (Rom.6.1−11) − nor the Pauline tradition can be held to be normative for the exploration of the motif of 'dying and rising'.

We have learned from the more recent studies of Late Antique religious figures, once classified as 'dying and rising' deities, the sorts of questions that might be brought, as well, to the early Christian data. Given the central conclusions of these studies, conclusions celebrated by so many students of early Christianity, we might seek, within the foreshortened period of time represented by the Christian data, evidence for an analogous process to that found in the Late Antique documents, that is to say, we might seek evidence of a shift from a figure clearly located within the sphere of the dead − a location, as will be argued in Chapter Five, by no means barren of soteriological implications[42] − to a figure held to transcend such a location, recognizing, in advance, that the specification of the myth and its soteriological dimensions will vary both within and between the several traditions.

As is well-known, if the theme of 'dying and rising' as a soteriological motif is present in some early Christ-cult traditions, it is notably lacking in others. 'Dying and rising' is entirely absent

---

[42] See Sfameni Gasparro, *Soteriology and Mystic Aspects in the Cult of Cybele and Attis*: xvi, 42−43, 45, 48, 59−60 and 125 who insists on this point with respect to Attis. This important monograph will be discussed further in Chapter Five.

in Q. There is good evidence for early martyrological interpretations of Jesus in which his death has soteriological implications
without any focus on a resurrection.[43] The problem of the lack
of a resurrection narrative in Mark is notorious. 'Dying and
rising' would be an impossible utterance for an early Christian
Docetist ... and so on. In terminology that will be introduced in
the next chapter, 'dying' traditions such as the martyrological
interpretations of Jesus seem more characteristic of locative (in
this case, Judaean) Christian cults; the Pauline emphasis on 'dying
and rising', more characteristic of these some Christian cults in
their utopian forms. *This same dual perspective – locative/utopian –
is characteristic of all of the Mediterranean religions in Late Antiquity,
and constitutes one basis for conceiving an analogical relationship
between these religions and early Christianities.* (See below, Chapter
Five.)

Informed by the more recent researches on the history of the
putative Mediterranean 'dying and rising' deities, it may be as
useful to see the notion of Christian 'dying and rising' as the
product of a complex developmental process in which it becomes
more interesting to ask about the historical circumstances that led
to the formation of the *Corpus Paulinum*, and, hence, to the
possibility of the wide dissemination of views associated with
Paul, or to the addition of the resurrection narrative in Mark than
it does to focus on the matter of Pauline 'origins'. While the
answers to such questions are far from uncontroversial, there is an
apparent convergence within the datings proposed by the most
plausible hypotheses. Both the formation of the *Corpus*[44] and the

---

[43] This theme, in connection with the quotation of a pre-Pauline tradition in Rom.
3.24–26, has been the focus of the important study by S. Williams, *Jesus' Death as Saving
Event: The Background and Origin of a Concept* (Missoula, 1975), in the series, HDR, 2. See
further the work on martyrological traditions by B. Mack and his students, summarized in
Mack's important recent book, *A Myth of Innocence: The Gospel of Mark and Christian
Origins*: 105–108, et passim. Mack's work is the first study of 'Christian origins' which
may be taken up, with profit, by the general student of *religion*. Mack's magisterial
contribution will be discussed in Chapter Five.

[44] This is not the place to expose fully this controversial subject. The evidence and
arguments concerning an earlier date are well summarized in C. L. Mitton, *The Formation
of the Pauline Corpus of Letters* (London, 1955). To the useful bibliograhical note on the
state of the question in W. Schmithals, *Paul and the Gnostics* (Nashville, 1972): 254–55,
n. 28, I would add H. Gamble, Jr., *The Textual History of the Letter to the Romans* (Grand
Rapids, 1977): 115–22 et passim, in the series, SD, 42. I doubt that 1 Clement can be used
to establish a first century *Corpus*. See, D. A. Hagner, *The Use of the Old and New*

addition to Mark[45] appear to be late products of the mid-second century, thus recapitulating the process that has been observed in the case of other Late Antique cults. Furthermore, while there has been an understandable concentration of scholarly effort on matters of source, redaction and tradition history in the study of the New Testament, the recent investigations into the claimed 'dying and rising' traditions raise the need for equal attention to issues of *reception history*.[46] That is

Testaments in Clement of Rome (Leiden, 1973), in the series, SNT, 34, who attempts the same (315–31). In my view, he successfully demonstrates use of 1 Corinthians (195–213) and possibly Romans (214–20), but is less convincing on citations from other members of the Pauline collection (220–30); this accords well with the general pattern in the Apostolic writings (see Mitton, *The Formation of the Pauline Corpus of Letters*: 21). Note the shrewd comment by H. Gamble, 'The Redaction of the Pauline Letters and the Formation of the Pauline Corpus,' *Journal of Biblical Literature*, 94(1975): 417, n. 36: 'It is certainly no coincidence that the three letters for which textual tradition attests variations in address (Romans, 1 Corinthians and Ephesians) are precisely the letters most often cited in early witnesses to the usage of Paul's letters.' This would suggest that such witnesses are more likely evidence for the independent circulation of these epistles prior to their collection. For negative evaluations of 1 Clement and the Pauline *Corpus*, see, among others, A. Harnack, *Die Briefsammlung des Apostels Paulus* (Leipzig, 1926): 72, n. 4; P. N. Harrison, *Polycarp's Two Epistles to the Philippians* (Cambridge, 1936): 299; and G. Zuntz, *The Text of the Epistles* (London, 1953): 14.

By contrast to the suggested date of c. 90, I would accept those scholars who connect the formation of the *Corpus Paulinum* with Marcion's *Apostolikon*, and adopt a mid-second century date. See the blunt statement in W. Bauer, *Rechtgläubigkeit und Ketzerei im ältesten Christentum*, 2nd ed., (Tübingen, 1964): 224, in the series, BHTH, 10 – English translation, *Orthodoxy and Heresy in Earliest Christianity* (Philadelphia, 1971): 221. See further, among others, H. von Campenhausen, 'Marcion et les origines du canon neotestamentaire,' *Revue d'histoire et de philosophie religieuses*, 20 (1966): 213–26, cf. Campenhausen, *Die Entstehung der christlichen Bibel* (Tübingen, 1968), English translation, *The Formation of the Christian Bible* (Philadelphia, 1972): 145, et passim, and the careful restatement of the issue in R. J. Hoffmann, *Marcion: On the Restitution of Christianity. An Essay on the Development of Radical Paulinist Theology in the Second Century* (Chico, 1984): 105–109, esp. 107, n. 29, in the series, AARDS, 46. While the early position of J. Knox, *Marcion and the New Testament: An Essay on the Early History of the Canon* (Chicago, 1942): 140–57 is well known, see his later article, 'Acts and the Pauline Letter Corpus,' *Festschrift Paul Schubert* (Nashville, 1966): 279–87, esp. 284–86.

[45] For the dating adopted, see, C. E. B. Cranfield, 'Mark, Gospel of,' *Interpreter's Dictionary of the Bible* (Nashville, 1962), 3:276; and the shrewd remarks of J. D. Crossan, 'Empty Tomb and Absent Lord,' in W. Kelber, ed., *The Passion in Mark* (Philadelphia, 1976): 144–45. W. R. Farmer, *The Last Twelve Verses of Mark* (Cambridge, 1974), in the series, SNTSM, 25, while adopting a contrary point of view, presents an invaluable review of the evidence and a rich bibliography.

[46] For an important beginning at the enterprise of reception history, see A. Lindemann, *Paulus im ältesten Christentum: Das Bild des Apostels und die Rezeption der paulinischen Theologie in der frühchristlichen Literatur bis Marcion* (Tübingen, 1979), in the series, BHTH, 47. Although he overemphasizes 'orthodox' comfort with Paul, he is no more successful

to say, we need to reflect on the verdict of A. Benoit, among others, when he writes after reviewing the second-century Christian literature:

> One is struck by an especially surprising fact: the baptismal themes of Paulinism are totally absent. Nowhere, in all of the patristic literature of the second century can one perceive the least echo of the mystery according to which to be baptised is to die and be resurrected with Christ ... [Paulinism] played no role in the development of baptismal theology in this period.[47]

While the Valentinian documents from Nag Hammadi have been held by some scholars to constitute an exception,[48] they serve, above all, to remind us how controversial the notion of resurrection was in the second century in notable contrast to its wider currency and acceptance in the third and fourth centuries.[49]

This is to argue that we must see the development of a richer and more widely spread notion of the 'dying and rising' of the central cult figure, alongside of the development of the implications of this for the cult member, in second to fourth century Christianities as well as in the other contemporary religions of Late Antiquity, as *analogous processes*, responding to parallel kinds

than Benoit (see below, n. 47) in discovering Paul's 'dying and rising' theme in the second-century literature.

[47] A. Benoit, *Le baptême chrétien au second siècle: La théologie des pères* (Paris, 1953): 227, in the series, EHPRS, 43. Benoit especially takes up the issue of the alleged presence of the Pauline theme in Ignatius (78–82). Cf. H.-Ch. Puech and G. Quispel, who cite part of this passage from Benoit, in M. Maline, H.-Ch. Puech, G. Quispel and W. Till, *De Resurrectione: Epistula ad Rheginium* (Zürich and Stuttgart, 1963): xiii, and go on to argue: 'As has been often observed, the "mystical" themes of Pauline theology, and in the first place, that of the participation of believers in the death and resurrection of Christ, remained without great impact on the ecclesiastical literature of the second century.'

[48] This Valentinian exception was first insisted on by H.-Ch. Puech and G. Quispel in their 'Introduction' to *De Resurrectione*: xiii, cf. xxxi. It has been taken up, from quite different perspectives, in W. C. van Unnik, 'The Newly Discovered Gnostic "Epistle to Rheginos" On the Resurrection,' *Journal of Ecclesiastical History* 15(1964): 142, 153–65; M. L. Peel, *The Epistle to Rheginos: A Valentinian Letter on the Resurrection* (Philadelphia, 1969): 133–39 et passim; E. H. Pagels, *The Gnostic Paul* (Philadelphia, 1975): 1–3, 28–30 et passim. See the cautions in the studies of B. Layton on Rheginus: Layton, *The Gnostic Treatise on the Resurrection from Nag Hammadi* (Missoula, 1979): 56–66, in the series, HDR, 12; Layton, *The Gnostic Scriptures* (Garden City, 1987): 316–17.

[49] See, among others, the valuable survey of second century diversity in van Unnik, 'The Newly Discovered Gnostic Epistle': 154–64.

of religious situations rather than continuing to construct genealogical relations between them, whether it be expressed in terms of the former 'borrowing' from the latter, or, more recently, in an insistence on the reverse.

Once this argument has been accepted, there are further entailments. The commonplace limitation of inquiry to the canon, indeed to the notion of written documents at all, is an essentially theological determination which must be set aside by the scholar of religion. While this has far-reaching implications for the usual sorts of research into Christian 'origins', here we need confine ourselves to the particular matter at hand where a parallel picture to that already developed from the literary record emerges from a consideration of early Christian archaeological data. For example, G. F. Snyder concludes, in his recent exemplary survey of the field:

> Jesus does not suffer or die in pre-Constantinian art. There is no cross symbol nor any equivalent. Christians did find themselves in difficult circumstances, including death. Yet the symbols show them being delivered from those circumstances, or at peace despite them. Their faith in Jesus Christ [as revealed iconographically] centers on his delivering power. Moreover, their Christology fits more the heroic figure of Mark (without a cross) than the self-giving Christ of the Apostle Paul ... From 180 to 400 artistic analogies of self-giving, suffering, sacrifice, or incarnation are totally missing. The suffering Christ on a cross first appeared in the fifth century, and then not very convincingly.[50]

No other archaeological data (inscriptions et al.) contradict this iconographical description.

Given these preliminary considerations, the question for historically oriented comparison can be reformulated, although its answer will be the work of a generation. If an increased focus on the 'dying and rising' of the central cult figure and some notion of a relationship between the individual cult member and the destiny of the deity is a parallel innovation of the late second to fifth centuries, in both the Late Antique cults of Attis and Adonis

[50] G. F. Snyder, *Ante Pacem: Archaeological Evidence of Church Life Before Constantine* (Mercer, 1985): 56 and 165.

and of Jesus, rather than a 'survival' of an archaic element in these
cults, then the issue becomes one of analogy (possibly even of
shared causality) and no longer one of genealogy. Quite different
older traditions, of varying degrees of antiquity and setting, have
been reinterpreted in a similar manner; possibilities latent in the
various traditions (e.g., the themes discussed throughout this
chapter in Paul; the question, though not the affirmation, of
Attis's continued existence, a century later, in Pausanias [Turchi,
no. 248])[51] have moved to centre-stage and have become manifest. The question is not 'which is first?', but rather, 'why both, at
more or less the same time?'

Although it is not possible to anticipate fully what the
character of the answer to this question will be, one strategem is
precluded, a continuation (or a return) to the Protestant apologetic historical schema of 'origins and corruptions' detailed in
Chapter One, a schema which, ironically, has become ecumeni-
cal, being adopted with apparent ease by Roman Catholic
scholars (such as Hugo Rahner) in recent years.[52] That is to say,
one cannot adopt as an historical model, that which was initially
developed as an ahistorical myth: the notion of a pristine church
during the first five centuries; followed by a period of ten
centuries consisting of an initial stage of 'mixture,' then total
(Roman) 'idolatry';[53] and, finally, a new age *in qua Deus*

[51] See the formulation with respect to latency in G. Thomas, 'Magna Mater and Attis,'
ANRW (1984), 2.17.3:1520, 'In the first century B.C. ... Attis has no cult; there is no hint
of his resurrection. But by the time of Pausanias, the germs of the idea of survival after
death are present, in that Attis' body is not to see corruption ... By Arnobius' time, the
myth had developed to the point where Cybele can entreat Zeus *ut Attis reuiuisceret*. This
prayer was granted in so far that Attis' hair should continue to grow and that his little
finger should live and retain its normal motion. The idea of resurrection is now present
potentially: only a slight effort would be needed from thenceforth to make it a real belief.
That this final step had been taken later in the same century is shown by Firmicus
Maternus, and the doctrine is accepted by the later Neo-Platonists.' While there is reason
to suspect this reconstruction of a relentless lineal development, Thomas makes clear the
notion of latent possibilities within a tradition becoming increasingly manifest.
[52] H. Rahner, *Greek Myths and Christian Mystery*, English translation, (London, 1963;
rp. New York, 1971): 24–27.
[53] Compare the Lutheran portrait in the *Magdeburg Centuries* summarized in Chapter
One (p. 14, n. 17) with a version of the same periodization in S. Goulart, *Catalogue testium
quo ante nostrem aetatem Papae reclamauerunt* (Lyon, 1597), 1:629–30. The latter interprets
Flacius's epitome, *Catalogus testium veritatis, qui ante nostrem aetatum reclamarunt papae*
(Basel, 1556), from a Calvinist point of view.

Ecclesiam iterum ad fontes revocavit[54] – and argue simply that the later Roman church syncretized as a result of its expansion or its entanglement with the ('pagan') empire, while the early church remained, miraculously, both more insulated and free – or some other version of the regnant Protestant mythos, even if it be expressed in the more 'scientific' dualisms of 'charisma and routinization' or 'sect and church'.[55]

The question before us is the possibility of a comparative inquiry in which the coexistence of early Christianity and the other religions of Late Antiquity within the same geographical and temporal spheres constitutes, from the point of view of both method and theory, a distraction. As has already been argued in Chapter Two, the enterprise of comparison, in its strongest form, brings differences together solely within the space of the scholar's mind. It is the individual scholar, for his or her own good theoretical reasons, who imagines their cohabitation, without even requiring that they be consenting adults – not processes of history, influence, or diffusion which, all too often, have been held to be both the justification for and the result of comparison. It is this analogical enterprise that will be taken up in the final chapter.

[54] Ph. Melanchthon, *De Luthero et aetatibus ecclesiae* (1548), in *CR* 11:786.

[55] See, J. Z. Smith, 'Too Much Kingdom/Too Little Community,' *Zygon*, 13(1978): 123–30.

V

On Comparing Settings

I

In April, 1949, G. Ernest Wright and F. V. Filson collaborated in offering the Haskell Lectures at Oberlin College on the subject, 'The Bible Against its Environment.'[1] The title, upon reflection, seems an odd one. After all, we have been trained, since elementary school, in a popular 'Darwinism' that tells us that extinction is the fate of organisms that fail to adapt to their environment.[2] Here, the same failure is adjudged a triumph. What makes all the difference is the problematic modern theological category of 'uniqueness'. (See above, Chapter Two.) Thus one may question the initial conjunction of two terms in Filson's description of early Christian teaching, that it was 'distinct and unique' (8). The one term is not synonymous with the other. 'Distinctness' is always relative, it is a matter of being different with respect to this or that characteristic or quality and, as such, invites the comparative enterprise. 'Uniqueness' is absolute, and, therefore, forbids comparison by virtue of its very assertion. Nor is it necessary to affirm the consequences of a denial of total singularity as posed by Filson when he insists that, if Christianity is not unique, then it is either an instance of 'plagiarism' or 'eclecticism' (8). These are surely not the only possibilities available for the description of intercultural relationships or analogies.

While Filson persistently uses the terminology of 'unique' (e.g., 18, 19, 20, 21), particularly with respect to theological

---

[1] The lectures were subsequently published in two volumes in the series, SBT. G. E. Wright, *The Old Testament Against its Environment* (London, 1950), SBT, 2 and F. V. Filson, *The New Testament Against its Environment* (London, 1950), SBT, 3. All citations are from the latter work.

[2] This appears to be recognized by Filson when he writes, 'No religious group can grow without sharing the media of communication and the framework of life with those to whom they go ... they cannot work if they are totally alien to it' (26). Note the missionary model being employed which, in older literature, usually results in some form of a theory of 'accomodation'.

affirmations as to the nature of Jesus, he also employs a rich vocabulary of 'difference'. For example, with respect to its Jewish 'environment', Christianity is 'distinctive' (9, 13), 'significantly different' (13), 'original' (9, 20, 22, n. 32), 'new' or 'novel' (21, 22, 22 n. 36 – here 'absolutely new' denies the relativism) did or did not 'parallel' (22) or was in 'opposition' (13, 21) to its environment.

This ambiguity with respect to 'uniqueness' and 'difference', especially as here applied to the relations between Judaism and early Christianity, is endemic to the field of Christian scholarship, expressive of the dual function, discussed in Chapter Three, that Judaism has been made to play in discourse on early Christianity, serving both as an insulating device against 'hellenism', and as an ancestor to be transcended.[3]

To raise the issue of the setting of early Christianities is to ask at the outset the question of comparison and, thereby, to deny any initial postulation of 'uniqueness'. Much will depend on the framing of the issue. The traditional vague terminology of 'Early Christianity,' 'Jewish,' 'Gentile,' 'Pagan,' 'Greco-Oriental,' etc. will not suffice. Each of these generic terms denote complex plural phenomena. For purposes of comparison, they must be disaggregated and each component compared with respect to some larger topic of scholarly interest. That is to say, with respect to this or that feature, modes of Christianity may differ more significantly between themselves than between some mode of

---

[3] Some of this ambivalence is displayed by Filson with respect to the topic treated in Chapter Three, the relation of early Christianity to the Septuagint. When speaking about Judaism, Filson drives a wedge between 'Palestinian and Hellenistic Judaism', arguing that it was the former, 'Palestinian and Pharisaic Judaism rather than ... Hellenistic Judaism' (12), which was influential. 'The influence of the LXX and of Philo are not determinative of the basic content [of early Christianity]' (12, n. 13; cf. 24). On the other hand, the 'New Testament writers' found in the Old Testament 'their one great source of religious vocabulary and concepts' (22). With respect to the 'Hellenistic' content of this or that book in the New Testament, Filson consistently argues, for their 'solid Jewish foundation' (31), claiming that, as a procedural principle, the scholar must first ask, 'are there other, more frequent, and more vital parallels in the Old Testament and in Judaism, so that recourse to Gentile parallels is not necessary to find the place of origin of New Testament ideas? Such is often the case.' But the second question urged on the scholar is, 'Can we explain the New Testament content by pointing to any or all of these parallels? Or do we have to find the creative and ruling center in the New Testament history itself, which *alone* can explain the nature and content of the New Testament gospel?' (29, emphasis added) It is only with respect to Christian apologetic manipulation of Judaism that the scholar can 'have it both ways'.

one or another Late Antique religion. The presupposition of 'holism' is not 'phenomenological', it is a major, conservative, theoretical presupposition which has done much mischief in the study of religious materials, nowhere more so than in the question of Christian 'origins'.[4]

Much work has been done in recent years on social[5] and literary[6] settings for early Christianities. While consensus has not been achieved, it is my sense that we are further along in comparative studies in these areas than we are when we turn to the older topic of religious settings. For in matters other than religion, difference rather than identity governs the comparisons; the language of 'uniqueness' is increasingly eschewed; and analogy rather than genealogy is the goal.[7]

The issue confronting the enterprise of religious comparison is not so much one of a lack of data,[8] as one of inadequate theory ranging from matters of classification to more complex matters of interpretation and explanation.

I would illustrate this with a theoretical issue that stands at the very heart of the comparison of the religions of Late Antiquity with modes of early Christianity and which affects the general scholarly imagination of religion. The issue is the ubiquitous category of soteriology.

While definitions of soteriology are varied, several themes recur within the scholarly literature. Soteriology is conceived as being primarily individual, it presupposes cosmic and anthropological dualism, and it is built around the notion of an absolute alternative: saved or not-saved, with the former often dichoto-

---

[4] Smith, *Map Is Not Territory*: 253–54, citing K. Mannheim, *Ideology and Utopia* (New York, n.d.; reprint): 274. See above, pp. 52–53.

[5] W. Meeks, *The First Urban Christians: The Social World of the Apostle Paul* (New Haven, 1982) provides an extensive bibliography.

[6] D. Aune, *The New Testament in its Literary Environment* (Philadelphia, 1987) provides a rich bibliography.

[7] For a stimulating and important first meditation on the issue of the gospel as a 'unique' form, see J. Meagher, 'The Implications for Theology of a Shift from the K. L. Schmidt Hypothesis of the Literary Uniqueness of the Gospels,' in B. Corley, ed., *Colloquy on New Testament Studies: A Time for Reappraisal and Fresh Approaches* (Macon, 1983): 203–33.

[8] Especially with the on-going publication of EPRO. See above, pp. 79, n. 38 and 102, n. 32.

mized into 'this-worldly' or 'other-worldly' salvation.[9] In the hands of many scholars, both past and present, it is primarily soteriological notions which supply an evolutionary scale that ranks religions, with Protestant Christianity often serving as the implicit or explicit norm or the culmination of the exercise. Thus, Robert Bellah and Joseph M. Kitagawa, among others, use soteriology as a major variable in proposing evolutionary classifications of religions.[10]

[9] See, for example, the recent comparative description of the topic by N. Smart, 'Soteriology: An Overview', in M. Eliade, ed., *The Encyclopedia of Religion* 7:418–23, which characterizes soteriology:

> The term 'soteriology' means 'doctrine of salvation' or, more concretely, the 'way of salvation' ... The term is usually used to refer to the salvation of individuals ... The implication of the idea is that human beings are in some kind of unfortunate condition and may achieve an ultimately good state either by their own efforts or through the intervention of some divine power ... The usual scheme in the major religions that take the idea of individual salvation seriously is to pose the question in terms of a finite series of alternatives: you either attain [your goal] ... or you don't. [7:418–19].

Smart, in the course of his article, ventures a few comparisons between early Christianity and the religions of Late Antiquity. The results are typical. 'Very commonly, there is a belief in a saviour God ... Examples of this idea are, in the ancient world, Isis, Mithra, and Christ' (7:418). 'The right performance of ritual may be central to soteriology. Thus the early Christian view of the sacrament of baptism implied that the neophyte, on entering the Christian community, dies like Christ and is resurrected with Christ. Provided there are no problems in the rest of the person's life, he is assured of ultimate salvation because of the ritual or sacramental union with Christ as victor over sin and death ... There are similar motifs in the old mystery religions, for example the direct participation in the ritual reenactment of the myth of Persephone at Eleusis, and in the rites of Isis' (7:420). 'The means of salvation may be closely tied to the figure of a spiritual leader ... In small-scale societies the figure of the shaman is often important in serving as the expert who provides healing and reenacts the death and resurrection [!] of the person who has experienced evil. In ancient Greek religion, there were mystagogues and leaders such as Pythagoras and Plotinus ... Such figures, whether shaman or mystic, serve as a bridge to the mythic idea of the saviour God who helps humans by himself taking on the human form' (7:421).

A most thoughtful, although very preliminary, treatment of 'salvation' as a comparative category is that by W. G. Oxtoby, 'Reflections on the Idea of Salvation', in E. J. Sharpe and J. R. Hinnels, eds., *Man and his Salvation* (Manchester, 1973): 17–38.

[10] R. Bellah, 'Religious Evolution', a lecture given in 1963 and printed in Bellah, *Beyond Belief: Essays on Religion in a Post-Traditional World* (New York, 1970): 20–50. For Bellah's schema, generalized, see, T. Parsons, *Societies: Evolutionary and Comparative Perspectives* (Englewood Cliffs, NJ, 1966), in the series, Foundations of Modern Sociology. Compare, J. M. Kitagawa, 'Primitive, Classical and Modern Religions: A Perspective on Understanding the History of Religions', in J. M. Kitagawa, ed., *The History of Religions: Essays on the Problem of Understanding* (Chicago, 1967): 39–65, in the series, Essays in Divinity, 1. See, further, the remarks on the taxonomy of religions and evolutionary theories of religion in Smith, *Imagining Religion*: 5–8.

With respect to the religious traditions of Late Antiquity, most especially the 'mysteries', this essentially Christian focus on soteriological matters has led to their classification as 'religions of salvation' (*Erlösungsreligionen*) with particular emphasis on cultic participation in the 'dying and rising' of their cult-deity. That is to say, for the purposes of comparison: 1) salvation is to be understood as a triumph over death; 2) if other salvation-traditions are to be paralleled to those of early Christianity, they must exhibit this mode of soteriology, most especially in the specific form of 'dying/rising'; 3) because early Christianity, as normative in the Pauline corpus, most clearly displays this element, the resurrection of Jesus, (in theological jargon, the 'post-Easter faith') and the participation in this resurrection by the Christian, becomes the *sine qua non* of Christianity[11] and, therefore, the central criterion which governs comparison of early Christianity as a religion with the religious traditions of Late Antiquity. 4) As we have seen in the previous chapter, the purported lack of this criterion in the other 'mysteries' became a warrant for denying the comparison.

While it is by no means clear that *any* of these theses can be sustained, for our purpose, the issue that requires examination is the understanding of religion as preeminently soteriological (often expressed in semi-popular functionalist sentences about fulfilling or responding to human 'needs') and in the specification of this soteriology in terms of either afterlife or triumph over death.[12] While often drifting into an explanation for religion, this is initially a taxonomic question.

The first point that needs reiteration, as stated in Chapter Four, is that in almost no case, when treating with the religions of Late Antiquity, do we investigate a new religion. Rather, almost

---

[11] See the passages cited from representative New Testament scholars in P. Perkins, *Resurrection: The New Testament Witness and Contemporary Reflection* (Garden City, 1984): 17–19, et passim. For the theological elaboration, see especially the work of Walter Kunneth, *Theologie des Auferstehung* 4th ed. (Munchen, 1951), and the useful, if prosaic, summary of Kunneth in M. Kwiran, *The Resurrection of the Dead: Exegesis of 1 Cor. 15 in German Protestant Theology from F. C. Baur to W. Kunneth* (Basel, 1972): 326–56, in the series, ThD., 1.

[12] I set aside, here, an effort to criticize the conventional wisdom that 'primitive' religions are not soteriological as this is not directly relevant to my theme. Nevertheless, from the standpoint of the generic study of religion, such a criticism must be made. See, Smith, *Map Is Not Territory*: 296–309, et passim.

every religious tradition that forms the focus of our research has had a centuries-old history. We study archaic Mediterranean religions in their Late Antique phases (see above, pp. 106–7). The interrelationship between these two, archaic and Late Antique, under rubrics such as persistence and change forms the primary object of our study.

In a series of articles concerned with persistence and change in Mediterranean religions, I have argued for the presence (there, and elsewhere) of two world-views, the 'locative' and the 'utopian'.[13] The former is concerned primarily with the cosmic and social issues of keeping one's place and reinforcing boundaries. The vision is one of stability and confidence with respect to an essentially fragile cosmos, one that has been reorganized, with effort, out of previous modes of order[14] and one whose 'appropriate order' must be maintained through acts of conscious labour. We may term such locative traditions, religions of sanctification. The soteriology of such a view is two-fold: emplacement is the norm, rectification, cleaning or healing is undertaken if the norm (expressed primarily, although not exclusively, in the language of 'boundaries') is breached.[15] While the governing language of such locative/sanctification traditions is often imperial, suggestive, among other things, of a rigid social stratification, there is an ideological insistence on a democracy of responsibility for maintaining the proper *loci*. As expressed in one text, the king-god maintains the distinctions between sky and earth; the divine king maintains the order of his cities and 'weeds

[13] For an elaboration of this taxonomy of 'locative/utopian', and its application to specific traditions and texts, see Smith, *Map Is Not Territory*: xi-xv, 67–207. Cf. Smith, 'Native Cults in the Hellenistic Period,' *History of Religions*, 11(1971): 236–49; 'Hellenistic Religions', *Encyclopaedia Britannica*, 15th ed. (1974), 8: 749–51; 'Towards Interpreting Demonic Powers in Hellenistic and Roman Antiquity', *ANRW*, 2.16.1 (1978): 425–39.

[14] Although this is not the context to develop this, it is imperative that the cosmogonies of these locative traditions should not be seen as creation from chaos, as has all too frequently been maintained in the scholarly literature, but rather be understood as asserting the royal prerogative of a new king-god to reorder a previous arrangement. As the new order is built out of the components of the old, the threat of a return to the previous order is constant; hence both celebration of the present ordered world and a constant need for its maintainance and repair are the chief cultic activities. This is the language of confidence, rectification, and healing which forms much of the soteriology of locative traditions.

[15] I appreciate Smart's linking of healing and soteriology (7:419) in his article cited above (n. 9).

out' rebellion; the householders or slaves weed their gardens of rebellious (i.e., out of place) plants.[16] Each of these actions is equivalent. In theory, it would be as serious for a slave to overlook weeds mixed with desirable plants in the field as it would be for the king-god to overlook mixture in the cosmos.

Within such a locative view, a frequent pedagogic mythologem narrates the adventures of the hero-who-fails, the hero who attempts, unsuccessfully, to transcend his or her placement and must learn to keep place: for example, Gilgamesh, Innana, and, in some traditions, Orpheus.

I take up only the first example, the complex traditions of Gilgamesh[17], for these have often been taken as expressive of the larger theme with which we have been concerned, the question of death.

Despite the manner in which the synthetic Gilgamesh epic is often introduced in Humanities courses, the generative problematic of the text is not the possibility of 'everyman' escaping death. The epic never yields on the point that it is death which distinguishes the realm of the human from the realm of the gods (Old Babylonian version, X.3.2–14; cf. Old Babylonian version III.4.5–8). Rather, the question is whether Gilgamesh, as a mixture, as a divine-king, 'two-thirds god, one-third man' (Late Akkadian version, I.2.1; IX.2.16), might escape the common lot of humankind, a question already explicitly formulated and negatively answered in the Sumerian 'Death of Gilgamesh', (l. 34). With relentless insistence, especially in the Late Akkadian version, each of the putative exceptions are passed in review and shown to have died. Dumuzi/Tammuz is dead, all that is left is the lamentations for him, 'year after year' (Late Akkadian version, VI.46–47). Not even Etana, the king of Kish who was translated to the sky by an eagle escapes. He, along with kings and priests, is seen in the land of the dead in Enkidu's portentous dream:

[16] I refer here to the Sumerian 'Creation of the Pick-axe', in S. N. Kramer, *Sumerian Mythology* (New York, 1961): 51–53, with the revisions proposed in T. Jacobsen, *Towards the Image of Tammuz*, (Cambridge, MA., 1970): 113–14.

[17] I have followed the translations by A. Heidel, *The Gilgamesh Epic and Old Testament Parallels*, 2nd ed. (Chicago, 1949) and S. N. Kramer and E. A. Speiser in J. B. Pritchard, ed., *Ancient Near Eastern Texts Relating to the Old Testament*, 2nd ed. (Princeton, 1955): 44–52, 72–99. I have relied, throughout, on the important discussion by J. H. Tigay, *The Evolution of the Gilgamesh Epic* (Philadelphia, 1982).

In the House of Dust, which I entered,
I looked at [rulers], their crowns put away;
I [saw princes], those (born to) the crown,
Who had ruled the land from days of yore.
[These doubl]es of Anu and Enlil were serving meat roasts
...
In the House of dust, which I entered,
Reside High Priest and acolyte,
Reside incantatory and ecstatic,
Reside the laver-anointers of the great gods,
Resides Etana ... (Late Akkadian VII.4.40–49).

The sole exception is the unrepeatable instance of Utnapishtim and his wife. They have been reclassified as wholly divine through the action of Enlil: they 'became like the gods' (ēmû kî ilāni, Late Akkadian XI.193–94) and have been placed 'far away'. To be human, regardless of the degree of admixture with the divine, is to die, as Gilgamesh finally learns. After he gains and loses the rejuvenating plant, he does not seek to recover it, even though it lies just a short distance away,[18] but rather returns to Uruk and becomes a proper, in-place ruler (as in the non-epic Sumerian tradition, he becomes, after death, a judge in the Underworld).[19] Indeed, the worst curse, within the Gilgamesh epic, that the enraged Ishtar can threaten is that she will raise the dead: 'I will raise up the dead, and they will devour the living/I will make the dead outnumber the living!' (Late Akkadian VI.99–100)[20]

While the relentlessness of the Late Akkadian version of Gilgamesh is extreme, the point is replicated throughout the archaic literature. The dead are different and are to be kept

[18] If Speiser's translation (in Pritchard, *Ancient Near Eastern Texts*: 96) of the late Akkadian XI.297 is correct.

[19] See W. G. Lambert, 'Gilgameš in Religious, Historical and Omen Texts and the Historicity of Gilgameš', in P. Garelli, ed., *Gilgameš et sa légende* (Paris, 1960): 39–56, in the series, CRRAI, 7. Lambert's suggestion (p. 51) that Gilgamesh's rulership in the Underworld was 'from the beginning considered a compensation for missing eternal life' is to be doubted.

[20] Note that this same threat occurs in the complex 'Descent of Innana/Ishtar' tradition (Tigay, *Evolution*: 173–74 and n. 33). This text, and Gilgamesh, are the two paradigmatic instances of the ancient Near Eastern hero-that-failed mythologem, expressive of the dangers of transgressing boundaries.

distinct from the living; to mix the two would be a disaster. Nowhere is this plainer than in the rules and rituals concerning clean/unclean. Whether we examine the literature of the ancient Near East, Israel, or the Greeks, the major cause of uncleanness, and that which serves as a model for all the other forms of distinction, is corpse pollution – the mixture, the contact, of the living and the dead.

In such locative traditions, what is soteriological is for the dead to remain dead. If beings from the realm of the dead walk among the living, they are the objects of rituals of relocation, not celebration.[21] Even the complex tradition of the 'Descent of Innana/Ishtar' to the Underworld, where she seeks to extend her reign illegitimately (from a locative point of view), and the subsequent necessity for a substitute in the figure of Dumuzi/ Tammuz, followed by the need, in turn, to substitute for him his sister, Geshtinanna, so that the siblings alternate with each other between the land of the living and the realm of the dead, is strong testimony to the notion of ordered location – here superimposing a temporal boundary upon a spatial one – and to the power of death appropriately to hold those who come within its sphere. The fact that for so long the narrative sequence was thought to be reversed, that scholars assumed that Innana/Ishtar descended to the Underworld in order to rescue Dumuzi/Tammuz (rather than her descent being the cause of his being in the Underworld) is equally strong testimony to the inability of modern scholars of religion to conceive of a soteriological pattern with respect to death that does not involve a triumph over it, leading them to impose the inappropriate category of 'dying and rising' gods upon such locative traditions.[22]

[21] See J. Z. Smith, 'Towards Interpreting Demonic Powers'. This older sense of impropriety may well govern Mt.27.52–53 where, simultaneous with the crucifixion, amidst other apocalyptic signs that the locative order has been destroyed (especially the power of its central symbol, the Temple), the dead break out of the graves and appear in Jerusalem. The Temple-veil marks the paradigmatic sacred/profane distinction; the division between the living and the dead marks the paradigmatic clean/unclean distinction. I doubt that this special Matthean passage ought to be read as a Christological interpretation of Ezekiel 37, esp. 37.12. See D. Senior, 'The Death of Jesus and the Resurrection of the Holy Ones', *Catholic Biblical Quarterly*, 38(1976): 320–26.

[22] See S. N. Kramer, 'Dumuzi's Annual Resurrection: An Important Correction to Innana's Descent', *Bulletin of the American Schools of Oriental Research*, 183(1966): 31, and his later treatments in Kramer, *The Sacred Marriage Rite: Aspects of Faith, Myth and Ritual*

The Sumero-Babylonian traditions, by and large, did not persist in Late Antique form, so we cannot judge how they might have been reinterpreted.[23] Fortunately, we have other Mediterranean traditions for which the 'long view' is possible. While Greece, in the dominant archaic traditions of Eleusis and Dionysus, offers an interesting contrast between the former, an indigenous 'mystery' bound to a particular place with an hereditary priesthood, and the latter, an ideologically foreign 'mystery' attached to no particular place, a 'voluntary association' with a more entrepreneurial leadership (in these respects more closely resembling the majority of the Late Antique 'oriental mysteries'), both of which, in the course of their complex history, exist in both locative and utopian forms,[24] I turn, instead, to the case of the cult of Cybele and Attis as this will allow us directly to join the comparative issues raised in the previous chapter.

II

The origins of the cult are not accessible to modern scholarship (despite attempts to connect Cybele with the Anatolian goddess, Kubaba).[25] This means that we encounter the religion *only* in a

in Ancient Sumer (Bloomington, 1969); Kramer and D. Wolkstein, *Inanna* (New York, 1983). A survey of older views may be found in G. Wagner, *Pauline Baptism and the Pagan Mysteries* (Edinburgh and London, 1967): 140–45, et passim.

[23] The motif of a threatened birth with respect to divine kingship, reinterpreted with respect to Gilgamesh, appears to persist in the well-known passage in Aelian, 12.21, although the identification is far from certain and may well be a transposition from another figure (Tigay, *Evolution*: 252–55). While it is beyond the scope of this study, it may be noted that there are texts which illustrate reinterpretations of archaic Babylonian materials in the Hellenistic period (see Smith, *Imagining Religion*: 90–96), and it should be recalled that both Stoicism, the most ubiquitous form of utopian cosmology in Late Antiquity, and modes of astrology, appear to have their roots in late Babylonian speculation.

[24] See now the splendid monograph on these two traditions in their locative form by W. Burkert, *Ancient Mystery Cults* (Cambridge, MA., 1987), based on his Harvard Lectures of 1982. While recognizing that both promise a 'privileged life beyond the grave', he is emphatic that, within the two mysteries, 'the catchword is not "rescue" or "salvation" but "blessedness"'. (21), and that, 'while it is tempting to assume that the central idea of all initiations should be death and resurrection, ... the pagan evidence for resurrection symbolism is uncompelling at best' (23). 'There is a dimension of death in all of the mystery initiations, but the concept of rebirth or resurrection of either gods or *mystai* is anything but explicit' (75).

[25] See, among others, the comprehensive article by E. Laroche, 'Koubaba, déesse anatolienne, et le problème des origines de Cybèle', in *Éléments orientaux dans la religion grecque ancienne*, Colloque de Strasbourg, 22–24 mai, 1958 (Paris, 1960): 113–28.

diasporic form, largely, although not exclusively, in Greece and Rome. At an early date (the seventh and fifth centuries B.C), it is already free from an attachment to a central sacred place, having apparently undergone several major changes in character, including the conducting of its business in a foreign language. Nevertheless, what we can discern reveals a cult that is thoroughly locative in character.

In a stunning monograph, first published in 1979 and revised in 1985, G. Sfameni Gasparro reexamined the 'soteriological' aspects of the cults of Attis and Cybele.[26] Gasparro begins her argument by noting the baleful influence a preoccupation with Christian origins has brought to the study of the 'mysteries'. It led:

> all too often to a simplification of the complex and multiple phenomena gathered together in the category of the 'mysteries', while at the same time precedence was given ... to those aspects or elements which would appear to lend themselves better, by analogy or by contrast, to a comparison with Christianity, especially in its Pauline formulation. (xiii–xiv)

This has led to the focus on the category of 'dying and rising' as the chief mode of soteriology (xv–xvi). Rather, Gasparro maintains, what these cults have in common is the notion, borrowing Bianchi's terminology (see above, p. 107, n. 40), of a god who is 'subject to vicissitudes which include crisis, disappearance, sometimes even death, but also a positive outcome' (xvi). It will be the specification of this 'positive' element in a deity who dies (but is not 'raised') that forms one of the interpretative foci of Gasparro's work.

She begins by providing a general typology. In some instances,

---

[26] G. Sfameni Gasparro, *Soteriology and Mystic Aspects in the Cult of Attis and Cybele* (Leiden, 1985), in the series, EPRO 103. All citations will be to this work. This represents a revised English translation of Gasparro, *Soteriologia e aspetti mistici nel culto di Cibele e Attis* (Palermo, 1979), in the series, GIUM, 1. See further, Gasparro, 'Interpretazioni gnostiche e misteriosofiche del mito di Attis', in R. van den Broek and M. J. Vermaseren, eds., *Festschrift G. Quispel* (Leiden, 1981): 376–411, in the series, EPRO, 91; 'Sotériologie et aspects mystiques dans le culte de Cybèle et d'Attis', in U. Bianchi and M. J. Vermaseren, eds., *La soteriologia dei culti orientali nell'impero Romano* (Leiden, 1982): 472–79, in the series, EPRO, 92; 'Significato e ruolo del sangue nel culto di Cibele e Attis', in F. Vattioni, ed., *Atti del Settimana di Studi Sangue e antropologia biblica nella letteratura cristiana (1982)* (Rome, 1983), 1:199–232.

this 'positive outcome' can be expresed in the form of an 'alternating rhythm of presence and absence', as, for example, in the case of the Eleusinian Kore-Persephone; less clearly in some traditions of Adonis and Dionysus. In some instances, this 'positive outcome' can be expressed in the 'acquisition of a new status beyond death'. Osiris, already in archaic tradition, would be the best example of this category.

In other instances, such as Attis, this 'positive outcome' is expressed in the notion of some sort of a 'survival in death' (xvi). This, conjoined with other features typical of the 'salvation' offered within locative traditions – especially purification (14–15, 87 and n. 11) and healing (86–89 and nn. 5–10, 12–13, 16) – constitute what may be quite properly termed the soteriology of the cult.[27]

Gasparro's most provocative pages are devoted to describing in what sense Attis's limited 'survival' in death might be taken as soteriological. Lifting out a characteristic catena of passages:

[A] form of survival after death is indeed accorded to him [Attis]; his body does not decay and his hair continues to grow while a finger remains in motion, a sign that Attis is not completely dead. So if we cannot talk of the youth's return to life or 'resurrection', in the mythical tradition ... [Attis] has an outcome which, even if it is characterized by *pathos* and by mourning, guarantees a positive prospect for Attis, since he is saved from complete annihilation. In this manner, the youth obtains a subsistence beyond death, or rather what we would be entitled to call a subsistence 'in death'. (42).

The case of Attis knows neither a periodic 'return' nor a form of 'revival' ... he dies once for all, as emerges from all the testimonies, with very few exceptions. Nevertheless, dead Attis is annually commemorated by funeral rites of lamentation ... In this manner the character is felt to be present in a ritually effective way and order returns after its disruptions. (45).

---

[27] See the citation from Burkert, above, n. 24. The interrelationship of the notion of *ex voto* cultic activities, healing, purification, salvation and the 'mysteries' is a most provocative element in Burkert's work. See, Burkert, *The Ancient Mysteries*: 12–29.

> [The manifestations of joy, later expressed in the *Hilaria*]
> do not of course express the idea of a 'resurrection' of Attis
> ... but rather the certainty of his survival, either in the form
> of physical incorruptability or in ... his constant presence in
> the cult beside the Great Mother ... His disappearance is
> neither total nor final. (59).

> [Attis appears] as 'surviving in death'. The pine tree of the
> March festivals does not express the idea of a periodic
> manifestation of the deity, but rather, in its quality as an
> evergreen, it reveals him as a *praesens numen* even in the
> concealment and fixity of death. (125)

Common to each of these interpretations is the notion that it is possible to have a satisfying formulation of a soteriological dimension to the death of a cult figure without invoking the notion of resurrection or 'rising'. The former is wholly appropriate within a 'locative' context; the latter would be inappropriate.

Despite this advance, Gasparro remains too wedded to a series of correlations between seasonal patterns and structures of fertility (e.g. xvii, 29, 43, 45, 48, 84). As I have already suggested in Chapter Four, this correlation has resulted in the mischievous distinction between 'mythic' – that is to say, cyclical, seasonal, 'nature' cults – and 'historical' religions, the decisive *differentium* which has been illegitimately used to separate early Christianity from the 'mystery religions'. But, there is more. The notion of 'seasonal' is, itself, a misleading scholarly misnomer ultimately based on the notion of myth as 'bad science' (Tylor, Frazer, et al.) which confuses a *correlation* with an identity. Ironically, in this instance, the very 'confusion' lifted up by scholars to classify primitive thought as 'magical' or 'pre-logical' has been more often characteristic of modern 'scientific' scholarship on religion itself![28]

As we have come to learn, at least since Durkheim, myths are not about nature.[29] They are not primitive attempts to explain

---

[28] See, J. Z. Smith, 'In Comparison A Magic Dwells', in, *Imagining Religion*: 20–22.

[29] See, among other passages, E. Durkheim, *Elementary Forms of the Religious Life* (New York, 1965): 391, 'But the seasons have only furnished the outer framework [*le cadre extérieur*] ...' Compare the blunt formulation by C. Lévi-Strauss, *The Savage Mind* (Chicago, 1966): 95, 'The mistake of Mannhardt and the Naturalist School was to think that natural phenomena are *what* myths seek to explain, when they are rather the *medium through which* myths try to explain facts which are themselves not of a natural but of a logical order'.

natural phenomena. Myths may think *with* natural objects or categories; they are almost never *about* natural objects or categories. Thus the seasons may serve as a medium for thinking about periodicity, regularity, order, distinction, transformation and place. This is an intellectual activity of classification, concomitant variation, correlation, and the like. It need not be equated with agrarian concerns or fertility cults. In the case at hand, I should like to argue that in the cultic relationship to Attis, *pathos* is transformed into *ethos*. A singular death has been transformed into pattern, and while the death, appropriately, cannot be overcome, its effects are, thereby, ameliorated. The land of the dead remains other than the realm of the living, but it is not entirely alienated from life. There is growth and movement, albeit in an attenuated fashion. And, there is memory which if undertaken in a ritualized context guarantees a sort of *presence* and, above all, a *confidence* in the face of inescapable death. This latter is, perhaps, best expressed in the numerous terracotta statuettes of Attis recovered from various necropoli (90–93).

The 'voluntary associations' characteristic of the 'mysteries' of Attis and Cybele share with other locative traditions the same essential 'pay off', expressed succinctly in the words of a third century Carthaginian Saturn-shrine: 'for trust assured and health secured' (*pro comperta fide et pro servata salute*).[30]

III

If one turns to early Christian data comparable to that used by Gasparro to reconstruct the soteriological dimensions of the Attis traditions – iconography, inscriptions and the like, rather than the literary corpus, recognizing that this non-literary data becomes identifiably Christian for us only towards the end of the second century (this lack of apparent distinction for the prior period being, in itself, a significant datum) – an analogous portrait emerges. We find a heterogenous collection of relatively small

---

[30] A. Besaouch, 'A propos de récentes découvertes épigraphiques dans le pays de Carthage', *Comptes rendus de l'Academie des Inscriptions* (1975): 112, as quoted in R. MacMullen, *Christianizing the Roman Empire* (New Haven, 1984): 4, see MacMullen's important note on *fides* and *salus* in this text (123–24, n. 10). The argument of Burkert (see above, n. 27) is likewise relevant.

groups, marked off from their neighbours by a rite of initiation
(chiefly, adult baptism), with their most conspicuous cultic act a
common meal, and a variety of other activities that would lead a
scholar to classify these groups as being highly focused on a cult
of the dead.

What is of most relevance to our enterprise is the interpretation
of the various pre-Constantinian Christian symbols, as well as the
inscriptional materials, proposed by the recent careful study of
the entire corpus by Graydon F. Snyder. [31] If one were to
characterize his interpretation in a word, it would be that the
soteriological dimension is largely cast in the locative language of
'confidence' rather than the utopian language of 'salvation'.
Viewed in terms of its archeological data – the data most
comparable to that from the 'mysteries' – early Christianity
appears as a relentlessly locative tradition, a religion of sanctification.

With respect to the limited corpus of early Christian symbols –
the lamb, the anchor, the vase, the dove, the boat, the olive
branch, the Orante, the palm, bread, the Good Shepherd, fish and
vine and grapes – Snyder argues:

> Among the symbols ... none signifies suffering, death, or
> self-immolation. All stress victory, peace, and security in the
> face of adversity. The Jesus iconography follows the same
> pattern. There is no place in the third century for a crucified
> Christ, or a symbol of divine death. (29, cf. 14–26)

The pictorial programme (esp. the Jonah cycle, Noah and
Daniel) are understood by Snyder, in their pre-Constantinian
form, largely to express peace amidst adversity (47, 49–50, 54)
and, in the case of Susanna, peace despite imminent death (51).
The iconography of Jesus largely depicts him as a youthful
wonder-worker and healer (56, 59). These symbols show the
early Christians being delivered from difficult circumstances 'or
at peace despite them' (56). 'Confidence ... now' is the watch-
word. Even in the case of the popular scene of the Resurrection
of Lazarus:

---

[31] G. F. Snyder, *Ante Pacem: Archaeological Evidence of Church Life Before Constantine*
(Mercer, 1985). All citations above will be to this work. Snyder provides a rich
bibliography which need not be repeated here.

It depicts the present reality of resurrection rather than belief in another world ... [The early Christians] ate with the dead, talked to them, asked for their assistance ... The resurrection motif supports neither a view of otherworldly immortality nor a view of end-time judgement and resurrection. The presence of the dead [within the community] was made possible through the redeeming act of the wonder-worker Jesus. These resurrected dead then were part of the extended Christian family. (61)

Within the funerary inscriptions, *in pace* is the most frequent formula, becoming a 'trademark' of the early Christian burial (122, 128). It has its initial locus as a drinking-salutation in the Christian meal for the dead (17, 128). The same is the case for the common injunction, *vibas*, 'live!' It too is a drinking-acclamation from the Christian meal for the dead. 'It is a wish that all is well' with the departed as he or she 'participates in the fellowship of the saints both living and dead' (126). Even the technical term, *depositum*, as applied to the buried remains, should be understood in its legal sense as an article for safe-keeping, rather than as suggesting some interim state of the soul prior to resurrection (127).

What the archaeological evidence has been leading to, recognizing the bias introduced by the data being largely funereal in character, [32] is the awareness that one of the most central cultic activities of Christians of this era concerns the dead undertaken in an act of eating together with the dead in an extended 'kinship meal', a '*koinonia* meal that did not recall the sacrifice of Jesus Christ' (16, 22, 65); and that the cemetery was one of the two centres of religious activity, different from the *domus ecclesiae*, but no less revelatory of early piety (83). In the cemetery, the early Christians celebrated their kinship with one another, with their familial and special dead.[33] 'We note from the graffiti that

---

[32] There is a problem of bias in the data due to the largely funereal nature of remains. See, however, Smith, *Imagining Religion*: 18.

[33] In this context, it may be of significance to recall that Paul's most extensive discussions of the resurrection of the dead – in 1 Thessalonians and 1 Corinthians, the earliest treatments of the topic in Christian literature – are *both* triggered by questions concerning the status of dead members of the community.

For the early presence of Christian cults of the dead, I am tempted by the argument by C. A. Kennedy, 'The Cult of the Dead at Corinth', in J. H. Marks and R. M. Good, eds.,

prayers were addressed to the dead on behalf of the living, various eating and drinking acclamations were made to the deceased, and the meal, the *refrigerium*, was eaten in honour of the birthday or death day of the deceased person' (83). If the fourth century memoria at Salona be accepted as witness to earlier praxis, as is likely, we gain a more concrete picture:

> The celebration was very social. It strengthened family relationships, either blood or primary, by including extended generations. The service itself included anointing of the stone or *mensa*, antiphonal singing, dancing.

The *refrigerium* meal most likely consisted of fish, bread or cakes and wine. The latter was poured in a depression with access to the tomb (90–91).

Synder's summary of the total corpus of third century funerary cult data is worth citing:

> The prayers and acclamations, such as 'In peace, In Christ, In God,' reflect the faith that the same peace that marked the faith community in life also marked the extended faith community with its extended family in death. There is no sign of a more sophisticated [!] immortality, nor does resurrection, at least as revivification or resuscitation play any role. (167).

The dead remain dead, in a sphere other than the living; but there is contact, there is continuity of relationship, there is memorialization, there is presence. From our vantage point, there is little difference if these be expressed in the notion that Attis's finger still moves, or in the notion that the pouring out of a trickle of wine on a grave stone nourishes the dead. Above all, both traditions witness to *pistis*, to *fides*, to a sense of confidence.

What then of the literary tradition, the New Testament and early Christian literature, which appears far more dramatic in its religious claims than the archaeological material just reviewed?

Festschrift Marvin F. Pope (Guilford, CT, 1987): 227–36 that the Corinthian cultic 'problem' included feasting with the dead and that *eidolothuton* should be translated as 'memorial meals for the dead', but the evidence he cites is far from secure. Kennedy's study does represent a welcome attempt to displace the ubiquitous apologetic 'corruption' model (see Chapter One) which argues that Christian meals for the dead are a late, third or fourth century 'pagan' innovation.

Or, phrasing the question another way: if the 'locative' model is one built on a notion of rectitude, then what of so abrupt a notion as resurrection which appears to shatter the structure of *ethos*? Here salvation is no longer a matter of 'walls and bulwarks' (Isaiah 26.1), but of breaking out or breaking free of all walls; sanctification is no longer the goal, but rather salvation as achieved through acts of rebellion and transcendence. I would characterize such a view as 'utopian' (see above, n. 13).

In the previous chapter, we have already noted the second to fourth century AD reinterpretations, within some of the 'mystery' cults, of archaic locative traditions of dead deities in new experimental modes which appear to testify to these deities returning to life. In the case of Attis, there are only scattered hints of this process. The majority of these occur in the context of purification – for example, the later stages of the understanding of the *Taurobolium* ritual, the introduction of the *Hilaria* festival (see above, pp. 101–2) – and would suggest the same sort of cultic reinterpretation of archaic tradition as is characteristic of Semitic baptizing groups in the first three centuries: the shifting from a language of 'dirt' to one of 'sin', from locative rituals productive of purgation to utopian goals of salvation (expressed, at times in the language of 'rebirth'), and a consequent lengthening of the time span for the efficacy of the ritual or the reduction of it to a 'once for all' permanent action. With more specific reference to Attis, there are various allegorical treatments of his myth – never by adherents to the cult – of either a neo-Platonic or physicalist nature, which harmonized his story (as well as the story of other deities) to either the saga of the descent and ascent of the soul (Sallustius, Julian), or to a seasonal cycle (the 'Naassene Sermon', Firmicus Maternus). In all these cases, we see the straining of locative traditions in a utopian direction. The only apparent testimony to a fully utopian reinterpretation of Attis – again, not by a cult member – is Damascius's report of Isidore's dream (see above, p. 102) where one receives 'salvation from Hades (*sōtērian ex Hadou*)'. It may be important to note, among other changes, the different socio-political context of this report. The cult of Attis, although far from its homeland, had been integrated into the locative religions of its host countries: Greece and Rome, although never without controversy, never quite losing its label as 'foreign'.[34] Now, in a post-Constantinian situation, it is, once more, estranged and marked as being profoundly alien. It is in this sort of setting that we might expect to find a more utopian language in the Attis traditions. It is only in this setting that we, in fact, find it. [35]

Although the temporal span is radically foreshortened, it was suggested in Chapter Four that an analogous process of shifting from a locative to a utopian view might be found, in an attenuated fashion, in early Christian materials. I would expand this latter hypothesis, drawing, in part, on the recent work of Burton Mack, *A Myth of Innocence: Mark and Christian Origins*, which, as in the case of Gasparro with respect to Attis, constitutes a radical and thorough-going revision of Christian materials.[36] In treating his work, I shall confine myself to his characterization of the mythology of the various Jesus and Christ movements, and ignore that which is, in fact, more provocative in his work: his correlation of mythology with processes of social formation and his careful reconfiguring of the Gospel of Mark. The setting aside of the first is a matter of some regret. But it is the case, at present, that we simply lack all but a very few responsible social analyses of 'mystery' traditions.[37] As these are developed, the possibility of analogies with respect to social formation may well prove more interesting than our present preoccupation with mythologoumena. As to the second, there is simply no analogue within the 'mysteries' to the careful and cunning construction of the Markan gospel, a statement that does not require a postulation that the gospel is unique. Besides, there is no parity between the

[34] For a profound meditation on the ambiguous status of the *Magna Mater* cult with respect to centrality and marginality, see F. Hartog, *Le miroir d'Hérodote: Essai sur la représentation de l'autre* (Paris, 1980): 80–83, 110–11, et passim.

[35] I am aware that, in this formulation, I am offering a tentative and, undoubtedly, partial causal explanation for the co-occurrence of the shift to utopian interpretations in the case of the Cybele-Attis cult, and of Paul (see below, pp. 141–2), in terms of alienation and *ressentiment*. However, as indicated above, it is my belief that the determination of such matters 'will be the work of a generation' (see above, pp. 113–4).

[36] (Philadelphia, 1988). While I rely heavily on Mack and quote his work extensively, I am aware that I use him to answer questions that are not his, and that I press his extraordinary work in directions with which he may not agree.

[37] The most sophisticated exception is R. L. Gordon, 'Mithraism and Roman Society: Social Factors in the Explanation of Religious Change in the Roman Empire', *Religion*, 2(1972): 92–121. See further, J. Z. Smith, 'The Social Description of Early Christianity', *Religious Studies Review*, 1(1975): 19–25.

data of the Attis traditions and the data for early Christianity. For the former, we have scattered inscriptional and monumental remains and the second-hand statements of others, for the latter we have a rich, first-hand, documentary and iconographic corpus. There is also no methodological equivalent, in the case of 'mystery' materials, to the sort of micro-criticism to which the Christian materials have been subjected. Nevertheless, analogies can be suggested.

Building the work of contemporary New Testament scholarship,[38] which takes as given a distinction between one family of 'movements in Palestine and southern Syria that cultivated the memory of Jesus as a founder-teacher' and another group of 'congregations in northern Syria, Asia Minor and Greece wherein the death and resurrection of the Christ were regarded as the founding events' (11), Mack makes plain that, among the former, there were a variety of early Jesus-movements which constructed thoroughly satisfying Jesus-myths without either a death or a resurrection. Without rehearsing his analyses, Mack lists five such groups: the earliest stratum of the Galilean 'Q' and its sayings traditions of 'aphoristic wisdom' (57–87); the Jerusalemite 'Pillar' tradition (88–90) and the Trans-Jordanian 'Family of Jesus' (90–91) about which little for certain is known; the 'Congregation of Israel', which was largely responsible for the early miracle stories, combining motifs drawn from narratives of Moses and Elijah with more general 'divine man' themes, and which laboured to relate their Jesus-traditions to the 'epic' traditions of Israel, while rejecting the claims of Second Temple Judaism to the same (91–93); and, finally, the 'Synagogue Reform' group, largely responsible for the early pronouncement stories, which staked out a claim for table-fellowship in close proximity to the synagogue and Pharasaic groups (94–96). Each of these traditions might be classified as essentially 'locative' in character, in tension, to be sure, with rival (Jewish and Christian) locative groups, but not challenging the essential lineaments of a world constituted by order and placement.

[38] The origin of this contrast, in its present form, may be traced back to W. Heitmüller, 'Paulus und Jesus', *Zeitschrift für die neutestamentlichen Wissenschaft* 13(1912): 320–37. For Heitmüller's use of this characterization with respect to a comparison of Paul and the 'mystery' cults, see Heitmüller, *Taufe und Abendmahl im Urchristentum* (Tübingen, 1911).

Setting aside for the moment the issue of Q, each of these other groups have an attribute in common which distinguishes them from the majority of the 'mystery' cults. They are not perceived, and do not perceive themselves, to be foreign (cf. 96). They are movements within an archaic religious tradition, advocating change, as that religion itself is undergoing change (often in analogous fashions). They are different, but not 'other', although the later history of some of these groups will test the elasticity of this boundary and, at times, break it, shifting the taxonomy in a radical fashion.

From this perspective, the internal history of Q becomes especially revealing. The earliest layers of the tradition, located within circles of itinerant Galilean preachers, consist essentially of aphorisms and other gnomic forms which most closely resemble Cynic materials. 'Cynic themes, images and attitudes pervade Q discourse in its first stages of collection' (69). Mack goes on to characterize this Cynic-style wisdom as more a matter of *mētis* than of *sophia*, a mode of wisdom that does not presume 'stable systems' but rather cleverness in dealing with specific situations. While, significantly, never including polemic against specific institutions, the clever sayings exploited differences between expectation or ideology and reality. 'Some incongruity, some conflict of interest ... would be exposed.' It is a rhetorical stance of marginality giving one an angle of vision on what is taken to be commonplace or self-evident (64, 68). From my perspective, it is important to insist that such an attitude is not at all foreign to locative traditions. It is professionalized in divination and common to the various sage and scribal figures throughout the archaic Mediterranean world. It depends on the notion that 'truth' is won, not given; that one can imagine a state other than the way things are, an imagination that requires both an acute diagnosis of the way things are, expressed in concrete terms, a faith in a discoverable notion of the way things ought to be, and a confidence in the possibility of rectification. As Mack argues, in a daring reinterpretation of the phrase 'kingdom of God' as being essentially Hellenistic rather than Israelitic, 'using metaphors such as king, overseer, physician, gadfly, teacher, Cynic's understood themselves to be "sent" by God to preside over the human situation. Epictetus [3.22.63, 76, 80] even refers to the Cynic's vocation as a "reign" (*basileia*)' (73). The process can be expressed in the language of healing or rectification; the result is health and security.

> The invitation would have been something like the Cynic's 'kingdom' that is, to assume the Cynic's stance of *confidence* in the midst of confused and contrary social circumstances. Simply translated, Jesus, 'message' [in Q] appears to have been 'See how it's done? You can do it also'. (73, emphasis added)

If this history can be imagined as the thrust of the Q-type traditions in the thirties and forties, a second stage begins to be apparent in the fifties and sixties. The call to adopt a standpoint of marginality

> turned into calls for repentance, then, finally, pronounce-ments of judgment and doom upon 'this evil generation' ... The language of the kingdom became apocalyptic and the figure of Jesus at the beginning was matched by the figure of the Son of Man to come at the end. (85, cf. 102–3)

Again, it is important to emphasize that there is nothing in apocalypticism inherently foreign to a locative point of view (witness archaic Egyptian and Babylonian proto-apocalyptic and apocalyptic materials).[39] Indeed, apocalyptic materials (them-selves often the product of scribal wisdom schools) depend on the very same creation myths which undergird the locative imagina-tion of the world. Social distance, in the apocalyptic tradition, is transformed into a more cosmic perspective, but the essential confidence is unshaken.

In the latest, tertiary stage of the Q-traditions, the more generalized language of 'this generation' became more and more focused on 'Israel, that is the Jews living in northern Palestine, as if the message pertained particularly to them' (85), and biographi-cal materials began to be developed. Within Q

> reflection on the rejection of the prophets in Israel's history had been applied to the experience of the Jesus 'prophets' and, by retrojection, to the teachings of Jesus about such

[39] See, Smith, *Map Is Not Territory*: 67–87 and Smith, *Imagining Religion*: 90–101.

rejection. But it had not been applied to Jesus ... As the Q
material was taken up by those who composed the gospels,
however, a theme found in certain Jewish literatures of the
time about Israel's rejection and killing of the prophets came
to be applied, not only to the failed mission of the Q
prophets, but to the fact that Jesus had been killed as well ...
It should be emphasized at this point that nowhere in this
tradition running from Q into the early stages of biographic
interest in Jesus is there any evidence for a view of Jesus'
death as a 'saving event', much less for thinking that Jesus
had been transformed by means of a resurrection. (86, cf. 87,
n. 7)

Indeed, if anything, such traditions would have led, eventually,
to a cult of the powerful dead, the 'tombs of the prophets' (Mt
23.29/Lk 20.47), the Jewish and Christian *martyria*, which are
thoroughly locative structures.

Thus far, there is a set of Jesus-traditions which either do not
focus on his death, or conceive of his death without attributing
either saving significance to the death or linking it to a resurrection. For these latter options – a significance to Jesus's death
without a resurrection or the development of a 'dying/rising'
myth with respect to Jesus – we must turn from the 'movements
in Palestine and southern Syria that cultivated the memory of
Jesus as a founder-teacher' to the 'congregations in northern
Syria, Asia Minor and Greece wherein the death and resurrection
of the Christ were regarded as the founding events' (11).

The pre-Pauline or non-Pauline Christ-cult, expressing its
consciousness of the transforming presence of Christ in the
community (100 and n. 2) employed three quite distinct languages. One focused on his death (without employing the notion
of resurrection) as having significance for the community;
another focused on both death and resurrection, with the latter
originally referring, not to the destiny of the community, but
only to its significance for Jesus (104). A third language appears to
have focused on the resurrection as having saving significance for
the members of the community, but appears to minimize the
death. The first two can be still classified as essentially locative
understandings; the third is potentially utopian.

The first language is that of martyrdom (105–13) – 'the oldest "christology"' (109, n. 8) – as seen most clearly in Romans 3.25–26. Drawing upon a variety of scholarly constructions, Mack argues that the basic structure is that of 'hellenized version of an old Jewish wisdom tale' in which a 'vulnerable righteous one' is 'actually killed' with 'vindication' taking place after death (105–7). This could be combined with the second language (e.g. Phil 2.9; Eph 4.10: cf. 1 Tim 3.16) in which the 'vindication' was understood to be Jesus's 'exaltation' or 'enthronement' (113, n. 11) – a language independent of resurrection – and his being 'awarded spiritual sovereignty over the 'kingdom' for which he died and those who belonged to his kingdom were understood to have been vindicated as right' (111). Mack points to the 'pre-Pauline kerygma in Rom. 4.25 where Jesus' resurrection was "for our justification"' (111). and to its more complex form in 1 Cor. 15:3–5 where the death is for the benefit of the community, but the resurrection 'applies only to Jesus' own transformation' (104, cf. 112, n. 10 cont). The third language is best illustrated by the Corinthian 'spiritists', who claim present experience of the power of resurrection.

In light of the above, consider the Pauline *locus classicus* for the question of 'dying and rising', Romans 6.1–11. What we have learned, in general, as to how to read the Pauline letters obtains here as well. The passage is neither a formulation of *kerygma* nor a disquisition on baptism. It is a well-formulated argumentative passage (a diatribe) with a particular audience in mind. Romans 6.1 poses, as a rhetorical question, an objection (libertinism) to the principle of Christian freedom announced in the previous sentence (5.20–21), an objection already bluntly raised, but left unanswered in Romans 3.8, and returned to, again, in 6.15. In order to answer the objection, Paul twice appeals to the community's 'knowledge' (6.3, 6), that is to say, to an earlier, non-Pauline tradition which had already connected the mythologem of Christ's 'dying and rising' with baptism, in a manner either similar to, or different from, the Corinthian spiritists' understanding of their 'already' possessing a resurrection body (1 Cor. 4.8; less clearly, 1 Cor. 15), an understanding from which they had deduced libertarian consequences. In an apparent attempt to correct this sort of interpretation, Paul restates their conviction that they now 'walk in newness of life' (6.4b) in terms of a future condition (6.5b, 8b). In so doing, Paul has most certainly altered his addressee's understanding of the motif of dying/rising. The experience of (Spirit?) baptism was not, as they maintained, a precise analogue to the myth of Christ. He was *now* risen, they were *not now* risen, but *will* rise at some future date; but, they were *already* dead to their previous condition.[40] It is possible that the emphasis on Christ's death (i.e., the strong link of dying and rising) is a Pauline motif, introduced at this point as a corrective to the Spiritist interpretation, and that the latter, by contrast, had held to a translation or enthronement of Christ without death, or had proclaimed his resurrection from the dead without deriving any soteriological implications from the death, but only, as is common in some pre-Pauline kerygmatic formulations, from the fact of his having been raised (e.g. 1 Thessalonians 1.9–10; Romans 1.3–4; 4.24 [in contrast to 4.25]; 8.11; 10.9).

Romans 6.1–11 establishes the presence of '(dying) and rising' motifs within some early hellenistic Christ-cults with which Paul had a problematic relationship.[41] The notion of 'dying and

---

[40] For the general interpretation of Rom. 6.1–11, I have drawn on, and been stimulated by, many of the exegetical insights in Tannehill, *Dying and Rising* (see below, n. 42), and in E. Käsemann, *An Die Römer*, 4th ed. (Tübingen, 1980) in the series, HNT, 8a; English transl., *Commentary on Romans* (Grand Rapids, 1980): 160–71, both of whom provide rich bibliography. For the special topic of the pre-Pauline tradition in this passage, see Tannehill: 7–14, et passim, and Käsemann: 161–63; see also, N. Gäumann, *Taufe und Ethik: Studien zu Römer 6* (Münich 1967): 39, in the series, BZET, 47, each of which asserts some relationship to the 'mystery' cults. Although the results are not convincing, see the lengthy attempt to sort out Paul from tradition in Romans 6 in P. Siber, *Mit Christus Leben: Eine Studie zur paulinischen Auferstehungshoffnung* (Zürich, 1971): 191–249, in the series, ATANT, 61. A somewhat similar connection between death and baptism appears in Mk. 10.38–9. While the framework is Markan, the passage appears to be non-Markan and certainly non-Pauline, although the arguments for its being either pre-Pauline or Palestinian are less convincing. See, among others, P. Lundberg, *La typologie baptismale dans l'ancien Église* (Uppsala, 1942): 223–24, in the series, ASNU, 10, and compare the strictures in O. Küss, 'Zur Frage einer vorpaulinischen Todestaufe', *Münchener Theologische Zeitschrift*, 4 (1953): 1–17; E. Lohse, *Martyrer und Gottesknecht: Untersuchungen zur urchristlichen Verkündigung vom Sühnetod Jesu Christi* (Göttingen, 1955): 116–29; R. Busemann, *Die Jüngergemeinde nach Markus 10: Eine redaktionsgeschichtliche Untersuchung des 10. Kapitels im Markusevangelium* (Bonn, 1983): 147–48, in the series BBB, 57, who relies on the unpublished work of P. Wolf, *Lieght in den Logien von der Todestaufe: Mk 10.38f., Lk. 12.49f.* (diss. Freiburg, 1973): esp. 36–48, which is unavailable to me.

[41] As an aside, I may note that such an interpretation renders futile the pseudo-biographical attempts of some scholars to demonstrate the implausibility of Paul having had personal contact with any 'mystery' cult. This is but one more example of the

rising' was not 'borrowed' from the 'mysteries' by Paul, as earlier scholars, such as Pfleiderer, had presumed, it was taken up by him, in a critical and imaginative fashion, from some early Christian traditions.

Paul interacts with these early Christian languages in complex ways, taking them up, modifying them, recasting them to meet his own distinctive understanding. (How distinctive can be measured by the fact that his controversies were fierce with both 'Judaizing' and 'Hellenizing' factions.)

What Paul does, here and elsewhere, beyond playing these various interpretations against one another, is to subject the Christ-traditions, from a perspective of alienation and *ressentiment*, to a thoroughly utopian understanding. Thus, in his hands, death and resurrection become not so much elements in the mythology of Christ as taxonomic principles to interpret both cosmology and anthropology, instituting radical dualism at all levels of the system. Death and resurrection become correlated with Paul's two aeons typology,[42] made more urgent by his apocalypticism, which does not seem to have been characteristic of the Christ-groups as a whole. At the anthropological level, the familiar dualities of flesh/spirit, law/freedom, etc, are all subsumed under the rubric of death/resurrection. Or, as Mack would have it, utilizing somewhat different terminology:

> Paul ... commited as he was to a conversionist mentality, fastened on the Christ event as if it were a formula to be applied to every personal and social ill. Christian self-definition took place in this application. The formula followed the sequence from death to resurrection, or from everything tyrannical, conflictual, judgmental, legal, constraining, traditional, old, past, and painful to release into the imagined realm of pure spirit. absolute power, free grace, and eternal transcendence ... The process of application can

strategem of using some construct of Judaism as an insulating device protecting early Christianity from 'contamination'. While this theme has been taken up in Chapter Three, see now the summary in Wiens, 'Mystery Concepts in Primitive Christianity': 1263–65, and the blunt formulation of the ideological point in Metzger, 'Methodological Consideration': 7–8.

[42] Emphasis on interpreting 'dying and rising' in Paul in relation to the two aeons has been the special contribution of R. Tannehill, *Dying and Rising with Christ: A Study in Pauline Theology* (Berlin, 1967), in the series, BZNTW, 32.

be viewed as a dislodgement of the Christ event from its
originally 'historical' placement, to become the sign mark-
ing every community event of exchange. (122)

Any pretence of remediation, of rectification, of healing and
sanctification is absent. What began as an expression of the clever
distance of the Cynic sage with respect to the work-a-day world
in the Jesus-traditions, or the testimony to a new and inclusive
community in the 'Spirit' within the Christ-traditions has now
taken a different and thoroughly utopian turn: 'a desire for
personal transcendence as if the world were not worthy unless
transformed' (123). It is a turn that will be developed in various
forms of gnosticisms (shorn largely of any relationship to myths
of death and resurrection), and which will be rejected by the bulk
of early Christian tradition.

Measured in this way, most of the 'mystery' cults and the non-
Pauline forms of Christian tradition have more in common with
each other.[43] Ironically, in the history of scholarship, misled by a
Protestant preoccupation with one or two allegedly 'sacramental'
passages in Paul, precisely the opposite has been presumed to be the

---

[43] Sensitized by comparisons to the Attis traditions, we might note other features as
well. Take, for example, the most narrow understanding of 'locative' as a particular locus.
What is striking about the majority of the 'mysteries' is their freedom from attachment to
a particular place. This is characteristic of all of the so-called 'Oriental mysteries' due to
their essentially diasporic character, and true of the wide-spread archaic 'mysteries' of
Dionysus as well. The major exception is the relentlessly locative Eleusis, but, even here,
there are signs of experiment such as the performance of the ritual in the 'Eleusis' of
Alexandria. (This is not uncontroversial, see Burkert, *Ancient Mystery Cults*: 37 and 147,
n. 44.) While the grave of Attis is known (e.g. Pausanias; note the curious 'empty-tomb'
story in Diodorus 3.59 which could have, but did not, give rise to a tradition of post-
mortem appearance and power as was the case, for example, with the analogous story of
Theagenes of Thasos in Pausanias 6.11.1–9), it appears to have given rise to no memorial
cult. Early Christian materials retain some measure of diversity. One might suppose that
the various Syro-Palestinian Jesus-traditions retained some sense of the location of Jesus's
death; but there is no sign of a cult. Nowhere, in the various formulations of Jesus's death
and/or resurrection in the Christ-traditions, is the event placed. Mark's empty-tomb story
may well be seen as a combination of these two. The locus is recognized, but relativized
from a cultic point of view. It no longer contains the body of the powerful dead. (For this
reason, the hypothesis that rituals of veneration of the tomb lie behind the Marcan account
must be rejected. See, among others, G. Schille, 'Das Leiden des Herrn: Die evangelische
Passionstradition und ihr Sitz im Leben', *Zeitschrift für Theologie und Kirche*, 52[1955]:
195–99; W. Nauck, 'Die Bedeutung des leeren Grabes für den Glauben an den
Auferstanden', *Zeitschrift für die neutestamentliche Wissenschaft* 47[1956]: 262.) Rather the
loci stressed (in Paul and the gospels) have shifted to the 'appearances'. For the later, post-
Constantinian, complex relationships of place/no place with respect to the Church of the
Holy Sepulchre, see Smith, *To Take Place: Toward Theory in Ritual*: 74–95, et passim.

case. The entire enterprise of comparison between the 'mystery' cults and early Christianities needs to be looked at again.

Nor is this all. The question is not merely one of a revised taxonomy, urgent as that may be, but of interests. The history of the comparative venture reviewed in these chapters has been the history of an enterprise undertaken in bad faith. The interests have rarely been cognitive, but rather almost always apologetic. As such, no other purpose for comparison has been entertained but that of genealogy. We have watched the genealogy of this genealogy unfold over four centuries in modes appropriate, perhaps, to the prophetic vocation and invective of an Ezekiel (16.3), but utterly unseemly within the academy. The variety of comparative endeavours, their theoretical goals and methodological entailments, as described in Chapter two, have not been recognized. Rather, the old Reformation myth, imagining a 'pristine' early Christianity centred in Paul and subjected to later processes of 'corruption', has governed all the modulations we have reviewed. As in the archaic locative ideology, the centre has been protected, the periphery seen as threatening, and relative difference perceived as absolute 'other'. The centre, the fabled Pauline seizure by the 'Christ-event' or some other construction of an originary moment, has been declared, a priori, to be unique, to be sui generis, and hence, by definition, incomparable. The periphery, whether understood temporally to precede or follow the Pauline moment, or, in spatial terms, to surround it, is to be subjected to procedures of therapeutic comparison. This is exorcism or purgation, not scholarship. The mythic model of radical conversion, that of wholly putting off the 'old man' and wholly assuming the 'new', has been inappropriately projected into the historical realm.

The Protestant hegemony over the enterprise of comparing the religions of Late Antiquity and early Christianities has been an affair of mythic conception and ritual practice from the outset. It has not yet become an affair of the academy. If this shift to the academy should occur, it will bring about a radical reformulation of the generative questions and a thorough revaluation of the purposes of comparison. A phenomenon will be privileged only with respect to its utility for answering a theoretical issue concerning the scholarly imagination of religion. 'Let him who has ears, hear!'

INDEX

The Louis H. Jordan Bequest

The will of the Rev. Louis H. Jordan provided that the greater part of his estate
should be paid over to the School of Oriental
and African Studies to be employed for the
furtherance of studies in Comparative Religion, to which his life had been devoted.
Part of the funds which thus became available
able was to be used for the endowment of a
Louis H. Jordan Lectureship in Comparative
Religion. The lecturer is required to deliver
a course of six or eight lectures for subsequent publication. The first series of lectures
was delivered in 1951.